Human Resource Excellence

Human Resource Excellence

An Assessment of Strategies and Trends

Edward E. Lawler III and John W. Boudreau

Stanford Business Books
An Imprint of Stanford University Press
Stanford, California

Stanford University Press
Stanford, California
©2018 by the Board of Trustees of the
Leland Stanford Junior University.

Special discounts for bulk quantities of Stanford Business Books
are available to corporations, professional associations, and other
organizations. For details and discount information, contact the
special sales department of Stanford University Press.
Tel: (650) 725-0820, Fax: (650) 725-3457

Printed and bound by CPI Group (UK) Ltd, Croydon, CR0 4YY

Library of Congress Cataloging-in-Publication Data
Names: Lawler, Edward E., III, author. | Boudreau, John W., author. |
     University of Southern California. Center for Effective Organizations.
Title: Human resource excellence : an assessment of strategies and trends /
     Edward E. Lawler III and John W. Boudreau.
Description: Stanford, California : Stanford Business Books, an imprint of
     Stanford University Press, 2018. | "This book is the result of the Center
     for Effective Organizations' (CEO's) eighth study of the human resources
     (HR) function in large corporations"—Preface and acknowledgements. |
     Includes bibliographical references.
Identifiers: LCCN 2017034879 | ISBN 9781503603912 (pbk. : alk. paper)
Subjects: LCSH: Personnel management. | Organizational effectiveness.
Classification: LCC HF5549 .L28854 2018 | DDC 658.3/01—dc23 LC
record available at https://lccn.loc.gov/2017034879

Typeset by Classic Typography in 10½/14 Palatino

CONTENTS

TABLES AND FIGURES

FIGURES

PREFACE AND ACKNOWLEDGMENTS

This book is based on the results of the eighth study of the human resources (HR) function in large corporations by the Center for Effective Organizations. Like the previous studies, it measures how the HR function and organizations are changing and what makes HR an effective strategic partner. This study also analyzes how organizations can more effectively manage their human capital. It gathered data on many of the same topics and the same companies that we studied in 1995, 1998, 2001, 2004, 2007, 2010, and 2013, and we have compared data from our earlier studies to data we collected in 2016 in order to measure changes. For the third time, in 2016 we collected data from multiple countries so that we can determine how corporations in the United States differ from those of other countries. Information on how the data for this study were collected are in appendix B, which also presents information on the characteristics of the sample. A copy of the questionnaire used in the study and the responses for the U.S. sample are in appendix C.

A number of individuals and organizations helped us with data collection. We offer special thanks to our research partners who helped us with data collection; we list them in appendix A.

We also thank Vivian Jimenez for her help in preparing the manuscript. Alice Yee Mark, Aaron Griffith, and Nora Hilton helped with the data collection and did a terrific job analyzing the data.

The Marshall School of Business in the University of Southern California deserves special thanks and recognition for its continuing support of the activities of the Center for Effective Organizations. In addition, we thank the corporate sponsors of the center for their support of the center and its mission; their support is vital to the overall success of the center and is directly responsible for enabling us to do the kind of research reported here. The center, which will celebrate its fortieth anniversary in 2018, has been and continues to be focused on doing research that improves organizational effectiveness.

Special thanks go to Susan Mohrman, who has made many contributions to this research effort. She and Ed did the first three surveys, and she worked with us on the fourth.

THE AUTHORS   *Edward E. Lawler III* is Distinguished Professor of Business and director of the Center for Effective Organizations in the Marshall School of Business in the University of Southern California (USC). He has consulted with over one hundred organizations on employee involvement, organizational change, and compensation and has been honored as a top contributor to the fields of organizational development, organizational behavior, corporate governance, and human resource management.

After receiving his Ph.D. from the University of California at Berkeley, Lawler joined the faculty of Yale University as assistant professor of industrial administration and psychology. Three years later he was promoted to associate professor.

Lawler moved to the University of Michigan in 1972 as professor of psychology and also became a program director in the Survey Research Center at the Institute for Social Research. He held a Fulbright Fellowship at the London Graduate School of Business. In 1978, he became a professor in the Marshall School of Business at USC. During 1979, he founded and became the director of the Center for Effective Organizations. In 1982, he was named professor of research at USC and in 1999 was named Distinguished Professor of Business.

Lawler has been honored as a major contributor to theory, research, and practice in the fields of human resources management, compensation, organizational development, and organizational effectiveness. Most recently, he was the eighth recipient of the Society of Industrial and Organizational Psychology (SIOP) Distinguished Scientific Contributions Award. SIOP includes information about the award recipients as entries in *The SAGE Encyclopedia of Industrial and Organizational Psychology* (2016).

He is the author or coauthor of over four hundred articles and fifty-one books. His most recent book, *Reinventing Talent Management: Principles and Practices for the New World of Work* (Berrett-Koehler), was published in spring 2017. His other books include *Corporate Stewardship: Achieving Sustainable Effectiveness* (Greenleaf Publishing, 2015); *Global Trends in Human Resource Management: A Twenty-Year Analysis* (Stanford University Press, 2015); *Effective Human Resource Management: A Global Analysis* (Stanford University Press, 2012); *The Agility Factor* (2014); *Management Reset: Organizing for Sustainable Effectiveness* (Jossey-Bass, 2011); *Useful Research: Advancing Theory and Practice* (Berrett-Koehler, 2011); *Talent:*

Making People Your Competitive Advantage (Jossey-Bass, 2008); *America at Work* (Palgrave-Macmillan, 2006); *The New American Workplace* (Palgrave-Macmillan, 2006); *Built to Change* (Jossey-Bass, 2006); *Human Resources Business Process Outsourcing* (Jossey-Bass, 2004); *Treat People Right* (Jossey-Bass, 2003); *Organizing for High Performance* (Jossey-Bass, 2001); *Corporate Boards: New Strategies for Adding Value at the Top* (Jossey-Bass, 2001); and *Rewarding Excellence* (Jossey-Bass, 2000). For more information, see http://www.edwardlawler.com and http://ceo.usc.edu .

John W. Boudreau, professor and research director at the University of Southern California's Marshall School of Business and Center for Effective Organizations, is recognized worldwide for breakthrough research on superior human capital, talent, and sustainable competitive advantage. He consults and conducts executive development with companies worldwide that seek to maximize their employees' effectiveness by discovering the specific strategic bottom-line impact of superior people and human capital strategies.

Boudreau has more than two hundred publications, including books such as *Lead the Work: Navigating a World beyond Employment*, with Ravin Jesuthasan and David Creelman (Wiley, 2015); *Global Trends in Human Resource Management: A Twenty-Year Analysis*, with Edward Lawler (Stanford University Press, 2015); *Investing in People*, with Wayne F. Cascio (Pearson, 2011); *Effective Human Resource Management: A Global Analysis*, with Edward Lawler (Stanford University Press, 2012); *Short Introduction to Strategic Human Resources* with Wayne Cascio (Cambridge University Press, 2012); *Transformative HR*, with Ravin Jesuthasan (Wiley, 2011); *Retooling HR: Using Proven Business Tools to Make Better Decisions about Talent* (Harvard Business School Press, 2010); and *Beyond HR: The New Science of Human Capital*, with Peter M. Ramstad (Harvard Business School Press, 2007).

Boudreau's large-scale research studies and focused field research address the future of the global HR profession, HR measurement and analytics, decision-based HR, executive mobility, HR information systems, and organizational staffing and development. His scholarly research has been published in *Management Science, Academy of Management Executive, Journal of Applied Psychology, Personnel Psychology, Asia-Pacific Human Resource Management, Human Resource Management, Journal of Vocational Behavior, Human Relations, Industrial Relations,* and *Journal of Human Resources Costing and Accounting*. Features on his work have appeared in *Harvard Business Review, Wall Street Journal, Fortune, Fast Company,* and *Business Week,* among others.

He is the recipient of the 2013 Michael Losey award from the Society for Human Resource Management for excellence in research that has contributed to the human resource profession. His research received the Academy of Management's Organizational Behavior New Concept and Human Resource Scholarly Contribution awards. He received the 2009 Chairman's Award from the International Association for Human Resources Information Management for lifetime achievement in HR information management. He is a Fellow of the National Academy of Human Resources, the Society for Industrial and Organizational Psychology, and the American Psychological Association.

Boudreau was the first visiting director of Sun Microsystems' unique Research and Development Laboratory for Human Capital. He has coauthored a best-selling textbook on HR management that reached its eighth edition and has been translated into a number of languages, including Chinese, Czech, and Spanish.

The recipient of the General Mills Award for teaching innovations at Cornell University, Boudreau founded the Central Europe Human Resource Education Initiative, connecting American HR professionals and academic researchers with faculty and students in the Czech and Slovak Republics. A strong proponent of corporate/academic partnerships, Boudreau helped to establish and then directed the Center for Advanced Human Resource Studies at Cornell University, where he was a professor for over twenty years, before his current position as research director for the Center for Effective Organizations, at the University of Southern California.

Boudreau is a strategic advisor to a wide range of organizations, including early-stage companies, global corporations, government and military agencies, and nonprofit organizations. He is a foundation trustee of the National Academy of Human Resources. He has served as a member of the board of advisors of the Human Resource Planning Society and WorldatWork. He chaired the advisory board of the California Strategic HR Partnership, a Silicon Valley HR executive consortium, and served as an advisor to the Saratoga Institute, a global source of human capital benchmarking and performance measures. He has been elected to the executive committees of the Human Resources Division of the Academy of Management and the Society for Industrial and Organizational Psychology.

Boudreau holds an undergraduate degree in business from New Mexico State University, a master's degree in management, and a Ph.D. in industrial relations from Purdue University's Krannert School of Management. For more information, see https://ceo.usc.edu/research-scientist/boudreau

Human Resource Excellence

CHAPTER 1

What HR Needs to Do

A changing workforce, global competition, advances in information technology, new knowledge, demands for sustainable organizational performance, and a host of other changes are forcing organizations to constantly examine and change how they operate. They are using new technologies, changing their structures, redesigning work, relocating their workforces, and improving work processes to respond to an increasingly demanding, unpredictable, and global competitive environment (Worley, Williams, and Lawler 2014). These important changes have significant implications for how their human capital can and should be managed and how their human resource functions can and should be designed and operated (Lawler 2017). But are organizations changing their human capital management policies, practices, and processes? Are they redesigning their HR functions?

Over the past decade, it has been difficult to find a management book or business magazine that does not point out how many of the changes in the business world have made human capital—people—an organization's most important asset. Human capital management has been the focus of a great deal of writing on finding, motivating, developing, and monitoring talent. The annual reports of many corporations in North America, Europe, Asia, and Australia argue that their human capital and intellectual property are their most important assets. In many organizations, compensation is one of the largest costs, if not the largest one. In service organizations, it often represents 70 to 80 percent of the total cost of doing business. Even when compensation accounts for very little of the cost of doing business, human capital has a significant impact on an organization's performance (Cascio 2000; Cascio and Boudreau 2011). Without effective human capital, organizations are likely to have little or no revenue. Even the most automated production facilities require skilled, motivated employees to operate and maintain them. Knowledge work organizations depend on employees to develop, use, and manage their most important asset: knowledge. Thus, although human capital does not appear on the balance sheet of corporations, it represents an increasingly large percentage of many organizations' market valuation (Lev 2001; Huselid, Becker, and Beatty 2005).

In an increasing number of organizations, having the best talent and talent management processes can be a continuing and difference-making source of competitive advantage. It can make companies more innovative and agile, better able to develop superior products and customer knowledge, and offer superior services (Worley, Williams, and Lawler 2014).

Role of the HR Organization

Because of the way that the business environment has changed, there are more and more ways the HR function can add value to an organization. For decades, it has added value primarily by performing administrative tasks. But two other roles that it can play make it possible for it to add greater value. Lawler (1995) has developed this line of thought by describing three roles HR can take on. The first is the familiar HR management role (figure 1.1).

The second is the role of business partner (figure 1.2). It emphasizes developing systems and practices to ensure that a company's human resources have the needed competencies and motivation to perform effectively. In this approach, HR has a seat at the table when business issues are discussed and brings an HR perspective to these discussions. When it comes to designing HR systems and practices, this approach explores creating systems and practices that support the business strategy. HR focuses on the effectiveness of the human capital management practices and process improvements in them, and it is expected to help implement changes and help managers effectively deal with people issues.

The business partner approach positions the HR function as a value-added part of an organization so that it can contribute to business performance by effectively managing what is the most important capital of most organizations: their human capital (Ulrich, Younger, Brockbank, and Ulrich 2011; Ulrich and Brockbank 2005; Lawler 2008). But this approach may not be one that enables the HR function to add the greatest value given the increasingly important role that talent plays in determining organizational performance. By becoming a strategic contributor, the third role (see figure 1.3), HR has the potential to add more value in situations where human capital performance can have a major impact on organizational performance (Lawler and Boudreau 2015).

Acting as a strategic contributor means that HR helps the organization develop its strategy. Not only does HR have a seat at the strategy table, it helps to set the table with information about organizational capabilities, talent analytics, and the labor market. It helps shape and enhance strategies by bringing human capital decision science to strategy discussions. It helps organizations operate in ways that help it perform well financially, socially, and environmentally.

A firm's strategy must be closely linked to its talent. Thus, the HR function needs to be positioned to play a major role in both strategy formulation and implementation. Expertise in attracting, retaining, developing, deploying, motivating, and organizing human capital is

AIMS	Support business.
	Provide HR services.
PROCESS	Build performance management capabilities.
	Develop managers: link competencies to job requirements and career development.
	Plan succession.
	Enhance organizational change capabilities.
	Build an organization-wide HR network.
PLANNING	HR and all other functions inspect business plans; inputs from HR may be added to the planning process.

Figure 1.1. HR management

AIMS	Line management owns HR as a part of its role.
	HR is an integral member of management teams.
	The culture of the firm evolves to fit with strategy and vision.
PROCESS	Organize HR flexibly around the work to be done (programs and projects, outsourcing).
	Focus on the development of people and organizations (road maps, teams, organizational design).
	Leverage competencies, manage learning linkages; build organizational work redesign capabilities.
PLANNING	An integral component of strategic and business planning by the management team.

Figure 1.2. Business partner

AIMS	HR is a major influence on business strategy.
	HR systems drive business performance.
PROCESS	Self-service for transactional work.
	Transactional work outsourced.
	Knowledge management.
	Focus on organizational development.
	Change management.
	HR processes tied to business strategies.
PLANNING	HR is a key contributor to strategic planning and change management.

Figure 1.3. Strategic contributor

critical to both. Ideally the HR function should be knowledgeable not just about the business and talent; it should also be the expert in organizational and work design issues so that it can help develop needed organizational capabilities and facilitate organizational change.

To be a strategic contributor, HR executives need, in addition to knowing HR, to have an in-depth knowledge of business strategy, organizational design, and change management, and they need to understand how integrated HR practices and strategies can support organizational designs and strategies. This role requires extending their focus beyond delivery of the HR services and practices that are associated with being a business partner to a focus on making decisions about talent, organizational design, and business strategy.

To be an effective strategic contributor, HR needs to offer a perspective that is often missing in discussions of business strategy and change: knowledge of the human capital factors and the organizational changes that are critical in determining whether a strategy can be effectively implemented. Many more strategies fail in execution than in their conception (Lawler and Worley 2006). What sounds good often cannot be implemented for a variety of reasons having to do with talent management and organizational design.

Despite compelling arguments in support of HR management as a key strategic issue in most organizations, our research and that of others finds that HR executives usually are not strategic partners and do not use data to guide their decision making (Lawler 1995; Brockbank 1999; Lawler, Boudreau, and Mohrman 2006; Lawler and Boudreau 2009, 2012, 2015). All too often, HR is largely an administrative function headed by individuals whose roles focus on cost control and administrative activities (Ulrich 1997; Lawler and Mohrman 2003; Boudreau and Ramstad 2005a; Lawler and Boudreau 2009, 2012, 2015). Missing almost entirely from the list of HR focuses in our global surveys of HR in large corporations are such key organizational challenges as improving productivity, increasing quality, facilitating mergers and acquisitions, managing knowledge, implementing change, developing business strategies, and improving the ability of the organization to execute strategies (Lawler and Boudreau 2015). Since these areas are critical determinants of organizational performance, the HR function has been missing a great opportunity to add value.

There is some evidence that the HR function is beginning to redefine its role in order to increase the value it adds. The first seven phases of this research program collected data in 1995, 1998, 2001, 2004, 2007, 2010, and 2013. The results showed evidence of some change in large

U.S. corporations, but there was more discussion of change than actual change (Lawler and Mohrman 2003; Lawler et al. 2006; Lawler and Boudreau 2009, 2012, 2015).

Creating Change

Describing the new role of HR is only the first step in transitioning the HR function to a role of business partner who contributes to organizational effectiveness. For decades, the HR function has been organized and staffed to carry out administrative activities. Changing that role will require a different mix of activities and people. It necessitates reconfiguring the HR function to support changing business strategies and organizational designs. It also requires the employees in the HR function to have very different competencies from those they traditionally have had (Ulrich, Younger, Brockbank, and Ulrich 2012).

It is clear that information technology is playing an increasingly important role in the future of the HR function (Lawler, Ulrich, Fitz-enz, and Madden 2004; Boudreau 2010). Administrative tasks that have been traditionally performed by the HR function can be done by employees and managers on a self-service basis. Today's information technology–based HR systems simplify and speed up virtually every administrative HR task: salary administration, job posting and placement, address changes, family changes, and benefits administration, for example. What is more, HR systems are increasingly cloud based, and with personal device technology, they can be accessed from virtually anywhere by anyone, thus making self-service possible, convenient, and efficient.

Perhaps the greatest value of the new HR systems results from enabling the integration and analysis of HR activities, thus guiding strategy development and implementation. Metrics can be easily tracked and analyses performed that make it possible for organizations to develop and allocate their human capital more effectively (Boudreau and Ramstad 2007; Lawler, Levenson, and Boudreau 2004).

It is increasingly possible to measure and analyze the effectiveness of many HR policies and practices. With big data and a strategic mind-set, HR can be a data-driven function that practices evidence-based management (Boudreau and Jesuthasan 2011). Business leaders can now be held accountable for HR results based on measures of turnover, employee attitudes, bench strength, and performance distributions.

A strong case can be made that HR needs to develop much better metrics and analytics capabilities. Our previous studies identified metrics as one of four characteristics of HR systems that lead to HR's being a strategic partner. Managers want measurement systems that inform their decisions about human capital. All too often, however, HR focuses on the traditional paradigm of delivering HR services quickly, cheaply, and in ways that satisfy their clients but fail to make a true strategic difference in an organization's performance (Boudreau and Ramstad 1997, 2003). The issue is how to use HR measures to make a true strategic difference in an organization's performance.

Boudreau and Ramstad (2007) have identified four critical components of a measurement system that drives strategic change and organizational effectiveness: logic, analysis, measures, and process. Measures certainly are essential, but without the other three components, they are destined to remain isolated from the true purpose of the HR measurement systems. Boudreau and Ramstad (1997) have also proposed that HR can make great strides by learning how more mature and powerful decision sciences have evolved their measurement systems in order to improve decision making. They identify three anchor points—efficiency, effectiveness, and impact—that connect decisions about resources such as money and customers to organizational effectiveness and that can similarly be used to understand HR measurement:

Efficiency asks, "What resources are used to produce our HR policies and practices?" Typical indicators are cost-per-hire and time to fill vacancies.

Effectiveness asks, "How do our HR policies and practices affect the talent pools and organizational structures to which they are directed?" It thus refers to the effects of HR policies and practices on human capacity (a combination of capability, opportunity, and motivation) and the resulting aligned actions of the target talent pools. Effectiveness includes trainees' increased knowledge, better-selected applicants, stronger qualifications, and performance ratings of those receiving incentives.

Impact poses the hardest question of the three: "How do differences in the quality or availability of different talent pools affect strategic success?" This question is a component of talent segmentation, just as a component of market segmentation concerns is for marketers: "How do differences in the buying behavior of different customer groups affect strategic success?"

Most HR measurement systems largely reflect the question of efficiency, though there is some attention to effectiveness as well through focusing on such things as turnover, attitudes and bench strength (Gates 2004). Rarely do organizations consider impact (such as the relative effect of different talent pools on organizational effectiveness). More important, it is rare that HR measurement is specifically directed toward where it is most likely to have the greatest effect: on key talent. Attention to non-financial outcomes and sustainability also needs to be increased, and strategic HR can affect these as well (Boudreau and Ramstad 2005a; Mohrman, O'Toole, and Lawler 2015).

The Emerging HR Decision Science

The majority of HR practices, benchmarks, and measures still reflect the traditional HR paradigm of excellence, defined as delivering high-quality HR services in response to client needs. Even as the field advocates more strategic HR, it is often defined as delivering the HR services that are important to executive clients: leadership development, competency systems, performance management systems, and so on. But this traditional service delivery paradigm is fundamentally limited because it assumes that clients know what they need. Market-based HR and accountability for business results should also be recognized as important (Gubman 2004). All too often, however, they amount to merely using marketing techniques or business results to assess the popularity of traditional HR services and their association with financial outcomes.

Fields such as finance have a different approach. They have augmented their service delivery paradigm with a decision science paradigm that teaches clients frameworks to make good choices. Significant improvements in HR decisions will be attained not by applying finance and accounting formulas to HR programs and processes, but by learning how these fields evolved into the powerful, decision-supporting functions they are today. Their evolution provides a blueprint for what should be next for HR. The answer lies not just in benchmarking HR in other organizations, but in evolving to be similar to more strategic functions such as finance and marketing.

In marketing, decision science informs decisions about customers. In finance, it informs decisions about money. In human capital, a decision science should inform decisions about organizational talent and decisions made within and outside the HR function. Boudreau and Ramstad (2005a, 2007) have labeled this emerging decision science "talentship" because it focuses on decisions that improve the stewardship of the hidden and apparent talents of current and potential employees.

We see some evidence that perspectives are changing. In the past, discussions of HR systems and measures often focused on providing elegant scorecards or showing the return on investment of HR programs. Today, HR systems and measures are more frequently described as supporting decisions and honing strategy. Of course, reality often remains far different from the hype, but the evolution is promising.

Strategic Focuses

Human resource organizations often exist in organizational environments that are as turbulent as the competitive environments in which organizations find themselves. As companies take measures to survive and prosper, they make changes and introduce strategic initiatives that change the organization, the competencies it has, the way it manages its human resources, and its expectations of and relationships to its employees (Boudreau, Jesuthasan, and Creelman 2015; Boudreau and Jesuthasan 2011; Lawler and Worley 2011). A key driver of an organization's approach to organizing and performing is its business strategy. Thus, in order to understand how the HR function operates and what makes it effective, it is important to examine how its characteristics are related to the strategic focuses of the organization in which it operates. We have done this in our past studies and do it in this study as well.

Table 1.1 shows the prevalence of seven strategic focuses that are often part of a company's business strategy. It also shows that in our U.S. sample, the items measuring strategic focus statistically factor into five types: growth, information, knowledge, sustainability, and innovation. The focus concerned with information was rated the highest strategy in all of our surveys, and the item on customer focus was the most highly rated single item in all of the surveys. There are a few significant differences in the data from the different surveys; however, there is no overall trend that shows some focuses consistently increasing and others decreasing. Instead the results suggest that the focuses vary in importance based on what is happening during a particular time period.

Table 1.2 presents the strategic focus data for each country in our 2016 study. Building a global presence is the focus that shows the largest differences. The European and U.S. companies have the greatest focus on it and Australia the least. Australia is the country that is the most different, with the lowest ratings in many areas. This differs from our previous survey. One explanation for this may be change in the nature of the Australian sample: it includes fewer large global corporations for the 2016 study.

The highest-rated focus in almost every country is customer, and growth is rated the lowest. The others vary from country to country.

On balance, the strategic focus data support the point that organizations exist in complex, dynamic environments and need a variety of strategic and organizational initiatives to position themselves to perform successfully. In order to add value and act as a strategic contributor, the HR function needs to help ensure that the organizational capabilities and competencies exist to cope with a dynamic environment and changing

Table 1.1. Strategic focuses, United States

Strategic Focus	Means							
	1995[1]	1998[2]	2001[3]	2004[4]	2007[5]	2010[6]	2013[7]	2016[8]
Growth	**3.1**	**3.4**	**3.0**	**2.9**	**3.1**	**3.0**	**3.2**	**3.1**
Building a global presence	3.4	3.2	3.0	2.9	3.1	3.1	3.2	3.0
Acquisitions	2.8[2]	3.5[1,4,6]	3.1	2.9[2]	3.2	3.0[2]	3.3	3.1
Information-based strategies	—	**4.0**	**4.0**	**3.9**	**3.8**	**3.8**	**3.7**	**3.9**
Customer focus	—	4.4	4.4[7]	4.4	4.4	4.3	4.1[3]	4.4
Technology leadership	—	3.6	3.5	3.4	3.2	3.3	3.3	3.5
Knowledge-based strategies	—	—	**3.3**	**3.4**	**3.3**	**3.3**	**3.2**	**3.4**
Talent management	—	—	3.7[7]	3.7	3.6	3.4	3.4[3]	**3.7**
Knowledge/intellectual capital management	—	2.9	2.9	3.1	3.1	3.2	3.0	3.2
Sustainability	—	—	—	—	**3.6**[7,8]	**3.6**[7,8]	**3.2**[5,6]	**3.2**[5,6]
Innovation	—	—	—	—	**3.6**	**3.4**	**3.3**	**3.5**
Social purpose	—	—	—	—	—	—	—	**3.2**
Agility	—	—	—	—	—	—	—	**3.5**

Note: Bold numbers are scale means. Empty cells indicate that the item was not asked in that year.

Response scale: 1 = little or no extent; 2 = some extent; 3 = moderate extent; 4 = great extent; 5 = very great extent.

[1,2,3,4,5,6,7,8] Significant differences between years ($p \le .05$).

Table 1.2. Strategic focuses, by country

Strategic Focus	Means				
	United States[1]	Canada[2]	Australia[3]	United Kingdom/ Europe[4]	China[5]
Growth	**3.1**[3]	**2.5**	**2.1**[1,4,5]	**3.1**[3]	**2.9**[3]
Building a global presence	3.0[3]	2.9	2.0[1,4,5]	3.4[3]	2.8[3]
Acquisitions	3.1[2,3]	2.0[1,4,5]	2.3[1]	2.9[2]	3.0[2]
Information-based strategies	**3.9**[3]	**3.8**	**3.4**[1]	**3.9**	**3.8**
Customer focus	4.4[5]	4.5[5]	4.0	4.3	3.9[1,2]
Technology leadership	3.5[3]	3.1	2.9[1,5]	3.5	3.7[3]
Knowledge-based strategies	**3.4**[3]	**3.3**[3]	**2.6**[1,2,4,5]	**3.5**[3]	**3.5**[3]
Talent management	3.7[3]	3.4[3]	2.6[1,2,4,5]	3.6[3]	3.5[3]
Knowledge/intellectual capital management	3.2[3]	3.3	2.6[1,4,5]	3.3[3]	3.4[3]
Sustainability	**3.2**[4]	**3.6**	**3.0**[4,5]	**3.8**[1,3]	**3.6**[3]
Innovation	**3.5**	**3.5**	**3.1**[5]	**3.7**	**3.7**[3]
Social purpose	**3.2**[5]	**3.3**	**3.4**	**3.5**	**3.9**[1]
Agility	**3.5**[3]	**3.3**	**2.8**[1]	**3.5**	**3.3**

Note: Bold numbers are scale means.

Response scale: 1 = little or no extent; 2 = some extent; 3 = moderate extent; 4 = great extent; 5 = very great extent.

[1,2,3,4,5] Significant differences between countries ($p \le .05$).

organizational focuses. It is important to look at how the HR function is performing and changing, as well as how it is being driven by companies' strategies.

Management Approaches

The management approach that organizations take varies widely and should influence what the HR function can and should do. In the 2007, 2010, 2013, and 2016 surveys, we asked the respondents how much their company used these five management approaches:

- *Bureaucratic*: hierarchical structure, tight job description, top-down decision making

- *Low-cost operator*: low wages, minimum benefits, focus on cost reduction and controls

- *High involvement*: flat structure, participative decisions, commitment to employee development and careers

- *Global competitor*: complex, interesting work; best talent; low commitment to employee development and careers

- *Sustainable*: agile design, focus on financial performance and sustainability

The first four of these approaches are described in more detail in O'Toole and Lawler (2006). The fifth, sustainable management, is fully described by Lawler and Worley (2011). As can be seen in table 1.3, sustainable management is the most frequently used in the U.S. companies studied, followed by high involvement. These results most likely are due to changes in the business environment as more and more organizations compete globally based on their talent and experience demands for sustainable performance.

The results from our international sample for 2016, shown in table 1.4, are similar to those of the United States: the majority of the companies in our international sample use the sustainable approach the most and the low-cost-operator approach the least.

In previous surveys, China was a noticeable outlier. In 2010 and 2013, it used the low-cost-operator and bureaucratic approaches the most and the high-involvement approach the least in comparison to the other countries. It was a relatively low user of the global competitor approach. The most obvious explanation for the tendency of China to use different management approaches was its level of economic and management development. The results for 2016 show that China is more similar to other countries, perhaps a result of the globalization of Chinese companies.

Table 1.3. Management approaches, United States

To what extent do the following approaches describe how your organization is managed?	2016 Percentages					Means			
	Little or No Extent	Some Extent	Moderate Extent	Great Extent	Very Great Extent	2007[1]	2010[2]	2013[3]	2016[4]
Bureaucratic (hierarchical structure, tight job descriptions, top-down decision making)	14.9	32.5	28.1	19.3	5.3	2.66	2.82	2.77	2.68
Low-cost operator (low wages, minimum benefits, focus on cost reduction and controls)	29.2	34.5	23.0	10.6	2.7	2.07	2.02	2.22	2.23
High involvement (flat structure, participative decisions, commitment to employee development and careers)	10.6	23.9	29.2	30.1	6.2	3.04	3.05	2.92	2.97
Global competitor (complex, interesting work; best talent; low commitment to employee development and careers)	23.0	23.0	28.3	20.4	5.3	2.55	2.66	2.94	2.62
Sustainable (agile design, focus on financial performance and sustainability)	3.5	15.0	36.3	39.8	5.3	—	3.33	3.24	3.28

Note: The empty cell signifies that the item was not asked in that year.

No significant differences between years ($p \le .05$).

Table 1.4. Management approaches, by country

To what extent do the following approaches describe how your organization is managed?	Means				
	United States[1]	Canada[2]	Australia[3]	United Kingdom/ Europe[4]	China[5]
Bureaucratic (hierarchical structure, tight job descriptions, top-down decision making)	2.7[3]	2.9[3]	3.7[1,2,4,5]	2.9[3]	3.0[3]
Low-cost operator (low wages, minimum benefits, focus on cost reduction and controls)	2.2	1.8[3,5]	2.6[2]	1.9	2.4[2]
High involvement (flat structure, participative decisions, commitment to employee development and careers)	3.0[3]	3.0[3]	2.2[1,2,4,5]	3.1[3]	3.0[3]
Global competitor (complex, interesting work; hire best talent; low commitment to employee development and careers)	2.6	2.3	2.0[4]	2.9[3]	2.5
Sustainable (agile design, focus on financial performance and sustainability)	3.3[3]	3.3	2.6[1,4]	3.5[3]	3.0

Response scale: 1 = little or no extent; 2 = some extent; 3 = moderate extent; 4 = great extent; 5 = very great extent.

[1,2,3,4,5]Significant differences between countries ($p \le .05$).

The results from Australia are surprisingly different from those obtained in 2013 when they were very much like the results from other developed countries in 2013. The results in 2016 show it to be different, with the bureaucratic approach dominating. Again, an explanation may be that the 2016 Australian sample included fewer large global corporations.

Throughout this book, we look at how U.S. corporations that use these five approaches operate. They do not include all possible management approaches, and we do not believe that any company is managed in one way. We use them because they provide a way to identify the overall management approach that large corporations take and how HR practices are related to the way a company is managed. Picking the right approach to management and then implementing it effectively are opportunities for the HR function to add significant value.

Nature of Work

The world of work is changing in where it is done, who does it, and how it is done and rewarded. As a result, the traditional model of work and employment is becoming less and less dominant.

Table 1.5 presents 2016 data on how prevalent some alternative approaches to organizing and getting work done are. Although none of them are dominant, the data show that the traditional employment model, which is based on full-time employees coming to a workplace and being rewarded by a standard package of benefits and cash, is far from universal. Between 10 and 33 percent of organizations report that they use each of the alternative work design and reward system approaches for over 40 percent of their work. Over 50 percent report that over 21 percent of the work in their organization is done by other than full-time employees. Sixty-five percent report that over 20 percent of their work is location and time dependent. This means HR must increasingly support organizations that are managing and trying to optimizing multiple work relationships (Boudreau et al. 2015).

The international data for nontraditional work arrangements are presented in table 1.6. All the countries except China are similar. China HR leaders report the greatest use of alternative designs. Many social, governmental, and economic differences that separate China from other

Table 1.5. Type of work, United States						
	Proportion of Work					
What proportion of the work in your organization is:	0%–20%	21%–40%	41%–60%	61%–80%	81%–100%	Means
Designed as projects and tasks that are done by other than traditional employees?	46.2	33.0	11.3	8.5	0.9	1.85
Location and time flexible rather than limited to a particular place and time?	35.8	31.1	19.8	10.4	2.8	2.13
Detached from the traditional employment relationship through, for example, contracts and platforms?	65.1	24.5	7.5	1.9	0.9	1.49
Carried out through collaborations and connections that cross your organizational boundary—for example, alliances and borrowing and loaning talent from other organizations?	64.2	16.0	12.3	7.5	0.0	1.63
Rewarded immediately on task completion, rather than on a traditional periodic or calendar basis?	70.8	14.2	10.4	2.8	1.9	1.51
Rewarded in an individualized way, rather than by similar rewards for all employees?	46.2	24.5	16.0	10.4	2.8	1.99
Rewarded with elements, beyond the traditional rewards of, for example, money, benefits, stocks, recognition?	59.0	21.0	8.6	9.5	1.9	1.74

Table 1.6. Type of work, by country					
	Means				
What proportion of the work in your organization is:	**United States[1]**	**Canada[2]**	**Australia[3]**	**United Kingdom/ Europe[4]**	**China[5]**
Designed as projects and tasks that are done by other than traditional employees?	1.8[5]	1.5[5]	1.9	1.7[5]	2.5[1,2,4]
Location and time flexible, rather than limited to a particular place and time?	2.1	1.9	2.1	2.3	2.3
Detached from the traditional employment relationship—for example, through contracts and platforms?	1.5[5]	1.3[5]	1.7	1.5[5]	2.1[1,2,4]
Carried out through collaborations and connections that cross your organizational boundary, such as alliances and borrowing and loaning talent from other organizations?	1.6[5]	1.2[5]	1.7[5]	1.7	2.3[1,2,3]
Rewarded immediately on task completion, rather than on a traditional periodic or calendar basis?	1.5[5]	1.2[5]	1.5[5]	1.2[5]	2.4[1,2,3,4]
Rewarded in an individualized way, rather than by similar rewards for all employees?	2.0[5]	2.3	1.8[5]	1.7[5]	2.6[1,3,4]
Rewarded with elements, beyond the traditional rewards of, for example, money, benefits, stocks, recognition?	1.7[5]	1.3[5]	1.7[5]	1.5[5]	2.3[1,2,3,4]

Response scale: 1 = 0%–20%; 2 = 21%–40%; 3 = 41%–60%; 4 = 61%–80%; 5 = 81%–100%.

[1,2,3,4,5]Significant differences between countries ($p \leq .05$).

countries undoubtedly have created this difference. It is striking that China is apparently already using work arrangements that other countries have started using only recently.

Organizational Design

Organizational design is a key factor in enabling organizations to develop capabilities and perform in ways that produce a competitive advantage. Organizational design is more than structure; it includes elements such as management processes, rewards, people systems, information systems, and work processes (Galbraith 2014). These elements must fit with the strategy and with each other in order for an organization to perform effectively.

Organizational designs involve complex trade-offs and contingencies. Clearly no single design approach fits all organizations. As new business models emerge—complex partnerships, globally integrated firms, customer-focused designs, and network organizations—new approaches and organizational forms need to be created to deal with the complex performance requirements that organizations must address. Furthermore, multibusiness corporations are recognizing that different businesses exist in different markets and face varying requirements. Consequently, variation in organizational design is increasing both within multibusiness corporations and between businesses (Galbraith

2014). Thus, for companies and HR functions, one size does not fit all situations. Different organizational forms require different HR contributions, and thus different HR functional designs and systems.

Contributing to effective organizational design is a major domain in which the HR function has the opportunity to add strategic value (Lawler 2008, 2017). Increasingly, the only sustainable competitive advantage is the ability to organize effectively, respond to change, and manage well (Mohrman, Galbraith, Lawler, and Associates 1998; Lawler and Worley 2006; Worley et al. 2014). Confirmation of this statement is provided by Lawler, Mohrman, and Benson's (2001) longitudinal study of the Fortune 1000, which shows a significant relationship between firm financial performance and the adoption of new management practices designed to increase a firm's capabilities. Further confirmation of this is provided by data showing that agile firms outperform all others over the long term (Worley et al. 2014).

Design of the HR Function

All parts of organizations—operating units and staff functions alike—need to be designed to deliver high value. For staff groups, this requires the development of a business model—a value proposition defining what kind of value they will deliver that the company is willing to pay for because their work strengthens company performance. It also requires them to determine how best to deliver their services.

The HR function must think about whether the elements of its design indeed create a high-performance organization—one capable of delivering maximum value while consuming the fewest possible resources. That means concentrating on the way HR organizes to deliver routine transactions services, traditional HR systems development and administration, and strategic business support.

HR must develop structures, competencies, customer linkages, metrics, management processes, rewards, and information technology to ensure that scarce resources are optimally deployed to deliver value. In addition to making sure its function is optimally designed, HR can add value by helping design the key features of the rest of the organization.

In many respects, it is useful to think of HR functions as multiple product businesses. They have customers, products and services, revenue, and competitors (self-service vendors and consulting firms). In order to exist, they need to perform in a way that makes them the "best buy."

Organizational design decisions for HR, as well as for companies as a whole, are made in response to four key questions:

- *Which activities should be centralized and leveraged, and which should be decentralized in order to provide focus on the unique needs of different parts of the organization?* Organizations are combining centralization and decentralization, trying to be big (coordinated) in functions such as purchasing when there is an advantage to being big and small (decentralized and flexible) in functions such as new product development when there are advantages to being small and agile.

- *Which functions should be performed in-house and which should be outsourced?* Companies should outsource when they can purchase high-quality services and products more inexpensively or reliably than they can generate internally.

- *Which functions should be hierarchically controlled, and which should be integrated and controlled laterally?* In some areas, organizations function in a lateral manner, integrating and creating synergies across various parts of the organization, creating cross-functional units to carry out entire processes, and collaborating with suppliers and customers. Organizations are searching for ways to leverage across business units while setting up organizational and management approaches that give the optimal levels of flexibility and control to various business units.

- *Which processes should be automated?* Increasing amounts of HR work (like the work of other disciplines) can use automation and artificial intelligence to enhance or even substitute for human workers, but what is it advantageous to have them do?

Traditionally HR (and many other staff groups such as information technology) has been organized in a hierarchical manner, and it has seen its mission as designing, administering, and enforcing adherence to HR policies and systems. As a result, all too often HR has been seen as an expensive and necessary evil that consumes resources disproportionate to the value that it adds to the organization. A number of changes in structure and process are being advocated for HR:

- Decentralizing business support to operating units in order to increase responsiveness

- Contracting with business units for the services that are to be delivered, and perhaps even requiring services to be self-funding as a way of ensuring that businesses get only the services that they are willing to pay for and that they see as contributing to business performance

- Creating efficient central services units or outsourcing transactional services, or both

- Creating centers of excellence that provide expert services, often in a consulting capacity

- Increasing the rotation of people within various staff functions and between staff and line, and having fewer lifelong careers within a narrow staff function, in order to broaden the perspectives of HR staff professionals and increase their awareness of business issues, as well as the depth of understanding of HR issues among line management

- Expanding the scope of the HR function to include communications and sustainability, to mention just two areas

Conclusion

The future of the HR function in organizations is uncertain (Boudreau 2016). On the one hand, if it does not change, it could end up being largely an administrative function that manages an information technology–based HR system and vendors who do most of the HR administrative work. On the other hand, it could become a driver of organizational effectiveness and business strategy. In many organizations, one of the key determinants of competitive advantage is effective human capital management. More than ever before, the effectiveness of an organization depends on its ability to address issues such as knowledge management, change management, and capability building, which could fall into the domain of the HR function. The unanswered question at this point is whether HR will rise to the occasion and address these issues.

In order to increase its contribution to organizational effectiveness, HR must rethink its basic value proposition, structure, services, and programs in order to address how it can add value in today's economy with new organizational forms, business strategies, and performance demands. It faces a formidable challenge in helping organizations deal with the human issues that are raised by large-scale strategic change. To deal with these challenges effectively, HR has to focus on how it is organized and its competencies and role in business strategy.

There is some evidence that the situation of HR is changing and that the function is beginning to redefine its role in order to increase the value it adds. Data collected in 1995, 1998, 2001, 2004, 2007, 2010, and 2013 found evidence of some change in large U.S. corporations, but there has been more talk of change than actual change (Lawler and Boudreau 2015). If this is true in the 2016 results examined in this book, it will be additional evidence that HR is not doing what it needs to do in order to be a key contributor to organizational effectiveness.

CHAPTER 2

What HR Does

- HR spends the majority of its time on services, controlling, and record keeping.

- How HR spends its time has not significantly changed since 1995.

- HR executives say that in the past, they spent more time on services, controlling, and record keeping than they do currently, but data from earlier surveys do not support this claim.

- HR is most likely to help boards in the United States and the United Kingdom/Europe with executive compensation and succession planning.

- Providing support to boards is clearly an area where HR could do more.

- HR in the United States and Europe gives the most help to its boards. The least is given in Australia.

- HR provides boards with little help on sustainability and board effectiveness.

- What HR does is related to the organization's management approach. For example, bureaucratic organizations have HR functions that spend more time on services, controlling, and record keeping.

- In contrast to prior surveys, the Chinese sample of HR leaders reported spending their time like all other countries studied.

A key issue for HR functions is how they divide their time between providing services and doing higher value-added business partner and strategic work such as working with boards. A major criticism of HR functions for decades has been that they are bogged down in administration and policing and as a result do not do the much-needed strategic talent management and organizational effectiveness work. The results of our previous surveys support this conclusion. They have consistently shown that HR functions spend over 50 percent of their time on service provision, auditing, and maintaining records.

Time Allocation

As with our previous surveys, respondents were asked to estimate the percentage of time that their HR function currently spends in carrying out five roles and how much time they spent on them five to seven years ago. Figure 2.1 shows that the U.S. respondents report the function currently spends the most time on service provision and as a strategic business partner. When the time spent on service provision is combined with the time spent on records and auditing/controlling, respondents report that 51 percent of their time is currently spent on administration and services.

The responses from Canada, Australia, United Kingdom/Europe, and China are very similar to the U.S. responses. The data from them in table 2.1 show only small differences among these countries and in comparison to the United States. The results for China show a much more

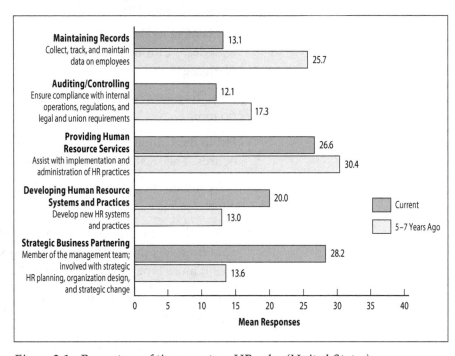

Figure 2.1. Percentage of time spent on HR roles (United States)

Table 2.1. Mean percentage of current time spent on various HR roles, by country					
HR Roles	United States[1]	Canada[2]	Australia[3]	United Kingdom/ Europe[4]	China[5]
Maintaining records: Collect, track, and maintain data on employees	13.1[3,5]	15.3	21.0[1]	16.7	19.3[1]
Auditing/controlling: Ensure compliance with internal operations, regulations, and legal and union requirements	12.1[5]	10.7[5]	13.7[5]	11.9[5]	17.9[1,2,3,4]
HR service provider: Assist with implementation and administration of HR practices	26.6	29.0	26.2	21.4	25.4
Development of HR systems and practices: Develop new HR systems and practices	20.0	18.3	17.2	17.2	17.4
Strategic business partner: Member of the management team; involved with strategic HR planning, organizational design, and strategic change	28.2[5]	26.7	22.0[4]	32.8[3,5]	20.0[1,4]
[1,2,3,4,5]Significant differences between countries ($p \leq .05$).					

similar pattern to that of the other countries than they have in the past. This may reflect the changing economic and political development in China, which perhaps is becoming more similar to Western countries. The China sample spent somewhat more time on auditing/controlling and somewhat less time providing services than the other countries.

When asked to look back and consider what HR's time allocation in their organizations was five to seven years ago, U.S. HR executives report a significant change in how their function's time is spent. A comparison between tables 2.1 and 2.2 shows that they now spend less time (52 percent versus 73 percent) on record keeping, auditing, and service provision and more time (27 percent versus 48 percent) on developing new HR systems and practices and being a strategic business contributor.

Our results from the other countries are very similar to those from the United States with respect to how they say HR spent its time five to seven years ago. A comparison between tables 2.1 and 2.2 shows that in all countries, HR leaders believe the time spent on strategy has increased over the previous five to seven years.

Before we conclude that this has actually occurred, it is important to compare the results for the United States from 1995, 1998, 2001, 2004, 2007, 2010, and 2013 with those from 2016. The U.S. data from the six earlier surveys are very similar to those collected in 2016 (see tables 2.3 and 2.4). There is no significant change in the responses to the question asking how time is spent now or in response to the question asking how time was spent five to seven years ago. In other words, there has been no major change in any of the responses about how time is spent from the 1995 study to the 2016 study. This raises serious questions about the validity of the reports by our respondents about the past.

HR Roles	United States[1]	Canada[2]	Australia[3]	United Kingdom/ Europe[4]	China[5]
Maintaining records: Collect, track, and maintain data on employees	25.7	22.4	33.0	26.6	26.6
Auditing/controlling: Ensure compliance with internal operations, regulations, and legal and union requirements	17.3[4]	14.4[5]	19.0[4]	11.5[1,3,5]	20.3[2,4]
HR service provider: Assist with implementation and administration of HR practices	30.4[5]	37.0[3,5]	24.3[2]	28.5	24.6[1,2]
Development of HR systems and practices: Develop new HR systems and practices	13.0	12.6	12.5	12.8	14.0
Strategic business partner: Member of the management team; involved with strategic HR planning, organizational design, and strategic change	13.6[4]	13.7	11.2[4]	20.6[1,3]	14.6

Table 2.2. Mean percentage of time spent five to seven years ago on various HR roles, by country

[1,2,3,4,5]Significant differences between countries ($p \leq .05$).

Table 2.3. Percentage of current time spent on various HR roles, United States

HR Roles	Means							
	1995[1]	1998[2]	2001[3]	2004[4]	2007[5]	2010[6]	2013[7]	2016[8]
Maintaining records: Collect, track, and maintain data on employees	15.4	16.1	14.9	13.2	15.8	13.6	15.2	13.1
Auditing/controlling: Ensure compliance with internal operations, regulations, and legal and union requirements	12.2	11.2	11.4	13.3	11.6	12.5	13.0	12.1
HR service provider: Assist with implementation and administration of HR practices	31.3[7]	35.0[5,7,8]	31.3[7]	32.0[7]	27.8[2]	30.4	25.7[1,2,3,4]	26.6[2]
Development of HR systems and practices: Develop new HR systems and practices	18.6	19.2	19.3	18.1	19.2	16.7[8]	19.0	20.0[6]
Strategic business partner: Member of the management team; involved with strategic HR planning, organizational design, and strategic change	22.0[8]	20.3[6,7,8]	23.2	23.5	25.6	26.8[2]	27.1[2]	28.2[1,2]

[1,2,3,4,5,6,7,8]Significant differences between years ($p \leq .05$).

Table 2.4. Percentage of time spent five to seven years ago on various HR roles, United States

HR Roles	Means							
	1995[1]	1998[2]	2001[3]	2004[4]	2007[5]	2010[6]	2013[7]	2016[8]
Maintaining records: Collect, track, and maintain data on employees	23.0	25.6	26.7	25.9	26.3	23.2	26.8	25.7
Auditing/controlling: Ensure compliance with internal operations, regulations, and legal and union requirements	19.5[4,5,6]	16.4	17.1	14.8[1]	15.2[1]	15.7[1]	17.2	17.3
HR service provider: Assist with implementation and administration of HR practices	34.3	36.4[7]	33.1	36.4[7]	33.0	32.8	28.6[2,4]	30.4
Development of HR systems and practices: Develop new HR systems and practices	14.3	14.2	13.9	12.6	13.5	14.4	13.2	13.0
Strategic business partner: Member of the management team; involved with strategic HR planning, organizational design, and strategic change	10.3	9.4[6,7]	9.1[6,7,8]	9.6[7]	12.1	13.9[2,3]	14.2[2,3,4]	13.6[3]

[1,2,3,4,5,6,7,8] Significant differences between years ($p \leq .05$).

It might be expected that the 2016 estimates of how things were five to seven years earlier would be somewhat in line with how things were said to be in our 2013 study, and especially in our 2010 study (six years ago), but they are not. Instead, rather than showing a change in time spent, the 1995, 1998, 2001, 2004, 2007, 2010, and 2013 results for how time is spent are the same as the results for 2016. This finding suggests that the HR executives who responded in 2016, as well as those who responded in those previous surveys, may have perceived more change in their organization than has actually taken place. In short, they may be guilty of wishful thinking and a selective memory.

What should we believe: Retrospective reports of the way things were or data from the past about the way things were at the time the data were collected? The answer is obvious: most individuals are much better at reporting how things are now than about what they were like years ago. Reports concerning the past often include changes that reflect favorably on the individual and what should have happened. In this case, it is possible that HR executives want to see themselves and their function as more of a strategic contributor now than they were in the past. This is quite likely, given the many books and articles that have called for this to happen and the advantages it offers those in the HR profession.

The stubborn lack of change in the reports of how time is spent is surprising and concerning: the results from 1995 are almost identical to those from 2016. As we stated in chapter 1, the world of work, organizations, and business has changed dramatically since 1995. Thus, it is surprising, even shocking, that how HR spends its time has not changed. Each time we have done our survey, we have expected to see some change in how HR spends its time, but no sign of change has appeared. The lack of change in HR despite massive social and economic changes makes us wonder whether anything can cause HR to spend more time on being a strategic contributor to organizational effectiveness.

It is worth noting that there is one explanation for the lack of change in the reports of how HR spends its time that suggests some progress. HR executives may have gained a much better understanding of what is involved in being a strategic contributor. As a result of their developing this understanding, they are setting a higher standard for what constitutes strategic work. If this raising of the bar is true, it could be that HR is doing more strategic partner work though it does not report any change in time allocation.

It is not too surprising that HR continues to report it has changed given the many calls for it to change, even though it may not have. We have seen this pattern recalling great change when in fact the data suggest no change occurred in each of our previous surveys. It raises the question of whether it indicates that HR executives believe they have made progress toward an objective they feel is important when in fact they have not. There is reason to believe that the need for accelerated change may not be totally lost on HR leaders. In fact, the Global Consortium to Reimagine HR, Employment Alternatives, Talent, and the Enterprise (CHREATE), which brought together over fifty chief HR officers and other thought leaders to look at the future of HR, revealed a common belief that the HR profession must disruptively accelerate to meet emerging challenges (Boudreau 2016).

Strategic Focuses

The relationships between the strategic focuses of an organization and how HR spends its time are shown in table 2.5. The correlations in the table show a clear pattern: maintaining records and auditing/controlling are negatively related to all the strategic focuses except growth, and the negative relationships for information-based and knowledge-based strategies and for innovation are statistically significant. We found similar results in our 2004, 2007, 2010, and 2013 studies. Apparently the weaker an organization's strategic focus on these areas is, the more the HR function spends its time maintaining records and auditing/controlling. Given the lack of a strategic focus, this may be the best way HR can spend its time in these organizations.

The time that the HR function spends on strategic business activities is positively related to three of the strategic focuses. Time spent on developing HR systems is positive but not significantly related to all five strategic focuses. Although the relationships are not strong, this finding suggests that HR becomes much more involved in strategic business activities when the organization has a strong strategic focus, regardless of what that focus is. This is supported by the strong relationship between the three strategic focuses (information, knowledge, and innovation) and HR's role as a strategic business partner. One implication of this finding is that in order for HR to become more strategic, organizations must strengthen their strategic focuses. One way for this to happen is for HR to provide leadership to the rest of the organization in becoming more strategic. If it can accomplish this, we believe there is a good chance that HR will spend more time on strategy and the development of HR systems that support their organizational strategy and less time on recording and auditing.

Table 2.5. Relationship of HR roles to strategic focuses, United States					
	Strategic Focuses				
HR Roles	**Growth**	**Information-Based Strategies**	**Knowledge-Based Strategies**	**Sustainability**	**Innovation**
Maintaining records	−.02	−.24*	−.32***	−.13	−.29**
Auditing/controlling	−.11	−.23*	−.14	−.10	−.22*
HR service provider	−.02	−.10	−.08	.10	−.01
Development of HR systems and practices	.18ᵗ	.06	.10	.04	.04
Strategic business partner	−.02	.31***	.28**	.02	.28**
Significance level: ᵗ$p \leq .10$, *$p \leq .05$, **$p \leq .01$, ***$p \leq .001$.					

Management Approaches

The management approach that organizations take has significant relationships to how HR spends its time. As shown in table 2.6, taking the bureaucratic approach is associated with spending significantly more time maintaining records and significantly less time developing HR systems and practices As might be expected, strategic business partnering is significantly higher in high-involvement organizations and maintaining records is significantly lower. The same pattern exists for sustainable management organizations, although the relationships are weaker. These results reinforce the point that what HR does is at least partially determined by the way an organization is managed: bureaucratic organizations, for example, have bureaucratic HR functions.

Board Help

HR expertise and information are critical to many of the issues that corporate boards deal with. They range from executive compensation to talent management and organizational effectiveness. When they face such issues, do boards call on HR? If they do, HR at least has a part-time seat at the most important decision-making table in the organization. If they do not, it is hard to see how HR can play a significant role with respect to many of the key strategic decisions that organizations make.

Table 2.7 shows the responses to a question about the type of help HR gives to boards in U.S. firms. The question was first asked in 2004, so there are data from 2004, 2007, 2010, 2013, and 2016. Executive compensation and succession have been and continue to be the two issues on which HR is most likely to be asked for help in U.S. corporations. This finding is not surprising, given that these are areas where HR functions traditionally should be able to provide help and where board members are likely to see HR as knowledgeable and a source of help.

Table 2.6. Relationship of HR roles to management approaches, United States					
	Management Approaches				
HR Roles	**Bureaucratic**	**Low-Cost Operator**	**High Involvement**	**Global Competitor**	**Sustainable**
Maintaining records	.37***	.14	−.45***	−.08	−.26**
Auditing/controlling	.11	.12	−.20*	−.07	−.21*
HR service provider	−.04	−.07	.02	.09	.12
Development of HR systems and practices	−.18^t	.01	.10	.07	.09
Strategic business partner	−.14	−.10	.31***	−.04	.10
Significance level: $^t p \leq .10$, *$p \leq .05$, **$p \leq .01$, ***$p \leq .001$.					

Table 2.7. HR extent of help to boards, United States										
	2016 Percentages					Means				
HR Extent of Help	Little or No Extent	Some Extent	Moderate Extent	Great Extent	Very Great Extent	2004[1]	2007[2]	2010[3]	2013[4]	2016[5]
Executive compensation	6.4	8.3	8.3	27.5	49.5	4.2	4.1	3.9	4.3	4.1
Addressing strategic readiness	18.3	14.7	30.3	26.6	10.1	2.8	2.8	2.8	2.8	3.0
Executive succession	6.4	6.4	19.3	22.9	45.0	3.8	3.8	3.7	4.0	3.9
Change consulting	17.4	19.3	29.4	22.9	11.0	2.6	2.7	2.6	2.7	2.9
Developing board effectiveness/corporate governance	31.2	14.7	29.4	22.0	2.8	2.5	2.5	2.2	2.4	2.5
Risk assessment	15.6	15.6	40.4	22.0	6.4	2.4[5]	2.6	2.6	2.6	2.9[1]
Information about the condition or capability of the workforce	9.2	12.8	22.0	33.9	22.0	3.3	3.3	3.2	3.0[5]	3.5[4]
Board compensation	23.9	15.6	17.4	18.3	24.8	3.4[3]	3.0	2.8[1,4]	3.2[3]	3.0
Sustainability	36.7	13.8	27.5	15.6	6.4	—	—	—	2.4	2.4

Note: Empty cells indicate that the item was not asked in that year.

[1,2,3,4,5]Significant differences between years ($p \le .05$).

It is disappointing to find that the organizational effectiveness issues of change consulting and strategic readiness receive such low ratings. These areas have average ratings at or below "asking for help to a moderate extent" (3.0). Particularly low are help with board effectiveness and sustainability.

There is positive news in the fact that "providing information about the condition or capability of the workforce" is the third most requested area and shows a significant increase from 2013 to 2016. This is an area where HR should have good information. It is also a critical organizational performance determinant and thus an area where a high rating is warranted. If HR performs well in areas like it and executive succession, it may well be asked for help in executing change and strategic readiness. So far, this does not seem to be happening. A comparison of the 2004, 2007, 2010, and 2013 results reveals few significant changes in these areas. In comparison to 2013, the 2016 data show significantly more use of HR with respect to workforce conditions. Overall, it is clear that in most companies, HR has its foot in the boardroom door, but that is all, and there is little evidence that this will change despite the accelerating rate of change in the nature of work and organizations.

International Results

The data from the other countries in the study (see table 2.8) are in general similar to the U.S. data, but with some interesting differences. This is not surprising since all of the countries have different board

Table 2.8. HR extent of help to boards, by country					
	Means				
HR Extent of Help	United States[1]	Canada[2]	Australia[3]	United Kingdom/ Europe[4]	China[5]
Executive compensation	4.1[3,5]	3.9[3]	2.7[1,2,4]	4.3[3,5]	3.3[1,4]
Addressing strategic readiness	3.0	2.9	2.6	3.3	2.9
Executive succession	3.9[3,5]	3.5[3]	2.4[1,2,4]	4.2[3,5]	3.0[1,4]
Change consulting	2.9[4]	2.8	2.9	3.5[1,5]	2.9[4]
Developing board effectiveness/ corporate governance	2.5	2.2[4]	2.1[4]	3.1[2,3]	2.7
Risk assessment	2.9	2.8	2.6	3.2	2.8
Information about the condition/ capability of the workforce	3.5	3.2	3.1	3.8	3.3
Board compensation	3.0[3]	2.3[4]	1.8[1,4,5]	3.5[2,3]	2.8[3]
Sustainability	2.4[4]	2.2[4]	2.0[4,5]	3.0[1,2,3]	2.8[3]

Response scale: 1 = little or no extent; 2 = some extent; 3 = moderate extent; 4 = great extent; 5 = very great extent.
[1,2,3,4,5]Significant differences between countries ($p \leq .05$).

structures and are subject to different regulations and laws. If anything is a surprise, it is that the differences among the developed countries are not greater. Boards in the United States and Canada seem to ask for the least help specifically with organizational development. Generally, across all of the areas, Chinese and Australian boards are rated as asking for the least help.

It is not surprising that the results from China are different. The Chinese sample includes government-owned firms, so it is somewhat surprising that the differences are not larger. Still, three differences stand out: corporate boards in China ask for less help with executive compensation, succession, and board compensation. This is in part due to the fact that these are the three areas where U.S. boards ask for a great deal of help. U.S. boards have evolved to expect HR help, but Chinese boards have not yet shown that expectation, even in these traditional HR strongholds. It seems quite likely that the different labor markets that U.S. and Chinese firms face, as well as the history of board governance in the two countries, accounts for this difference.

Strategic Focuses

The relationship between the help provided to the board and the strategic focuses of organizations is shown in table 2.9. When strategies have a more direct relationship to human capital, including knowledge-based, information-based, sustainability, and innovation strategies, boards ask

Table 2.9. Relationship of strategic focuses to board help, United States					
HR Extent of Help[a]	**Strategic Focuses**				
	Growth	**Information-Based Strategies**	**Knowledge-Based Strategies**	**Sustainability**	**Innovation**
Executive compensation	.18[t]	.13	.34***	.12	.19*
Addressing strategic readiness	.06	.35***	.45***	.28**	.36***
Executive succession	.16[t]	.29**	.42***	.11	.27**
Change consulting	.08	.31***	.48***	.24*	.22*
Developing board effectiveness/corporate governance	.05	.20*	.29**	.33***	.12
Risk assessment	.00	.24*	.42***	.38***	.30***
Information about the condition/capability of the workforce	.08	.32***	.50***	.32***	.37***
Board compensation	.14	.11	.29**	.21*	.12
Sustainability	.15	.22*	.40***	.57***	.24*

[a]Response scale: 1 = little or no extent; 2 = some extent; 3 = moderate extent; 4 = great extent; 5 = very great extent. Significance level: $^{t}p \leq .10$, $^{*}p \leq .05$, $^{**}p \leq .01$, $^{***}p \leq .001$.

for help in these areas. Somewhat surprisingly, the lowest relationships are with growth. Overall, it seems that boards with a strong organizational effectiveness–driven strategy are high users of HR help.

The use of HR help for board compensation shows the weakest relationships to many of the strategic focuses, probably because all organizations, regardless of strategy, typically need support with board compensation. Help with information on workforce readiness is strongly related to four of the focuses. Also strongly related are strategic readiness, succession, change consulting, risk assessment, and sustainability, a result that likely reflects the close connection between these strategies and workforce performance issues. Not all of the relationships are strong, but it does seem that the more an organization has a strategic focus other than growth, the more likely its board is to rely on help from HR.

Management Approaches

Table 2.10 shows the relationship between management approaches and board help. The strongest relationships are with the high-involvement approach, the sustainable approach, and the low-cost-operator approach. The more that the high-involvement and sustainable approaches to management are used, the more active HR is with the board. This finding makes good sense and reinforces the point that when organizations take talent seriously as a source of competitive advantage, HR organizations

Table 2.10. Relationship of management approaches to board help, United States					
	Management Approaches				
HR Extent of Help[a]	**Bureaucratic**	**Low-Cost Operator**	**High Involvement**	**Global Competitor**	**Sustainable**
Executive compensation	−.03	−.07	.21*	.28**	.19*
Addressing strategic readiness	−.07	−.08	.31***	.14	.28**
Executive succession	−.03	−.09	.20*	.24*	.17^t
Change consulting	−.05	−.26**	.30**	.04	.28**
Developing board effectiveness/corporate governance	.10	−.13	.21*	.11	.22*
Risk assessment	.01	−.11	.26**	.08	.26**
Information about the condition/capability of the workforce	−.02	−.24*	.29**	.16^t	.20*
Board compensation	.15	−.25**	.14	.17^t	.10
Sustainability	.04	−.19*	.32***	.14	.37***

[a]Response scale: 1 = little or no extent; 2 = some extent; 3 = moderate extent; 4 = great extent; 5 = very great extent. Significance level: $^t p \leq .10$, *$p \leq .05$, **$p \leq .01$, ***$p \leq .001$.

can and do play a more important role (Lawler 2008, 2017). Also supporting this conclusion are the many negative relationships between the bureaucratic and the low-cost-operator approaches and how active HR is with the board. This finding probably reflects the fact that these approaches focus on cost and compliance more than talent development and management. Overall, in organizations pursuing bureaucratic or low-cost operator strategies, there appears to be a significant headwind against HR being asked to help the board.

Conclusion

HR has not significantly changed how it allocates its time since we began this research in 1995. In all of the countries we studied, it remains a function that spends the majority of its time on services, controlling, and record keeping. HR executives have consistently reported that they spend more time providing strategic services than they did five to seven years ago, but our longitudinal data do not support that conclusion. Our data on management approaches and strategy provide one likely reason why there has not been much change: the management approaches and strategies that call for changes in how HR operates are only now gaining market share.

HR has a limited role when it comes to supporting boards. Its major support areas are executive compensation and succession. In most areas, its level of support has not changed. An organization's management approach has a strong relationship to the overall level of support HR provides to boards. That support is highest in high-involvement and sustainable management organizations and low in bureaucratic and low-cost-operator organizations. Providing support to boards is clearly an area where HR could do more. There is little doubt that if it did more with boards, HR could play a larger role in formulating and implementing business strategies and determining organizational performance. The key question at this point is what it needs to do in order to do more.

Our findings that HR has not changed how it spends its time and that it spends relatively little time on strategy and board support make it particularly important that throughout this book, we focus on HR's strategic role. We need to establish what it can and should be. We also need to determine what changes are needed in order to make change happen and what the advantages are when HR performs a more strategic role.

CHAPTER 3

The Strategic Role of HR

- In most U.S. organizations, HR is a full partner in or has an input role to business strategy. This is a significant change from 2013.

- HR plays a larger role in strategy when organizations have a strong strategic focus and practice high-involvement management and sustainable management.

- HR's strategy activities typically involve organizational diagnosis and change rather than strategic direction decisions (mergers, new business, options, and choices).

- HR does not have a major role in most organizations' sustainability activities.

- HR executives believe that sustainability should be built into HR processes such as selection and training, but they report that in their organization it is not.

- HR executives report that HR should be much more active in the design of sustainability programs.

- The more HR is involved in sustainability activities, the larger is its role in corporate strategy.

- HR's strategy activity is related to its strategic role but not to organizational performance.

The involvement that an organization's HR function has in the development and implementation of strategy—how much and what kind—is a critical determinant of its influence and the value it adds. There is a growing consensus among executives and researchers that human capital needs to be given more and better-informed consideration because it should be an important determinant of what strategies an organization can and should pursue (Boudreau 2010; Cascio and Boudreau 2012; Cascio, Boudreau, and Church, 2017; Lawler 2008, 2017). It also should be a key determinant of how a strategy is pursued.

Types of Involvement

HR's involvement in business strategy can take a variety of forms. Figure 3.1 shows that in 2013 and 2016, virtually all HR functions reported involvement in business strategy. However, in over 59 percent of the companies studied, HR is less than a full partner in the eyes of their HR executives and managers. When the 2013 data are compared to those of 1998, 2001, 2004, 2007, and 2010, there is no statistically

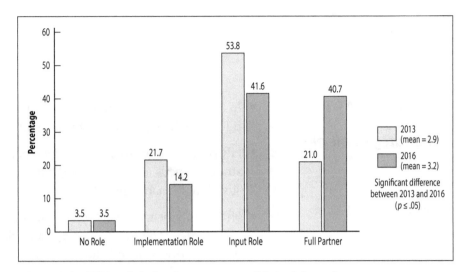

Figure 3.1. HR's role in business strategy (United States)

significant change in the extent to which HR reports being involved in business strategy (see Lawler and Boudreau 2012 for data from 1998 to 2010). However, the 2016 results show a significant increase in the number of organizations where HR is a full partner. Thus, the data suggest that the HR function is becoming more of a strategic partner in more organizations, though still is not in most.

International Results

The international data in table 3.1 show that results from Canada and the United Kingdom/Europe are similar to those in the United States in that HR typically has an input role or acts as a full partner. Canada and the United Kingdom/Europe report slightly less frequently having no role or an implementation role. As in prior surveys, China is different from the United States, Canada, and the United Kingdom/Europe: it reports acting as a full partner far less frequently and having the other three roles somewhat more frequently. The Australian sample of HR leaders described a strategic role midway between China and the United States, United Kingdom/Europe, and Canada samples. The Australia results are different from prior surveys, which we attribute to the 2016 Australian sample being from smaller organizations than before.

At the bottom of table 3.1 are the mean ratings on a scale that assigned 1 = no role, 2 = implementation role, 3 = input role, and 4 = full partner. The mean ratings generally support the comparisons we have just described. This 4-point scale is used in other chapters to define HR's strategic role and explore its relationship to the other variables in the survey.

Table 3.1. HR's role in business strategy, by country					
	Percentages				
Role in Strategy	United States[1]	Canada[2]	Australia[3]	United Kingdom/ Europe[4]	China[5]
No role	3.5	0.0	8.8	2.7	11.5
Implementation role	14.2	5.6	20.6	2.7	15.6
Input role	41.6	47.2	47.1	51.4	55.2
Full partner	40.7	47.2	23.5	43.2	17.7
Mean	3.19[5]	3.42[3,5]	2.85[2]	3.35[5]	2.79[1,2,4]

[1,2,3,4,5] Significant differences between countries ($p \leq .05$).

Table 3.2. Strategic focuses and HR's role in business strategy, United States					
	Strategic Focuses				
Role in Strategy	Growth	Information-Based Strategies	Knowledge-Based Strategies	Sustainability	Innovation
No role[1]	2.9	3.4	3.3	2.5	2.5
Implementation role[2]	3.0	3.3[3,4]	2.8[4]	3.0	2.7[3,4]
Input role[3]	3.1	4.0[2]	3.3[4]	3.2	3.6[2]
Full partner[4]	3.0	4.1[2]	3.8[2,3]	3.4	3.8[2]

Response scale: 1 = little or no extent; 2 = some extent; 3 = moderate extent; 4 = great extent; 5 = very great extent.

[1,2,3,4] Significant difference ($p \leq .05$) from one other role in strategy.

Strategic Focuses

The role that HR plays in the strategy process is related to its organization's strategic focus. As can be seen in table 3.2, when HR has a full partner role, all of the strategic focuses except growth are higher. The strongest relationship is with innovation. Overall, when HR plays a stronger role in strategy, there is more likely to be a greater strategic focus on information, knowledge, sustainability, and innovation. It appears that these strategic focuses create greater opportunity and demand for a strong HR strategic role.

Management Approach

Table 3.3 shows the relationship between HR's role in strategy and an organization's management approach. It shows that when HR has a full partner role in strategy, high-involvement management and sustainable management are the most common management approaches. Indeed, the results show a statistically significant pattern where the high-involvement approach is less evident when HR plays a role other than full partner. In low-cost-operator and bureaucratic companies, we see the opposite pattern; these strategies are more prominent in organizations where HR plays no role in strategy compared to where HR is a full partner. These findings are not surprising; they fit well with how these approaches think about the role of people. With high-involvement and sustainable management, people are front and center, whereas in the others, they are "something to be dealt with." These results do raise an interesting question about causation: Does this relationship exist because the HR full partner role leads to high involvement and sustainable management or the reverse? It is a question that the data cannot answer, but our view is that the major direction of causation is from the management style to role of HR. That said, the reverse no doubt is true in some companies.

Table 3.3. Management approaches and HR's role in business strategy, United States

Role in Strategy	Management Approaches				
	Bureaucratic	Low-Cost Operator	High Involvement	Global Competitor	Sustainable
No role[1]	3.8	2.7	2.7	3.0	3.7
Implementation role[2]	2.9	2.1	2.3[4]	2.4	3.1
Input role[3]	2.8	2.1	2.7[4]	2.5	3.1
Full partner[4]	2.3	2.3	3.5[2,3]	2.8	3.5

Response scale: 1 = little or no extent; 2 = some extent; 3 = moderate extent; 4 = great extent; 5 = very great extent.
[1,2,3,4] Significant difference ($p \leq .05$) from one other role in strategy.

Table 3.4. Business strategy activities, United States

Activities	Means					Correlation with HR Role in Strategy
	2004[1]	2007[2]	2010[3]	2013[4]	2016[5]	
Help identify or design strategy options	2.9	3.0	2.8	2.7	2.9	.61***
Help decide among the best strategy options	3.0	3.1	2.9	2.8	3.0	.62***
Help plan the implementation of strategy	3.6	3.8	3.6	3.5	3.8	.58***
Help identify new business opportunities	2.0	2.2	2.0	1.9	2.3	.44***
Assess the organization's readiness to implement strategies	3.5	3.5	3.2	3.3	3.5	.51***
Help design the organization structure to implement strategy	3.8	3.9	3.6	3.7	4.0	.50***
Assess possible merger, acquisition, or divestiture strategies	2.9	3.0	2.7	2.9	3.0	.39***
Work with the corporate board on business strategy	2.6	2.9[4]	2.6	2.4[2,5]	2.8[4]	.43***

Response scale: 1 = little or no extent; 2 = some extent; 3 = moderate extent; 4 = great extent; 5 = very great extent.
[1,2,3,4,5] Significant difference ($p \leq .05$) between years.
Significance level: [†]$p \leq .10$, *$p \leq .05$, **$p \leq .01$, ***$p \leq .001$.

Strategy Activities

The role that HR plays in strategy can be realized through a wide variety of activities, from strategy design and decision making to diagnosing and preparing the organization for the strategy. Table 3.4 presents data on the extent to which HR leaders report engaging in several of these activities.

HR executives report that they are particularly likely to be involved in assessing organizational readiness, designing an organization's structure, and planning for the implementation of strategy. They are less likely to be involved in new business opportunities, work with the board, and the design strategy options. Overall, most HR tends to be more involved in assessment and implementation, after strategies are determined. Assessment and implementation are logical areas for HR, so it is not surprising that they are rated as areas of frequent involvement. A comparison of the 2004, 2007, 2010, 2013, and 2016 data shows no significant changes in HR's involvement in strategy activities in these years, which is consistent with the findings reported in chapter 2 that HR has not changed its time allocation during this period, despite the significant and accelerating changes in organizations and society.

The right-most column of table 3.4 also shows the relationship between HR strategy activities and HR's role in strategy. Not surprisingly, all the strategy activities show a positive and significant relationship with the strength of HR's partnership role in strategy. Notably, the two activities most strongly associated with HR's strategic role are identifying/designing strategy options and deciding among those options. Yet these two items are also far less extensively reported by HR than assessing readiness, designing structure, and implementing strategy. This suggests that a strong HR role in strategy is associated with taking on activities that are less reactive and occur earlier in the strategy process.

International Results

The international data in table 3.5 show many similarities across countries. HR is most frequently involved in assessing readiness, designing structure, and implementing strategy and less involved in identifying options and opportunities and deciding among them in all countries. HR is the least active in China, and Australia is more similar to China than the United States, United Kingdom/Europe, and Canada.

Strategic Focuses

The numerous, significant positive associations between a company's strategic focus area and HR strategy activities are shown in table 3.6.

Table 3.5. Business strategy activities, by country

Activities	Means				
	United States[1]	Canada[2]	Australia[3]	United Kingdom/ Europe[4]	China[5]
Help identify or design strategy options	2.9	3.3[5]	2.7	3.1[5]	2.6[2,4]
Help decide among the best strategy options	3.0[5]	3.3[5]	2.9	3.2[5]	2.5[1,2,4]
Help plan the implementation of strategy	3.8[3,5]	3.6[5]	3.2[1]	3.8[5]	3.1[1,2,4]
Help identify new business opportunities	2.3	2.1	1.9	2.3	2.2
Assess the organization's readiness to implement strategies	3.5[3,5]	3.4[5]	2.8[1]	3.3[5]	2.7[1,2,4]
Help design the organization structure to implement strategy	4.0[5]	3.9[5]	3.4	3.8[5]	3.2[1,2,4]
Assess possible merger, acquisition, or divestiture strategies	3.0[3,5]	2.6	2.1[1,4]	3.0[3,5]	2.3[1,4]
Work with the corporate board on business strategy	2.8[5]	2.7	2.4	3.1[5]	2.4[1,4]

Response scale: 1 = little or no extent; 2 = some extent; 3 = moderate extent; 4 = great extent; 5 = very great extent.

[1,2,3,4,5] Significant differences between countries ($p \leq .05$).

Table 3.6. Relationship of business strategy activities to strategic focuses, United States

Activities	Strategic Focuses				
	Growth	Information-Based Strategies	Knowledge-Based Strategies	Sustainability	Innovation
Help identify or design strategy options	.02	.47***	.45***	.25**	.37***
Help decide among the best strategy options	−.07	.49***	.52***	.19*	.41***
Help plan the implementation of strategy	.00	.47***	.55***	.19[t]	.49***
Help identify new business opportunities	.02	.37***	.43***	.28**	.30***
Assess the organization's readiness to implement strategies	.00	.31***	.50***	.25**	.20*
Help design the organization structure to implement strategy	.12	.46***	.52***	.17[t]	.41***
Assess possible merger, acquisition, or divestiture strategies	.31***	.42***	.50***	.11	.32***
Work with the corporate board on business strategy	.08	.34***	.48***	.15	.30***

Response scale: 1 = little or no extent; 2 = some extent; 3 = moderate extent; 4 = great extent; 5 = very great extent.

Significance level: [t] $p \leq .10$, * $p \leq .05$, ** $p \leq .01$, *** $p \leq .001$.

Three of the strategic focuses—information, knowledge, and innovation—are significantly associated with HR's active involvement in all of the business strategy activities. The sustainability focus is significantly related to most of the activities. The generally positive relationship between HR strategy activity and the strength of many of the strategic focuses is not surprising: in order to perform most of these strategy activities effectively, HR needs the guidance of a well-articulated strategy.

Growth is unrelated to most strategy activities, with the exception of assessing mergers and divestitures. It is a bit surprising that a strategic focus on growth has a weak or no relationship to all but one of the strategy activities of the HR function while three others—innovation, information, and knowledge—have strong, positive relationships to virtually all of the activities. It is impossible to examine this discrepancy more closely and explain it with the data that we have.

Management Approach

The relationships between business strategy activities and management approaches are shown in table 3.7. The pattern of relationships paints a clear picture: in organizations that adopt the low-cost-operator and

Table 3.7. Relationship of business strategy activities to management approaches, United States					
	Management Approaches				
Activities	**Bureaucratic**	**Low-Cost Operator**	**High Involvement**	**Global Competitor**	**Sustainable**
Help identify or design strategy options	−.12	.11	.40***	.03	.38***
Help decide among the best strategy options	−.21*	.04	.41***	−.04	.36***
Help plan the implementation of strategy	−.14	.03	.39***	.04	.39***
Help identify new business opportunities	−.17ᵗ	.14	.31***	−.01	.38***
Assess the organization's readiness to implement strategies	−.22*	−.11	.50***	.07	.29**
Help design the organization structure to implement strategy	−.10	−.03	.35***	.11	.21*
Assess possible merger, acquisition, or divestiture strategies	−.26**	−.04	.27**	.18ᵗ	.29**
Work with the corporate board on business strategy	−.08	.01	.27**	.11	.23*
Response scale: 1 = little or no extent; 2 = some extent; 3 = moderate extent; 4 = great extent; 5 = very great extent. Significance level: ᵗp ≤ .10, *p ≤ .05, **p ≤ .01, ***p ≤ .001.					

bureaucratic management approaches, HR less frequently engages in strategy activities, with some negative relationships reaching statistical significance. The opposite is true of the extent to organizations that use the high-involvement or sustainable approaches: the stronger these approaches are, the more frequently HR is active in both strategy creation and implementation. Overall, how an organization is managed clearly makes a difference in HR's strategy activities, but it is not certain why. Is it because the management approach shapes the HR function, or vice versa? Our view is that in most cases, it is the former because high-involvement and sustainable management approaches offer an encouraging environment for HR strategy activities, while low-cost-operator and bureaucratic approaches are neutral or discouraging.

HR Strategy

Historical data on the type of HR strategy, as well as the relationship between HR strategy type and HR's role in strategy, are presented in table 3.8. The results from 2004, 2007, 2010, 2013, and 2016 are similar for three of the activities. However, three do show a significant increase. Data on supporting change management, integrated strategy, and data-based decision are all significantly higher in 2016. This is an important result because it suggests that HR is increasing the role it plays in making organizations more effective. It is also notable because it is a rare example of change, since 2007.

With respect to the absolute level of these HR strategy types, it is important to note that none of the mean scores are particularly high. The highest is 3.6 while most are less than 3.0 on a 5-point scale. It appears that to a moderate extent, HR drives change management, develops a human capital strategy that is integrated with business strategy, and provides HR data to support change management.

HR is not particularly active in the use of data and analytics. Data-based talent strategy, data-based decision making, and analytical support for business decisions are the lowest-rated HR strategies in table 3.8. However, data-based decisions do show an upward trend in 2016. This finding is consistent with growing interest in HR analytics, big data, and the importance of human capital.

HR executives in 2007 said that all of the items in table 3.8 were activities they would increase, and as of 2016 they had increased them somewhat. In 2007, all of the strategy items were rated near the top of the scale (2.6 or greater on a 3-point scale) in terms of the future focus of the HR organization. Apparently these items represent the way that HR planned to be involved in the strategy process, but change has been slow. When and to what extent these activities will be put in place is a

Table 3.8. HR strategy, United States

HR Strategy	Means					Correlation with HR Role in Strategy (2013)
	2004[1]	2007[2]	2010[3]	2013[4]	2016[5]	
Data-based talent strategy	2.7	2.6	2.7	2.5	2.7	.31***
A human capital strategy integrated with business strategy	3.2	3.3[4]	3.0	2.9[2,5]	3.3[4]	.50***
Provides analytical support for business decision making	2.9	2.8	2.8	2.6	2.9	.43***
Provides HR data to support change management	3.2	3.0	3.0	2.8	3.1	.47***
HR drives change management	3.4	3.2	3.1[5]	3.1[5]	3.6[3,4]	.54***
Makes rigorous data-based decisions about human capital management	2.7	2.6	2.7	2.4[5]	2.9[4]	.43***
HR is involved in decisions about whether and where to use project-based, freelance, and platform gigs in order to get work done	—	—	—	—	2.8	.41***
Provides direction and services for workers who are not covered by a traditional employment relationship (e.g., contract, gig, platform workers)	—	—	—	—	2.6	.29**

Note: Empty cells indicate that the item was not asked in that year.

Response scale: 1 = little or no extent; 2 = some extent; 3 = moderate extent; 4 = great extent; 5 = very great extent.

[1,2,3,4,5] Significant differences between years ($p \leq .05$).

Significance level: [†]$p \leq .10$, *$p \leq .05$, **$p \leq .01$, ***$p \leq .001$.

major question. The comparison between 2013 and 2016 does show a significant increase in three of the activities and the other three show a small increase.

The correlations between the current activity levels and HR's overall role in strategy are also presented in table 3.8. All are high. The data-based talent strategies item has the lowest correlation among the old items, but it is still highly significant. Why this relationship is relatively weak is not entirely clear given that it is potentially an important part of the strategy process. One possibility is that effective measurement systems require not just data but sound analytics, good logic, and attention to change management processes (Boudreau and Ramstad 2006). It may be that today's HR data focus primarily on the quality of measures but do not sufficiently reflect the other elements of a complete data-based decision strategy.

Two new strategy activities, both involving nontraditional work relationships, were added to the 2016 survey. They are in the bottom two rows of the table. Their average ratings are among the lowest of all the strategy items, suggesting that HR typically has a less than moderate involvement in decisions involving whether and where these relationships are used and in providing services to these workers. Given the growing importance of this type of work relationship, a strong argument can be made for HR to be more involved (Boudreau, Jesuthasan, and Creelman 2015). Notably, the relationship between these two items and HR's role in strategy is positive and statistically significant. The level of the correlations suggests that the relationship is somewhat stronger for HR being involved in decisions about these workers, relative to providing services to these workers.

What the results in table 3.8 do show is a clear pattern of the types of underused HR activities that are related to having a role in strategy. They provide a useful set of practices that HR organizations should consider adopting in order to play an important role in strategy formulation. It is encouraging that some of them are increasingly being used.

The international data on HR strategy are similar to the U.S. data. They show significant differences only with respect to Australia, which has the lowest ratings on most HR strategy items.

Strategic Focuses

Table 3.9 shows the relationship between an organization's strategic focuses and its HR strategy approaches. Most of the items show strong significant relationships with the extent of strategic focus on information, knowledge, sustainability, and innovation. The growth strategic focus is significantly related to only one of the HR strategy approaches: integrating human capital strategy with business strategy. The consistent pattern across most of the strategic focuses reinforces the point that when organizations have a clear strategic focus, HR is likely to be actively engaged in strategic HR.

Table 3.9. Relationship of current HR strategy to strategic focuses, United States					
	Strategic Focuses				
HR Strategy	**Growth**	**Information-Based Strategies**	**Knowledge-Based Strategies**	**Sustainability**	**Innovation**
Data-based talent strategy	.17^t	.36***	.52***	.26**	.33***
A human capital strategy integrated with business strategy	.19*	.46***	.61***	.30***	.42***
Provides analytical support for business decision making	.11	.49***	.49***	.31***	.38***
Provides HR data to support change management	.05	.51***	.48***	.31***	.38***
HR drives change management	.17^t	.49***	.57***	.16^t	.33***
Makes rigorous data-based decisions about human capital management	.14	.43***	.51***	.22*	.35***
HR is involved in decisions about whether and where to use project-based, freelance, and platform gigs in order to get work done	.16^t	.35***	.45***	.18^t	.35***
Provides direction and services for workers who are not covered by a traditional employment relationship (e.g., contract, gig, platform workers)	.18^t	.16^t	.32***	.11	.13
Response scale: 1 = little or no extent; 2 = some extent; 3 = moderate extent; 4 = great extent; 5 = very great extent. Significance level: $^tp \leq .10$, $^*p \leq .05$, $^{**}p \leq .01$, $^{***}p \leq .001$.					

Perhaps the most interesting results in the table concern the pattern of strong correlations between the information-based, the knowledge-based, and the innovation-based strategies and the HR strategy items. An organization that has a knowledge-based or information-based strategy is particularly likely to emphasize the role of HR processes and measures—as it should, since talent is a particularly critical asset in organizations with these strategies. This finding is further confirmation of the future importance of HR strategic activities since more and more organizations are developing information- and knowledge-based strategies.

Management Approach

The human capital strategy approaches in table 3.10 are mostly significantly and positively correlated with two of the five management approaches: high involvement and sustainable. It is not surprising that the HR strategy approaches are more extensively used when organizations are high involvement and sustainable, given their emphasis on talent and human capital. In contrast, it is interesting that most of the HR strategy approaches are negatively correlated with the low-cost-operator and bureaucratic management approaches. This once again highlights the large difference in how different management approaches treat talent and the HR function. High involvement and sustainability seem to create fertile ground for active HR strategy, while low-cost-operator and bureaucratic approaches seem to create headwinds.

Table 3.10. Relationship of current HR strategy to management approaches, United States					
	Management Approaches				
HR Strategy	**Bureaucratic**	**Low-Cost Operator**	**High Involvement**	**Global Competitor**	**Sustainable**
Data-based talent strategy	−.05	−.13	.32***	.12	.34***
A human capital strategy integrated with business strategy	−.26**	−.20*	.54***	.12	.42***
Provides analytical support for business decision making	−.03	−.06	.34***	.09	.41***
Provides HR data to support change management	−.09	−.09	.40***	.03	.30***
HR drives change management	−.38***	.01	.46***	.08	.38***
Makes rigorous data-based decisions about human capital management	−.06	−.03	.32***	.16	.32***
HR is involved in decisions about whether and where to use project-based, freelance, and platform gigs in order to get work done	−.39***	−.13	.45***	.18ᵗ	.33***
Provides direction and services for workers who are not covered by a traditional employment relationship (e.g., contract, gig, platform workers)	−.24**	.11	.24*	.15	.22*

Response scale: 1 = little or no extent; 2 = some extent; 3 = moderate extent; 4 = great extent; 5 = very great extent.

Significance level: $^t p \leq .10$, $^* p \leq .05$, $^{**} p \leq .01$, $^{***} p \leq .001$.

Sustainability

The future of corporations increasingly depends on their addressing the social and environmental challenges that affect their economic activity. Corporate social and environmental responsibilities need to shift from being a peripheral add-on strategy focus and risk-avoidance activity to being integrated into how companies operate and their business strategies (Mohrman and Lawler 2014; Mohrman, O'Toole, and Lawler 2015). Society is increasingly demanding that corporations develop sustainably and operate in ways that meet the needs of the present without compromising the ability of future generations to meet their needs. This definition of sustainable performance was originally articulated in a 1987 United Nations report, *Our Common Future* (Brundtland 1987), and has become the dominant definition of sustainability.

Leading companies have made strides in embedding the triple bottom line of financial, environmental, and social sustainability in their operating and reporting practices. However, it is not clear how many have fully incorporated social and environmental responsibility into their business strategies, financial decision making, performance goals, reward systems, and employment processes (Mohrman and Lawler 2014).

Companies are finding that corporate social responsibility is now a major factor in attracting, hiring, and retaining top talent. Some organizations have created an employer brand that addresses this need and are providing employees with meaningful ways to participate in the transition to sustainability. HR functions can play a major role in implementing corporate sustainability by building it into HR strategy, policy, and practices. They also can help organizations manage the changes that are required in order for them to be sustainably effective. HR professionals can play a central role in change management, culture change, organizational design, and competency building, all critical to a sustainable business strategy.

In many respects, sustainability has always been active in organizations' community and charitable activities. HR has also had a major role in determining and assessing how its organization's employees are treated, a key part of an organization's social sustainability.

HR Role

The responses to the survey's questions about HR's role in sustainability activities, first asked in 2013, show that HR does not play a major or leadership role in these activities of most corporations. As can be seen in figure 3.2, most HR executives in our 2013 and 2016 surveys say that they play either a minor role or an active support role; less than

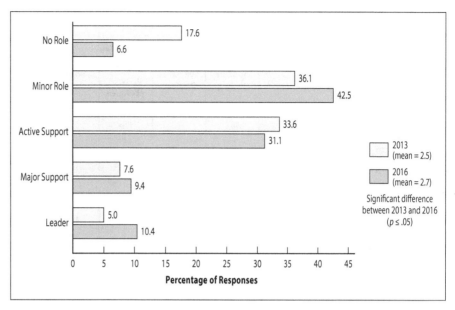

Figure 3.2. HR's role in sustainable activities (United States)

20 percent say they play a major support or leader role. The slight increase from 2013 to 2016 is statistically significant.

The roles that HR executives say they play are dramatically different from those they say they should play. Most of these executives believe that HR should at least be in an active support role, and close to a majority say that they should be either a major supporter or a leader of sustainability.

Table 3.11 provides data on the kind of role HR plays in sustainability activities and how much it directly supports the sustainability performance objectives of the companies. Two of the statements in the table are paired so we can compare what HR does and what HR thinks it should do. On these questions, the gap between what HR feels it should do with respect to sustainability and what it actually does is very large in the direction of HR not doing enough.

The scores for what it does average around the middle of the scale (neither agree nor disagree). They consistently fall short of doing what is needed to make HR a positive force when it comes to sustainability. For example, the first statement refers to whether sustainability performance and competencies *are* explicitly built into HR processes. Only a little over 30 percent of the executives believe that is true of their company. But when it comes to whether they feel that it *should* be true, almost 70 percent feel that it should be true. Although the gap between "should be" and "is" is not as large as it is for building sustainability

Table 3.11. Sustainability activities, United States

Sustainability Activities	2016 Percentages					2013 Means	2016 Means	2016 Correlation with HR Role in Strategy
	Strongly Disagree	Somewhat Disagree	Neither Disagree nor Agree	Somewhat Agree	Strongly Agree			
Sustainability performance and competences *are* explicitly built into HR processes such as selection, rewards, and development.	18.3	22.9	17.4	31.2	10.1	2.8	2.9	.23*
Sustainability performance and competences *should be* explicitly built into HR processes such as selection, rewards, and development.	3.7	11.9	15.6	38.5	30.3	3.8	3.8	.05
HR *is involved* in the design of sustainability initiatives and programs.	10.2	20.4	20.4	35.2	13.9	3.1	3.2	.34***
HR *should be involved* in the design of sustainability initiatives and programs.	2.8	5.5	23.9	36.7	31.2	3.8	3.9	.12
HR *provides* support and expertise in organization design issues that impact sustainability.	6.5	3.7	24.3	46.7	18.7	3.3	3.7	.36***
	No Role	Minor Role	Active Support	Major Support	Leader	2013 Mean	2016 Mean	2016 Correlation with HR Role in Strategy
HR's role in sustainability is:	6.6	42.5	31.1	9.4	10.4	2.5	2.7	.29**

Significance level: $^!p \le .10$, $^*p \le .05$, $^{**}p \le .01$, $^{***}p \le .001$.
Significant differences between years ($p \le .05$).

into HR programs, there is also a gap with respect to whether HR is involved in the design of the sustainability initiatives. Whether it provides support and expertise in organizational design relative to sustainability shows an increase from 2013 to 2016. This appears to be the area where HR has an active role in an issue with an impact on sustainability.

Perhaps the best way of summarizing the data presented in figure 3.2 and table 3.11 is that HR executives believe that HR should play a significant role in the design and implementation of sustainability activities and that sustainability should be a key part of the company's HR systems. However, when it comes to whether that is currently true, the answer is no. It is particularly telling that the lowest score in table 3.11 is on sustainability being built into HR processes, the area where HR has the best chance to influence sustainability practices and results.

The correlations in table 3.11 between HR's role in sustainability activities and in strategy are positive. It appears that when HR plays a major role in sustainability, it is also a player in corporate strategy. In many respects, this is not surprising since a key issue in many organizations' corporate strategy is sustainability. Therefore, if HR is involved in sustainability activities, this work naturally will lead to being involved in corporate strategy too. Similarly, if it is involved in corporate strategy, it is likely to be involved in discussions about sustainability because it can be a key piece of an organization's business strategy.

Overall, the data on HR and sustainability clearly show that HR is not a major player in sustainability but that it would like to be and feels that it should be. It has a lot to offer if it has expertise in change management, organizational design, and the design of HR systems that support sustainability. Clearly sustainability expertise and activities go hand-in-hand with HR being a more powerful and involved strategic partner in corporations. It does not appear that HR has to give up anything when it comes to being a strategic partner by being heavily involved in a corporation's sustainability activities. Indeed, quite the contrary appears to be true: they go together and represent a positive opportunity for HR. Given the low level of activity that HR currently reports with respect to sustainability, this appears to be an area where it can move forward, improving how the company functions but positioning itself to be a stronger business strategy partner.

International Results

HR's active role in sustainability does vary significantly in the countries surveyed (table 3.12), with Australia much lower than the others. HR is active in all countries except Australia when it comes to providing

Table 3.12. Sustainability activities, by country					
	Means				
Sustainability Activities[a]	**United States[1]**	**Canada[2]**	**Australia[3]**	**United Kingdom/ Europe[4]**	**China[5]**
Sustainability performance and competences *are* explicitly built into HR processes such as selection, rewards, and development.	2.9[3,5]	3.0	2.3[1,4,5]	3.4[3]	3.5[1,3]
Sustainability performance and competences *should be* explicitly built into HR processes such as selection, rewards, and development.	3.8	4.0	4.0	4.3	3.8
HR *is involved* in the design of sustainability initiatives and programs.	3.2	3.3	2.7[4,5]	3.6[3]	3.3[3]
HR *should be involved* in the design of sustainability initiatives and programs.	3.9	4.1	3.9	4.4[5]	3.7[4]
HR *provides* support and expertise in organization design issues that impact sustainability.	3.7	3.9[3]	3.1[2,4]	4.0[3]	3.5
HR's role in sustainability is:[b]	2.7	2.6	2.3[4,5]	3.1[3]	3.0[3]

[a]Response scale: 1 = strongly disagree; 2 = somewhat disagree; 3 = neither disagree nor agree; 4 = somewhat agree; 5 = strongly agree.
[b]Response scale: 1 = no role; 2 = minor role; 3 = active support; 4 = major support; 5 = leader.
[1,2,3,4,5]No significant differences between countries ($p \le .05$).

support and expertise in organizational design issues that affect sustainability. In all countries, there is a belief that HR should be involved in sustainability activities. United Kingdom/Europe is the strongest in this belief.

There is only one significant difference between countries with respect to what HR sustainability activities should be and not many nearly significant differences either. We expected the "should be involved" scores in China to be lower than in Europe and the United States, where there is more environmental regulation and legislation, and they are slightly lower with respect to design.

Strategic Focuses

The relationship between the role of HR in sustainability and the strategic focuses of organizations is shown in table 3.13. The highest correlations in the table are with the sustainability strategic focus.

All of the correlations between HR's role in sustainability activities and the degree to which an organization has a sustainability focus are significant, and all are higher than they were in 2013. The highest correlation is between sustainability performance competencies explicitly built in to HR processes and the degree to which a company focuses on sustainability. This is an obvious connection point, and it shows that HR has adjusted its activities to fit the business strategy of a sustainability-oriented organization. Apparently organizations that have a strong

Table 3.13. Relationship of sustainability activities to strategic focuses, United States					
	Strategic Focuses				
Sustainability Activities[a]	Growth	Information-Based Strategies	Knowledge-Based Strategies	Sustainability	Innovation
Sustainability performance and competences *are* explicitly built into HR processes such as selection, rewards, and development.	.03	.17[t]	.32***	.55***	.15
Sustainability performance and competences *should be* explicitly built into HR processes such as selection, rewards, and development.	−.01	.01	.10	.41***	−.13
HR *is involved* in the design of sustainability initiatives and programs.	.09	.17[t]	.31***	.47***	.15
HR *should be involved* in the design of sustainability initiatives and programs.	.09	.07	.13	.33***	−.04
HR *provides* support and expertise in organization design issues that impact sustainability.	.12	.32***	.35***	.40***	.32***
HR's role in sustainability is:[b]	.05	.14	.20*	.51***	.21*
[a]Response scale: 1 = strongly disagree; 2 = somewhat disagree; 3 = neither disagree nor agree; 4 = somewhat agree; 5 = strongly agree.					
[b]Response scale: 1 = no role; 2 = minor role; 3 = active support; 4 = major support; 5 = leader.					
Significance level: [t]$p \leq .10$, *$p \leq .05$, **$p \leq .01$, ***$p \leq .001$.					

strategic focus on sustainability find a greater opportunity for HR's role to be a strongly supportive one when it comes to sustainability activities. The second highest correlation with knowledge-based strategies. This may reflect the need to attract and manage educated talent.

Management Approach

There is a positive correlation in table 3.14 between the degree to which an organization has a management approach that focuses on sustainable performance and the degree to which sustainability is part of HR processes. Here, there is an alignment between what HR is doing and the way the organization is being managed. However, the correlations are relatively low compared to what might be expected if an organization's HR function was committed to a sustainable management approach.

As can be seen in table 3.14, there is no significant relationship between HR's belief that it should engage in various sustainability support activities and the degree to which an organization has a sustainable management approach. This is surprising, but it may be that HR executives believe HR should participate in sustainability activities and support it regardless of their organization's strategy.

The results in table 3.14 do show a number of significant correlations between the high-involvement management approach and HR's role in sustainability. The more an organization takes this approach, the more HR seems to participate in sustainability initiatives and programs. In

Table 3.14. Relationship of sustainability activities to management approaches, United States					
	Management Approaches[b]				
Sustainability Activities[a]	**Bureaucratic**	**Low-Cost Operator**	**High Involvement**	**Global Competitor**	**Sustainable**
Sustainability performance and competences *are* explicitly built into HR processes such as selection, rewards, and development.	−.16[t]	−.16[t]	.39***	.06	.33***
Sustainability performance and competences *should be* explicitly built into HR processes such as selection, rewards, and development.	.03	.01	.16[t]	.01	.05
HR *is involved* in the design of sustainability initiatives and programs.	−.15	−.03	.36***	.03	.35***
HR *should be involved* in the design of sustainability initiatives and programs.	.00	.12	.09	.10	.20*
HR *provides* support and expertise in organization design issues that impact sustainability.	−.19[t]	−.22*	.35***	.07	.27**
HR's role in sustainability is:[c]	−.10	.01	.30**	−.02	.33***
[a]Response scale: 1 = strongly disagree; 2 = somewhat disagree; 3 = neither disagree nor agree; 4 = somewhat agree; 5 = strongly agree.					
[b]Response scale: 1 = little or no extent; 2 = some extent; 3 = moderate extent; 4 = great extent; 5 = very great extent.					
[c]Response scale: 1 = no role; 2 = minor role; 3 = active support; 4 = major support; 5 = leader.					
Significance level: [t]$p \leq .10$, *$p \leq .05$, **$p \leq .01$, ***$p \leq .001$.					

some respects, this is not surprising and probably reflects the people side of the triple bottom line. High-involvement management focuses on the people side of organizations. Thus, in an organization with a high-involvement management approach, it is not surprising that HR would be engaged in sustainability practice installation and change management design.

What is surprising in table 3.14 is that there is not a stronger relationship between the two "should be" items and the high-involvement approach to management. None of these correlations are significant. Apparently the HR executives surveyed do not necessarily think that HR should emphasize sustainability in their HR systems simply because their organization has a high-involvement approach to management. And as we noted earlier, even when organizations have a sustainable management approach, HR executives do not necessarily think that HR should be more active in the design of sustainability activities.

The correlations between HR's role in sustainability activities and the management approach of the organization are surprisingly low. There is a significant, but not high, correlation between the degree to which an organization's management approach focuses on sustainable performance and the degree to which HR plays a role in the organization's sustainability activities. A similar correlation exists for the relationship to high-involvement management. It is surprising that the relationship with sustainable management is not higher given that a management approach focusing on sustainability should send a message to the HR function that it should be a major player in the organization's sustainability activities. The fact that this does not seem to be true may be a significant contributor to HR's not being the business partner that it would like to be. Clearly it needs to play a role in the organization that supports the way that it is managed if it wants to be seen as a strategically relevant part of the organization.

Conclusion

Overall, the data suggest that HR has a considerable way to go when it comes to adding value as a strategic contributor. In most organizations, it is making some progress but is not yet a major contributor to the business strategy process. This is particularly true in the case of organizations in China. The low level of strategy involvement there is not surprising given its level of economic development. It is surprising and disappointing in the case of the other countries.

The data suggest that HR is making some progress in the United States. Overall the 2016 results are slightly better than the 1998 results. However, our data suggest that HR has not become a major strategic business contributor or made a major commitment to developing HR strategy. This is true even though a number of business changes have occurred that would seem to be ones that would lead to HR being more of a strategic partner.

In most companies, HR is not very active in sustainability activities, although HR executives feel it should be significantly more so. This is true in all the countries studied. The areas where HR executives think it should provide more support are the design of sustainability programs, organizational design, change management, and the way business is conducted. HR executives also believe that sustainability should be built into such HR processes as selection, rewards, and development. Not surprising, HR is more involved in sustainability activities when an organization has it as a strategic focus. Finally, it is important to note that when HR is active in sustainability, it is much more likely to play a significant role in strategy. Certainly HR can be a contributor to strategy if it does the right things.

On the encouraging side, HR executives report being active in a number of areas that are directly tied to the strategic direction of the business. These range from human capital recruitment and development through organizational design and strategy development. The challenge for HR is to increase the degree to which it is involved in strategy-related activities so that it can become a full partner in the high-value-added area of business strategy. One finding that suggests this might happen is the higher level of strategy activities in knowledge-based and information-based organizations. As more and more organizations in developed countries focus on knowledge and information, HR may start engaging in more strategy activities. Another encouraging finding is the high level of strategy activities in high-involvement firms. These too are likely to increase in the developed world. This finding once again makes the point that HR's role is tied to, and most likely determined by, the organization's overall strategy and management approach.

CHAPTER 4

HR Decision Science

- Decision science sophistication relates significantly to HR's strategic role.

- All decision science activities are rated at moderate levels, with educating business leaders particularly low rated, a similar pattern since 2007.

- HR's value added through services and decision support has a stronger correlation with HR's strategic role than value added through compliance.

- Levels of decision science sophistication were generally rated lower in Australia than in other countries, particularly in areas other than compliance and delivering services.

- China's ratings of decision science sophistication for the first time were similar to those of other countries and significantly higher than Australia's.

- Bureaucratic and low-cost operation management approaches are negatively related to decision science sophistication, while high-involvement and sustainable approaches are positively related.

- Strategic focuses on information, knowledge, sustainability, and innovation were positively related to decision science sophistication, while a focus on growth was not related.

Decision science provides a framework of principles and decision rules, based on valid evidence, to guide leaders' strategic choices (Boudreau and Ramstad 2007). A classic example of decision science in management is portfolio theory in finance, which informs decision frameworks such as return on investment, return on equity, and diversification of investments. A striking feature of these frameworks is that their objective is not solely to improve the quality of decisions about financial resources, but to improve the validity and consistency of the mental models that leaders use when they consider such decisions. The key issues are not only the overall sophistication and quality of decisions, but also the quality of the principles underlying those decisions.

Similar to the finance discipline, higher-quality human capital decisions occur if HR professionals and other managers have valid and logical frameworks that help them understand how human capital affects sustainable organizational effectiveness and if they are educated and held accountable for using that understanding to identify and make vital choices that involve strategic human capital. For HR to be a truly transformative function, leaders must use valid principles to guide their decisions (Boudreau and Jesuthasan 2011). The state of HR's decision science, however, is far less mature than those of finance, marketing, and some management disciplines. Despite the importance of HR decision science, little research describes the decision frameworks that HR and other business leaders use or the quality and prevalence of the systems that are used to educate business leaders (Boudreau 2012). This chapter presents findings on the quality of human capital decisions and the relationship between decision quality and the strategic role of HR.

Quality of Decisions about Talent and Human Capital

Table 4.1 shows the results of questions that ask about the quality of decision making by non-HR and HR leaders when it comes to human capital and, by comparison, other important resources. The first item poses the fundamental question of whether their organization excels in the competition for critical talent. HR leaders rate their organization as moderately effective in competing for key talent. This rating has remained virtually the same since 2007, when we first posed the question.

For the item that taps the definition of talentship—"decisions that depend on or affect human capital are as rigorous, logical, and strategically relevant as decisions [about more tangible] resources" (Boudreau and Ramstad 2007), the average rating is just above the midpoint. While not high, it is significantly higher than in 2007 and 2013. This suggests that HR leaders may be finding business leaders more motivated and

Table 4.1. HR decision making, United States					
	Means				**2016 Correlation with HR Role in Strategy**
Decision Making	**2007[1]**	**2010[2]**	**2013[3]**	**2016[4]**	
We excel at competing for and with talent where it matters most to our strategic success.	3.2	3.1	3.2	3.2	.35***
Business leaders' decisions that depend on or affect human capital (e.g., layoffs, rewards) are as rigorous, logical, and strategically relevant as their decisions about resources such as money, technology, and customers.	2.9[4]	3.0	2.8[4]	3.3[1,3]	.32***
HR leaders have a good understanding about where and why human capital makes the biggest difference in their business.	3.2	3.3	3.2	3.6	.48***
Business leaders have a good understanding about where and why human capital makes the biggest difference in their business.	3.2	3.1	3.1	3.3	.47***
HR systems educate business leaders about their talent decisions.	2.5	2.4	2.2[4]	2.7[3]	.38***
HR adds value by ensuring compliance with rules, laws, and guidelines.	3.5	3.4	3.2[4]	3.6[3]	.13
HR adds value by delivering high-quality professional practices and services.	3.6	3.6	3.4	3.7	.46***

Response scale: 1 = little or no extent; 2 = some extent; 3 = moderate extent; 4 = great extent; 5 = very great extent.

[1,2,3,4] Significant difference ($p \leq .05$) between years.

capable of incorporating the rigor they use with other resources to their decisions about human capital.

The third and fourth items in table 4.1 refer to talent segmentation. They ask whether HR leaders and business leaders understand where and why human capital makes the biggest difference in their business. These items, which receive moderate ratings (virtually the same as in the past survey), display some of the strongest positive correlations with HR's strategic role. This suggests that talent segmentation, particularly a deep understanding of where there is pivotal return on improved performance, may be both a result of and perhaps a precursor to a stronger strategic role for HR.

If business leaders are to learn to make sound talent decisions, the HR systems they use should educate them about the quality of those decisions in the same way that management systems in finance, marketing, and operations management provide clear feedback regarding managers' decision quality (Boudreau and Ramstad 2007; Boudreau 2010). Yet the fifth item in table 4.1, regarding HR systems for educating business leaders, suggests that such education remains stubbornly low. The 2016 results mirror the results from the previous surveys. Once again this question has the lowest ratings among the decision science questions. Yet the correlation between this question and HR's strategic role is positive and significant in every wave of the survey, just as it is in 2016. There is a significant and apparently untapped opportunity to improve how well HR systems educate leaders about talent decisions. One potential gain resulting from this education is a stronger strategic role for HR.

Finally, the last three items in table 4.1 ask about how HR adds value. Boudreau and Ramstad (2007) suggest that mature professions evolve to a balance of adding value through compliance, services, and decision support. The table shows that HR executives believe that HR adds value to a moderate or great extent in all three areas. However, the overall level of value actually added by HR leaves room for improvement in all three areas. The correlation pattern with HR's role in strategy is notable: it shows a strong association between HR executives' perceptions of HR's strategic role and the value added by HR through services and decision support. When it comes to value added through compliance, however, the correlation with HR's strategic role is much lower and not significant. This may be because compliance is an expected basic outcome and that improving it makes little difference to the quality of HR's strategic contributions or that it is not seen as a distinguishing element compared to high-quality services and decision support.

Overall, managers have increased their awareness of the importance of human capital and their role in nurturing and deploying it. HR data, analytics, and scorecards have become more available, providing a basis for improved decisions. However, there is a great deal that managers still do not know about talent segmentation, and the rigor of their decisions has room to improve. HR executives have said for decades that when it comes to sound principles of human capital decisions, "Our business leaders don't know what they don't know." This appears still to be the case.

HR executives, who see room for improvement, may need to provide tangible examples of more sophisticated human capital decision principles. As with the development of the decision sciences of marketing and finance, one would hope to see an HR decision science develop that makes it clear that competing effectively with and through human capital requires leaders, both inside and outside HR, who are not satisfied with the traditional HR service delivery paradigm. They need to realize that it must be extended to include making better decisions about human capital where it matters most to strategic success (Boudreau and Ramstad 1997, 2005a, 2005b, 2005c, 2007). Our 2016 survey suggests some progress in this arena, but it appears to be quite slow.

International Results

Table 4.2 presents the international results. In past surveys, the Chinese ratings were significantly lower than those of the other countries. Many of the differences were statistically significant. In 2016, the results are different.

Table 4.2. HR decision making, by country					
	Means				
Decision Making	United States[1]	Canada[2]	Australia[3]	United Kingdom/ Europe[4]	China[5]
We excel at competing for and with talent where it matters most to our strategic success.	3.2[3]	3.2[3]	2.2[1,2,4,5]	3.4[3]	2.9[3]
Business leaders' decisions that depend on or affect human capital (e.g., layoffs, rewards) are as rigorous, logical, and strategically relevant as their decisions about resources such as money, technology, and customers.	3.3[3]	3.4[3]	2.3[1,2,4,5]	3.1[3]	2.9[3]
HR leaders have a good understanding about where and why human capital makes the biggest difference in their business.	3.6[3]	3.4	2.8[1,4,5]	3.6[3]	3.5[3]
Business leaders have a good understanding about where and why human capital makes the biggest difference in their business.	3.3[3]	3.2	2.5[1,4,5]	3.3[3]	3.5[3]
HR systems educate business leaders about their talent decisions.	2.7[2,3]	2.0[1,5]	1.9[1,5]	2.6	3.0[2,3]
HR adds value by ensuring compliance with rules, laws, and guidelines.	3.6	3.3	3.3	3.5	3.3
HR adds value by delivering high-quality professional practices and services.	3.7[5]	3.7	3.2	3.8[5]	3.2[1,4]
HR adds value by improving talent decisions inside and outside the HR function.	3.7[3,5]	3.8[3,5]	2.8[1,2,4]	3.8[3,5]	3.2[1,2,4]
Response scale: 1 = little or no extent; 2 = some extent; 3 = moderate extent; 4 = great extent; 5 = very great extent. [1,2,3,4,5]Significant differences between countries ($p \le .05$).					

The pattern of ratings for every country is very similar to the results for the U.S. sample reported. Most ratings fall near the midpoint of the scale, with the exception of the degree to which HR systems educate business leaders about their talent decisions, which is rated lower. The one exception is China, which rates this item somewhat higher than the first two items, but the pattern is generally similar. Thus, the conclusions reached for the United States seem to hold for all the national samples in the survey. There appears to be a solid but not exemplary level of talent decision science utilization in all of these countries, with opportunities for improvement, particularly in how well HR systems educate business leaders about their decisions.

In past surveys, China appeared to be at an earlier stage of HR development when it came to advancing a decision science. In the 2016 survey, however, Australian HR leaders rated themselves lower than most other countries on all the items, except those dealing with compliance and service delivery. While the China ratings of the first two items are slightly lower than those of the United States, Canada, and United Kingdom/Europe as before, the Chinese ratings of these items were significantly higher than those of Australia in 2016. Chinese HR leaders also rated higher on the item about educating business leaders about their HR decisions.

Overall, the rating pattern is similar across countries, suggesting that decision quality is moderately high but slow to change. In 2016 we see evidence that China's ratings match those of other countries for the first time.

HR Decision Science Sophistication and HR's Role in Strategy

The correlations between the HR decision science questions and the perception of HR's role in strategy in table 4.1 show a similar pattern to earlier surveys: many significant and positive correlations between the ratings of the decision science items and HR's role in strategy. One correlation was not significant: between HR's value added through compliance. Generally, where decision science principles are rated highly, so is HR's role in strategy.

We do not know the causal direction of the strong relationships found with strategy involvement. Our belief is that when HR managers and their business leaders are better on all elements of the HR decision science, organizations achieve high HR strategy involvement. Alternatively, the causal direction may go from strategic role to HR decision science sophistication. This interpretation is consistent with the situation that we often see in organizations, where a handful of HR executives are highly skilled at talent segmentation and strategic insights. Often they developed this ability through fortuitous career opportunities to observe and participate in business strategy development and implementation. This interpretation argues for efforts to get HR executives more involved in strategy as a way to build and convey the HR decision science.

Developing the decision science capability of managers outside HR may lead to HR strategic involvement. Our results suggest that some HR executives already have opportunities for full partnership in strategy development and implementation, but in general, HR executives do not rate highly the decision science capability of non-HR managers. Improving the decision science capability of managers outside HR may make them more effective at working with strategically involved HR executives.

Strategic Focuses

The relationships between the extent to which organizations are pursuing different strategic focuses and their ratings of the elements of a sophisticated HR decision science are shown in table 4.3. Clearly, the pattern of significant associations varies greatly among the different strategic focuses.

Table 4.3. Relationship of HR decision making to strategic focuses, United States					
	Strategic Focuses				
Decision Making	Growth	Information-Based Strategies	Knowledge-Based Strategies	Sustainability	Innovation
We excel at competing for and with talent where it matters most to our strategic success.	.17	.33***	.61***	.27**	.49***
Business leaders' decisions that depend on or affect human capital (e.g., layoffs, rewards) are as rigorous, logical, and strategically relevant as their decisions about resources such as money, technology, and customers.	.08	.37***	.46***	.26**	.35***
HR leaders have a good understanding about where and why human capital makes the biggest difference in their business.	.00	.34***	.28**	.07	.21*
Business leaders have a good understanding about where and why human capital makes the biggest difference in their business.	.08	.38***	.42***	.13	.31***
HR systems educate business leaders about their talent decisions.	.18^t	.34***	.41***	.20*	.16
HR adds value by ensuring compliance with rules, laws, and guidelines.	.07	.04	.24*	.33***	.09
HR adds value by delivering high-quality professional practices and services.	.00	.36***	.48***	.21*	.39***
HR adds value by improving talent decisions inside and outside the HR function.	.11	.41***	.54***	.26**	.42***
Response scale: 1 = little or no extent; 2 = some extent; 3 = moderate extent; 4 = great extent; 5 = very great extent. Significance level: $^t p \le .10$, $^* p \le .05$, $^{**} p \le .01$, $^{***} p \le .001$.					

All but one strategic focus show multiple significant correlations with most of decision science items. The exception is a focus on growth, which shows no significant correlations. This pattern has consistently been present in our earlier surveys as well. This suggests that how strongly an organization emphasizes growth has little to do with the level of these HR decision science activities.

A focus on sustainability showed few correlations with these decision science items in the 2013 survey, but this changed in 2016, where we see significant correlations for all items except the two about HR and business leaders understanding where and why human capital makes the biggest difference. The results for sustainability now resemble more closely the results for all other strategies except growth, perhaps because as the focus on sustainability matures, the value of high-quality human capital decisions becomes more apparent.

The correlations for the innovation strategy have generally increased compared to both 2007 and 2013. In 2007, pursuing innovation was not strongly associated with excellence in the human capital decision science, but in 2010, this changed and the association has increased in the two surveys since. This certainly is consistent with the reality that talent quality is needed in order for innovation to occur. Possibly, in earlier times of innovation, organizations focused on more traditional resources such as technology, alliances, and intellectual property protection, but as innovation has become more difficult and competitive, the importance of human capital and high-quality talent decisions has become more apparent.

The results for items reflecting HR leaders' and business leaders' understanding of talent segmentation (where and why human capital makes the biggest difference), as well as the three items reflecting how HR adds value, show a significant pattern change from 2007 to 2016. In 2007, these items were generally not correlated with the different strategic focuses, though a few correlations with the knowledge-based strategic emphasis were significant. The 2010 data show strong correlations with these items across all strategies except growth, and this pattern seems to be sustained in the 2016 results. Such a generalized shift suggests that HR decision science quality may be becoming a more generalized factor in a broad array of strategic focuses.

The pursuit of a growth strategy, however, is not highly correlated with the talent items. It may be that the dogged pursuit of growth motivates a focus on more traditional roles for HR than in supporting decisions and educating leaders. It may be that organizations pursuing growth strategies have not internalized the connection between high-quality talent decisions and strategy success. The sustainability focus showed a similar result, but it is now changing, suggesting that in the future, the value of decision science quality will become more strongly correlated with a growth focus.

It is also notable that HR's ability to add value through compliance has the lowest correlation with the strategic focuses, whereas delivering high-quality services and improving talent decisions often correlates significantly. Again, compliance is seen as table stakes (the minimum acceptable value) rather than as a differentiating factor when it comes to HR being an important contributor. The exceptions are for the knowledge-based and sustainability focuses, where value through compliance is positively associated. This may reflect increased regulatory complexity or scrutiny in organizations pursuing these focuses, which depend more on laws and regulations concerning intellectual property and environmental protection.

Management Approaches

Table 4.4 shows the relationship between the HR decision-making items and the five management approaches. In general, the results suggest that the level of HR decision science is much more strongly positively associated with the high-involvement and sustainable management approaches than with the other three approaches. This is consistent with the idea that in the high-involvement approach, there is a major reliance

Table 4.4. Relationship of HR decision making to management approaches, United States					
	Management Approaches				
Decision Making	**Bureaucratic**	**Low-Cost Operator**	**High Involvement**	**Global Competitor**	**Sustainable**
We excel at competing for and with talent where it matters most to our strategic success.	−.43***	−.21*	.54***	.12	.41***
Business leaders' decisions that depend on or affect human capital (e.g., layoffs, rewards) are as rigorous, logical, and strategically relevant as their decisions about resources such as money, technology, and customers.	−.36***	−.16ᵗ	.46***	.06	.42***
HR leaders have a good understanding about where and why human capital makes the biggest difference in their business.	−.31***	−.03	.35***	−.02	.24*
Business leaders have a good understanding about where and why human capital makes the biggest difference in their business.	−.37***	−.05	.45***	−.01	.31***
HR systems educate business leaders about their talent decisions.	−.24*	−.19*	.37***	.07	.44***
HR adds value by ensuring compliance with rules, laws, and guidelines.	−.09	−.27**	.24*	−.02	.14
HR adds value by delivering high-quality professional practices and services.	−.24**	−.12	.29**	.04	.21*
HR adds value by improving talent decisions inside and outside the HR function.	−.37***	−.13	.38***	.09	.31***
Response scale: 1 = little or no extent; 2 = some extent; 3 = moderate extent; 4 = great extent; 5 = very great extent. Significance level: ᵗp ≤ .10, *p ≤ .05, **p ≤ .01, ***p ≤ .001.					

on talent alignment, commitment, and trust at all levels of the organization and that it demands business leaders attend to talent and human capital issues. It is also consistent with the idea that sustainability-focused approaches have a higher level of attention to outcomes that go beyond the traditional financial and competitive growth outcomes. The three other approaches (bureaucratic, low cost, global) may rely on a more traditional approach in which leaders outside HR may be held less accountable for making high-quality HR decisions because they focus on more traditional resources and perceive that their results depend less on effective talent management.

The results for the other management approaches are quite different from those for the sustainable and high-involvement approaches. The correlations are nonsignificant for global competitors, meaning that there is little relationship with the extent or quality of the HR decision science items. An emphasis on the bureaucratic or the low-cost-operator approach is negatively associated with all the HR decision science items, a pattern that was present in our 2007 survey, became stronger in the 2010 survey, and is quite pronounced in the 2016 survey.

Indeed, the results for the bureaucratic approach show a striking and significant *negative* relationship with all of the decision science items, which suggests that a bureaucratic approach discourages excellence and value in these areas. When the focus is highly bureaucratic, it may be that leaders have little time for and see little value in making high-quality human capital decisions. Notably, the item about adding value through compliance is the only one that is not negatively associated with the bureaucratic approach, suggesting that rule compliance is tolerated.

For organizations that approach management with a bureaucratic model, we surmise that issues of human capital and workforce management are delegated to a formal HR function and are managed largely through formal systems. This is not to say that such systems are unsophisticated or inattentive to human capital issues, but they are generally not as much designed to enhance talent decisions as they are to ensure that proper processes are followed. This is somewhat supported by the fact that the item assessing whether HR adds value through compliance is less negatively correlated than the other items with the bureaucratic management approach.

Low-cost-operator strategies place a premium on efficiency and low overhead, which often means lean budgets for HR, which is often seen as overhead. It also may create a focus that regards talent as a cost, not an asset. Thus, for HR executives, a least-cost-possible approach to talent may mean accepting that the organization will not excel in the talent competition and that the resources to build, use, and disseminate an HR decision science will be limited.

Finally, it is notable that the global competitor approach consistently falls between the strong human capital decision emphasis of the high-involvement and sustainable approaches and the negative human capital decision emphasis of the bureaucratic and low-cost-operator approaches. This is consistent with the results of our surveys since 2007. We surmise that organizations with the global competitor approach may use a combination of HR decision-making approaches given the diversity of their operations and workforces. It also may mean that human capital decision management is not a major focus for them.

Conclusion

HR executives rate human capital decision making both inside and outside HR as moderately effective. Thus, there is significant room for improvement. An important finding is the striking similarity between HR leaders' perceptions of business leader talent decision sophistication and HR's role in strategy. It would appear that there is synergy between HR's strategic role and non-HR executives' ability to make strong decisions about talent and HR.

The HR decision science facility of organizations appears to vary with the strategy they pursue. It is more sophisticated when they pursue information-based, knowledge-based, sustainability, and innovation business strategies than when they pursue growth strategies. It is also more sophisticated in high-involvement and sustainable management approaches. This suggests that business leader sophistication and HR contribution is higher in strategies where the line of sight between human capital and business outcomes is strong and managers' talent decisions are clearly tied to business and strategic results. High-involvement and sustainable management organizations create a culture and values that emphasize not just HR's capability to manage the workforce well but that it is the responsibility of all leaders to do so.

Generally our findings argue strongly for the strategic value of organizations to have a strong human capital decision support capacity both within and outside their HR functions. There is much room for improvement, as the average ratings of decision quality in 2016 are still close to the midpoint of the rating scale, as they were in earlier surveys. The 2016 results provide strong evidence of the positive association between an organization's decision science capacity and HR's role in strategy, particularly in organizations pursuing management approaches and strategies that are workforce intensive and high involvement.

CHAPTER 5

HR Organization and HR Skills

- The design of HR functions has changed. Centers of excellence have become more common, as has self-service.

- The degree to which HR practices vary within an organization has decreased.

- HR does little to develop HR talent by rotating people into, within, and out of the function.

- Results suggest that what HR needs to do to become more of a strategic contributor is to establish centers of excellence and develop HR talent.

- HR professionals suffer from a skills deficit that limits their role in business strategy development and implementation.

- Ratings of HR skills show only a moderate level of satisfaction.

- Satisfaction with the skills of HR staff has increased in many areas since 1995.

- Satisfaction with HR skills is lowest in China.

- HR skills satisfaction is closely related to HR's involvement in business strategy.

- HR skill satisfaction is highest in organizations that have knowledge-based strategies.

The organizational and operational approaches that an HR function employs have a major impact on what it is able to do and how well it performs. This chapter examines the practices, structures, and talent development that have been suggested as potential ways for HR to become more of a business partner and, in some cases, a strategic contributor.

HR Organizing Approaches

The survey grouped HR organizing approaches into three scales based on a statistical analysis: HR service units, decentralization, and HR talent development. The items and the U.S. mean responses to them are shown in table 5.1. The organizational practices and talent management that HR uses the most are those concerned with decentralization and HR service units. A comparison of the results from 1995 to 2016 shows a significant increase in the use of HR centers of excellence. Most of this change appears to have occurred between 1995 and 2004, when the business partner model of HR became popular and organizations

Table 5.1. HR organization, United States

HR Organization	Means								Correlation with HR Role in Strategy
	1995[1]	1998[2]	2001[3]	2004[4]	2007[5]	2010[6]	2013[7]	2016[8]	
HR service units	**3.0**[4,5,6,7]	**3.2**	**3.3**	**3.5**[1]	**3.5**[1]	**3.4**[1]	**3.4**[1]	**3.3**	.39***
Centers of excellence provide specialized expertise.	2.5[2,3,4,5,6,7,8]	3.1[1]	3.1[1]	3.3[1]	3.4[1]	3.3[1]	3.5[1]	3.4[1]	.39***
Administrative processing is centralized in shared services units.	3.5	3.4	3.4	3.7[8]	3.5	3.5	3.4	3.2[4]	.24*
Decentralization	**3.3**[6,8]	**3.3**[6,8]	**3.3**[6,8]	**3.1**	**3.1**	**2.9**[1,2,3]	**3.0**	**2.8**[1,2,3]	−.09
Decentralized HR generalists support business units.	3.6	3.9[8]	4.0[8]	3.9	3.7	3.6	3.6	3.4[2,3]	.17[t]
HR practices vary across business units.	2.9[4,5,6,7,8]	2.6	2.6	2.3[1]	2.5[1]	2.3[1]	2.4[1]	2.2[1]	−.35***
HR talent development	**2.1**	**2.2**	**2.1**	**2.2**	**2.1**	**2.0**	**2.0**	**2.1**	.32***
People rotate within HR.	2.6	2.8	2.8	2.8	2.7	2.5	2.7	2.8	.28**
People rotate into HR.	1.8	1.8	1.8	1.8	1.7	1.8	1.7	1.9	.23*
People rotate out of HR to other functions.	1.8	1.9[7]	1.9[7]	1.9[7]	1.8	1.8	1.6[2,3,4]	1.8	.26**

Note: Bold numbers are scale means.

Response scale: 1 = little or no extent; 2 = some extent; 3 = moderate extent; 4 = great extent; 5 = very great extent.

[1,2,3,4,5,6,7,8]Significant differences ($p \le .05$) between years.

Significance level: [t]$p \le .10$, *$p \le .05$, **$p \le .01$, ***$p \le .001$.

felt the need for greater HR expertise. There has been little evidence of recent change.

The use of corporate centers of excellence complements the use of decentralized HR generalists by giving them a source for expert help. Growth in the use of these centers of excellence is consistent with the idea of HR being a business partner since it can provide a higher level of business-relevant HR expertise. Having HR processing centers can help HR be a business partner as well, since it can free HR professionals from doing administrative work.

Decentralized generalists who support the business units of a company are a particularly popular practice. This configuration is a possible way to position HR as a business partner by getting it close to the customers, though it has decreased in popularity in recent years, as has decentralization overall.

The degree to which HR practices vary across business units has a relatively low rating that is even lower in 2016 than it was in 1995. This finding suggests that while there may be dedicated HR leaders who are supporting businesses, their role is not to tailor HR practices to those businesses but rather to work with centers of excellence and HR service units in order to deliver common services to their parts of the organization.

The use of common practices most likely reflects efforts to simplify and achieve scale leverage in HR activities and the tendency for companies to engage in fewer unrelated businesses. Corporations may gain economies of scale when they use the same HR practices in all units, particularly in the case of transactions and the creation of self-service HR activities (those carried out by employees and managers outside the HR department) based on information technology.

The HR talent development practices are the least used ones shown in table 5.1, with no change from 1995 to 2016. Employee rotation into and out of HR in particular is infrequent and in fact has declined over the years. This lack of rotation is potentially a major problem for the HR function because it means that its members are likely to remain a separate group with a limited perspective on how their organization as a whole operates. Furthermore, they are unlikely to be involved in or deeply knowledgeable about the business. There also appears to be relatively little rotation within HR, a practice that creates silo careers and does little to help HR employees develop an understanding of the total HR function.

There are multiple significant relationships between the way that HR is organized and the role it plays in strategy. HR talent development and HR service units are significantly related to HR's role in strategy. This result confirms that HR needs to have good talent, perform its own operations effectively, and have the expertise and services that meet the needs of the business.

Having decentralized HR generalists has a low but positive relationship to HR's role in strategy. This finding provides weak support for the view that the best way to make HR more of a contributor to strategy is to put it close to the business. However, the significant negative correlation with having HR practices that vary across business units suggests that this works against having HR play a role in strategy, most likely because it typically exists when there is not a strong corporate HR function that can influence corporate strategy.

International Results

The international data on HR organization in table 5.2 show, with a few exceptions, that the results for China are different from those of the other

Table 5.2. HR organization, by country

HR Organization	Means				
	United States[1]	Canada[2]	Australia[3]	United Kingdom/Europe[4]	China[5]
HR service units	**3.3[5]**	**3.3**	**3.0**	**3.6[5]**	**2.8[1,4]**
Centers of excellence provide specialized expertise.	3.4[3,5]	3.4[5]	2.6[1,4]	3.7[3,5]	2.7[1,2,4]
Administrative processing is centralized in shared services units.	3.2	3.3	3.3	3.6[5]	2.9[4]
Decentralization	**2.8**	**2.5**	**2.6**	**3.1**	**3.0**
Decentralized HR generalists support business units.	3.4	3.3	2.7[4]	3.7[3]	3.2
HR practices vary across business units.	2.2[5]	1.8[3,5]	2.5[2]	2.4	2.8[1,2]
HR talent development	**2.1[3]**	**1.8[5]**	**1.6[1,5]**	**2.1**	**2.4[2,3]**
People rotate within HR.	2.8[2,3]	2.1[1,5]	1.9[1,4,5]	2.8[3]	2.8[2,3]
People rotate into HR.	1.9	1.7[5]	1.6[5]	1.7	2.2[2,3]
People rotate out of HR to other functions.	1.8[5]	1.6[5]	1.4[5]	1.7[5]	2.3[1,2,3,4]

Note: Bold numbers are scale means.

Response scale: 1 = little or no extent; 2 = some extent; 3 = moderate extent; 4 = great extent; 5 = very great extent.

[1,2,3,4,5] Significant differences ($p \leq .05$) between years.

countries. It is a low user of almost all organizing structures and practices. The largest difference between China and the other countries is in HR service units. China uses centers of excellence and administrative processing service units much less frequently than most of the other countries in the study do. None of the countries studied scored highly on developing HR talent through cross-functional rotation, with Canada and Australia scoring the lowest. The most common type of rotation is within HR. The small amount of rotation into and out of the HR function may help explain why HR often is not seen as business knowledgeable.

Strategic Focuses

Table 5.3 shows the relationships between the strategic focuses and the HR organization. The use of service units is significantly associated with all but one of the strategic focuses. HR talent development is also strongly associated with multiple strategic focuses. Only decentralization is not related to these focuses. It seems that the HR organizational designs in table 5.3 fit the strategic focuses of most organizations.

Three of the strategic focuses—knowledge-based, information-based, and innovation —are significantly related to HR organizational design. Sustainability has a lower, though significant, relationship with them. Given their reliance on talent, this is hardly surprising since these designs are supportive of effective talent management.

Table 5.3. Relationship of the HR organization to strategic focuses, United States					
	Strategic Focuses				
HR Organization	Growth	Information-Based Strategies	Knowledge-Based Strategies	Sustainability	Innovation
HR service units	−.02	.38***	.40***	.17^t	.35***
Decentralization	.09	−.17^t	−.13	−.13	−.05
HR talent development	.11	.32***	.49***	.25**	.27**

Response scale: 1 = little or no extent; 2 = some extent; 3 = moderate extent; 4 = great extent; 5 = very great extent.
Significance level: $^t p \le .10$, $^* p \le .05$, $^{**} p \le .01$, $^{***} p \le .001$.

Management Approach

A few of the relationships between an organization's management approach and the organizing structure of its HR organization are significant (table 5.4). The high-involvement approach is related to the development of HR talent, as is the sustainability approach. This is not surprising since these management approaches rely heavily on talent as a source of competitive advantage.

HR Skills

The skills and knowledge of the members of an organization's HR function are an important determinant of what it does and how well it performs (Ulrich, Brockbank, Johnson, Sandholtz, and Younger 2008). Much of the high-value-added work HR does is knowledge work that requires considerable expertise in a wide variety of areas. In today's rapidly changing global economy, the knowledge and skill requirements for the members of an organization's staff functions are continuing to evolve just as they are for the firm's core business and technical units. The key issues for HR are the skills and knowledge HR professionals need and the current level of their skills and knowledge.

Skill Importance

In 2007, we asked HR executives to rate the importance of a variety of HR skills and knowledge (Lawler and Boudreau 2009). For survey length reasons, we did not ask this question in 2010, 2013, or 2016 but we did ask about skill satisfaction. Table 5.5 shows the results of a statistical analysis that yielded four factors and one item. There is some similarity between our factors and the HR competencies that Ulrich and his partners have identified (Ulrich, Brockbank, Johnson, Sandholtz, and Younger 2008; Ulrich, Younger, Brockbank, and Ulrich 2012). However, ours are more focused on the content knowledge that HR executives need, while theirs include personal traits (e.g., "credible activist"), and as a result there are significant differences.

Table 5.4. Relationship of the HR organization to management approaches, United States

HR Organization	Management Approaches				
	Bureaucratic	Low-Cost Operator	High Involvement	Global Competitor	Sustainable
HR service units	.04	−.04	.19*	.09	.20*
Decentralization	.01	−.05	−.06	.17^t	−.04
HR talent development	−.17^t	−.04	.39***	.16^t	.31***

Response scale: 1 = little or no extent; 2 = some extent; 3 = moderate extent; 4 = great extent; 5 = very great extent.

Significance level: $^tp \le .10$, $^*p \le .05$, $^{**}p \le .01$, $^{***}p \le .001$.

Table 5.5. Importance of HR skills, United States, 2007

Skills and Knowledge	Percentages			Means	
	Not Important	Somewhat Important	Very Important	HR Executives	Managers
HR skills				**2.7**	**2.7**
HR technical skills	1.0	26.8	72.2	2.7	2.9^1
Process execution and analysis	2.1	29.2	68.8	2.7	2.5^1
Interpersonal dynamics				**2.8**	**2.7^1**
Team skills	0.0	12.4	87.6	2.9	2.7
Interpersonal skills	0.0	14.4	85.6	2.9	2.8
Consultation skills	1.0	20.6	78.4	2.8	2.6
Coaching and facilitation	1.0	22.7	76.3	2.8	2.7
Leadership/management	1.0	15.5	83.5	2.8	2.7
Business partner skills				**2.6**	**2.6**
Business understanding	0.0	7.2	92.8	2.9	2.8
Strategic planning	0.0	38.1	61.9	2.6	2.4^1
Organization design	3.1	53.6	43.3	2.4	2.7^1
Change management	0.0	20.6	79.4	2.8	2.8
Cross-functional experience	8.2	51.5	40.2	2.3	2.2
Global understanding	18.6	39.2	42.3	2.2	2.2
Communications	0.0	19.6	80.4	2.8	2.9
Metric skills				**2.4**	**2.3**
Information technology	9.3	55.7	35.1	2.3	2.0^1
Metrics and analytics	5.2	48.5	46.4	2.4	2.4
Data analysis and mining	6.2	48.5	45.4	2.4	2.3
Managing contractors/vendors	12.4	58.8	28.9	**2.2**	**2.1**

Note: Bold numbers are scale means.

^{1}Significant difference ($p \le .05$) between HR executives and managers.

Although there is some variation in how highly they were rated, most of the skills were rated high in importance. The skills that were rated particularly high include business understanding and skills having to do with interpersonal dynamics and change management. HR executives rated business understanding, team skills, and interpersonal skills highest and metrics skills and managing contractor skills lowest in importance. The relatively low rating of metrics skills is concerning because it is an area of growing importance and certainly is one that HR functions need to have. Of course, these data were collected in 2007. In the years since then, much more attention has been focused on metrics, big data, and information technology. As a result, if we had collected data in 2016, we might have seen metrics skills rated higher.

Overall, these results support the argument that HR professionals need to have a range of business skills; it is not enough for them to just be good HR technicians. They must understand the business and what makes it effective and help design the organization, develop teams and leaders, and support change efforts.

Satisfaction with HR Skills

Table 5.6 shows the level of satisfaction with the skills of the HR staff as rated by HR executives in 2016. Not surprisingly, as was true in past surveys, one of the highest levels of satisfaction is with HR technical skills. The other highest level of satisfaction is with skills in interpersonal dynamics: team skills, interpersonal skills, consultation skills, and leadership/management skills. This is also an area where the individual skills show an increased level of satisfaction when the 2016 data are compared to earlier data.

All of the business partner skill areas show significant increases in satisfaction, clearly a positive for HR, which must have these skills in order to be a business partner. The data are encouraging, but it is important to note that the level of satisfaction with business skills and interpersonal skills is just above neutral.

It is encouraging that HR professionals understand business better than they did in the 1990s; however, they still do not appear to bring substantive business expertise to the table. This deficit clearly must change if HR is to influence an organization's strategic direction. It is a critical weakness with respect to HR's performing as an effective strategic contributor. Fixing this deficit requires going well beyond simple business acumen to being able to create a truly unique perspective on strategy through the lens of HR and human capital.

There is a low satisfaction level with metrics and information technology skills and no significant increase in the level from 2004 to 2016.

Apparently HR managers are not improving their skills in this critical area. Metrics skills are particularly critical in terms of HR's ability to play a major business strategy role. Bringing data and performing data analyses are critical to many business decisions; thus, it is particularly important that HR executives have good skills in these areas.

Table 5.6. Satisfaction with skills of HR staff, United States

Skills and Knowledge	Means								Correlation with HR Role in Strategy
	1995[1]	1998[2]	2001[3]	2004[4]	2007[5]	2010[6]	2013[7]	2016[8]	
HR technical	—	—	—	**4.0[8]**	**3.7**	**3.8**	**3.7**	**3.7[4]**	**.36*****
Interpersonal dynamics	**3.3[3,4,5,6,7,8]**	**3.1[3,4,5,6,7,8]**	**3.6[1,2]**	**3.7[1,2]**	**3.6[1,2]**	**3.6[1,2]**	**3.5[1,2]**	**3.8[1,2]**	**.44*****
Team skills	3.3[3,4,5,6,7,8]	3.2[3,4,5,6,7,8]	3.7[1,2]	3.7[1,2]	3.7[1,2]	3.6[1,2]	3.7[1,2]	3.8[1,2]	.39***
Interpersonal skills	3.7[3,4,5,8]	3.5[3,4,5,6,7,8]	4.0[1,2]	4.1[1,2]	4.0[1,2]	3.9[2]	3.9[2]	4.1[1,2]	.34***
Consultation skills	3.0[4,8]	2.9[3,4,5,6,8]	3.3[2]	3.4[1,2]	3.3[2]	3.3[2]	3.1	3.5[1,2]	.34***
Leadership/ management skills	3.0[4,5,6,7,8]	2.9[3,4,5,6,7,8]	3.3[2,8]	3.5[1,2]	3.5[1,2]	3.5[1,2]	3.4[1,2,8]	3.8[1,2,3,7]	.38***
Business partner	—	—	—	**3.0**	**3.0**	**3.1**	**2.9[8]**	**3.3[7]**	**.43*****
Business understanding	3.0[3,4,6,8]	2.9[3,4,5,6,7,8]	3.3[1,2]	3.3[1,2]	3.2[2]	3.4[1,2]	3.3[2]	3.4[1,2]	.38***
Cross-functional experience	2.9	2.8[8]	2.9	2.9	2.8	3.0	2.8[8]	3.2[2,7]	.35***
Strategic planning	—	2.8	2.9	3.0	2.9	3.0	2.7[8]	3.1[7]	.38***
Organization design	—	2.7[4,8]	2.8[8]	3.1[2]	3.0	3.0	2.9[8]	3.3[2,3,7]	.45***
Global understanding	—	2.6[8]	2.7	2.8	2.8	2.9	2.9	3.0[2]	.24*
Change management	—	—	3.1	3.3	3.2	3.2	3.1[8]	3.5[7]	.23*
Metrics[a]	—	—	—	**2.8**	**2.8**	**3.0**	**2.8**	**3.0**	**.34*****
Information technology	—	—	3.1	3.0	2.9	3.0	3.0	3.1	.21*
Metrics and analytics	—	—	—	2.7	2.7	2.9	2.6	2.9	.36***
Sustainability	—	—	—	—	—	—	**2.8[8]**	**3.1[7]**	**.30****
Social media	—	—	—	—	—	—	**2.8**	**3.0**	**.22***
Globalization	—	—	—	—	—	—	**2.8**	**3.0**	**.16[t]**
Risk management	—	—	—	—	—	—	**3.0[8]**	**3.3[7]**	**.37*****
Organization culture	—	—	—	—	—	—	—	**3.8**	**.35*****
Workplace branding	—	—	—	—	—	—	—	**3.4**	**.27****

Note: Empty cells indicate that the item was not asked in that year. Bold numbers are scale means.

[a] Scale for metrics skills recalculated for pre-2016 surveys.

Response scale: 1 = very dissatisfied; 2 = dissatisfied; 3 = neither; 4 = satisfied; 5 = very satisfied.

[1,2,3,4,5,6,7,8] Significant difference ($p \leq .05$) between years.

Significance level: [t]$p \leq .10$, *$p \leq .05$, **$p \leq .01$, ***$p \leq .001$.

The four new items added to the 2013 survey—sustainability, social media, globalization, and risk management—are all areas of increased importance in today's business environment. None of them received high satisfaction ratings despite the fact that a great deal of attention has been focused on their importance. However, two of them do show a significant increase from 2013 to 2016. In chapter 3, we presented data suggesting that HR is not active in the sustainability area, so this result is not surprising. The same cannot be said for social media, globalization, and risk management, which are important issues for most organizations and areas where human capital is front and center. HR executives need to improve these skills. Two new skills satisfaction areas that were added in 2016, culture and branding, received relatively high satisfaction scores. This is not surprising since these have been and continue to be areas where HR is active.

International Results for HR Skill Satisfaction

Except for China, the skills satisfaction results for the other countries are very similar to those for the United States (see table 5.7). No other country stands out as having a particularly high or low level of skills satisfaction in all areas.

As was true in 2013, China has lower satisfaction levels with HR technical skills, interpersonal dynamics skills, and some business partner skills. As was true in 2010 and 2013, it has similar satisfaction levels with respect to metrics skills. The United States and Canada have the most positive scores across all areas.

Generally, the absolute level of satisfaction with skills is low for all countries. This is particularly true for business partner and metrics skills, areas where HR professionals in all countries need to improve.

Satisfaction with HR Skills and HR's Role in Strategy

The relationship between HR skills satisfaction and HR's role in strategy is shown in table 5.6. The correlations for HR technical skills, interpersonal dynamics, business partner skills, and metrics skills are statistically significant. The six business support areas (sustainability, social media, globalization, risk management, culture, and branding) are also related to HR's role in strategy, but some are at a lower level. The significant positive correlations between HR technical skills and HR's role in strategy support the view that HR technical skills are required in order to get involved in business strategy. The correlations of role in strategy with skills in interpersonal dynamics and business partner skills were expected to be high, given that they are truly the foundation for contributing to business strategy from both an implementation and

Table 5.7. Satisfaction with skills of HR staff, by country					
	Means				
Skills and Knowledge	United States[1]	Canada[2]	Australia[3]	United Kingdom/ Europe[4]	China[5]
HR technical skills	**3.7**	**3.9**	**3.8**	**3.5**	**3.4**
Interpersonal dynamics	**3.8[5]**	**3.9[5]**	**3.6**	**3.8[5]**	**3.3[1,2,4]**
Team skills	3.8[5]	4.0[5]	3.7	4.0[5]	3.3[1,2,4]
Interpersonal skills	4.1[5]	4.1[5]	3.7	4.1[5]	3.5[1,2,4]
Consultation skills	3.5	3.9[5]	3.5	3.3	3.1[2]
Leadership/management skills	3.8[5]	3.9[5]	3.4	3.7[5]	3.2[1,2,4]
Business partner skills	**3.3**	**3.3**	**3.0**	**3.3**	**3.0**
Business understanding	3.4	3.4	3.5	3.5	3.2
Cross-functional experience	3.2	3.1	3.0	2.9	3.2
Strategic planning	3.1	3.4	2.9	3.2	3.0
Organization design	3.3	3.4	3.0	3.2	3.1
Global understanding	3.0[5]	3.1	2.6	3.3[5]	2.6[1,4]
Change management	3.5[5]	3.7[5]	3.1	3.5[5]	2.9[1,2,4]
Metrics skills	**3.0**	**2.9**	**2.5[5]**	**2.6**	**3.0[3]**
Information technology	3.1[3,4]	3.1	2.6[1]	2.6[1]	3.0
Metrics and analytics	2.9	2.7	2.4[5]	2.6	3.1[3]
Sustainability	**3.1**	**3.1**	**2.6**	**3.1**	**2.9**
Social media	**3.0**	**2.9**	**2.5**	**2.7**	**3.0**
Globalization	**3.0[5]**	**2.9**	**2.5**	**3.1[5]**	**2.4[1,4]**
Risk management	**3.3**	**3.4**	**2.8**	**3.2**	**3.1**
Organization culture	**3.8[3,5]**	**4.0[3,5]**	**3.2[1,2]**	**3.6**	**3.3[1,2]**
Workplace branding	**3.4**	**3.7[3,4]**	**3.0[2]**	**3.0[2]**	**3.3**

Note: Bold numbers are scale means.

Response scale: 1 = very dissatisfied; 2 = dissatisfied; 3 = neither; 4 = satisfied; 5 = very satisfied.

[1,2,3,4,5] Significant differences between countries ($p \leq .05$).

a development point of view. The correlations with metrics skills are not as high as the others, but they are significant. These skills certainly are potentially useful in strategy development and implementation, so it is not surprising that they are related.

The relatively low correlations for social media and globalization are not surprising. Although they are important factors in strategy development, they are not core HR issues and as a result are most likely not key to HR's playing a role in strategy development. However, the fact that they are related suggests that HR can play a larger role in strategy development by developing them.

Table 5.8. HR professionals with necessary skills, United States								
Have Skills	**Percentages**							
	1995	**1998**	**2001**	**2004**	**2007**	**2010**	**2013**	**2016**
None	0.0	0.0	0.0	0.0	0.0	0.0	0.9	0.0
1%–20%	0.0	1.7	4.7	2.1	2.0	6.3	1.8	0.9
21%–40%	18.6	15.1	18.9	12.4	17.3	16.0	17.7	16.4
41%–60%	34.9	38.7	33.1	37.1	33.7	29.7	37.2	32.7
61%–80%	37.2	40.3	33.1	34.0	36.7	35.4	36.3	32.7
81%–99%	8.5	4.2	10.1	11.3	10.2	11.4	6.2	16.4
100%	0.8	0.0	0.0	3.1	0.0	1.1	0.0	0.9
Mean[a]	**4.38**	**4.30**	**4.25**	**4.49**	**4.36**	**4.33**	**4.25**	**4.50**

[a]Response scale: 1 = none; 2 = 1–20 percent; 3 = 21–40 percent; 4 = 41–60 percent; 5 = 61–80 percent; 6 = 81–99 percent; 7 = 100 percent.

No significant differences ($p \leq .05$) between years.

HR's Skill Levels

Despite the increase in satisfaction with HR skills in some areas, the percentage of HR professionals with the necessary overall skills did not change significantly from 1995 to 2016 in the judgment of HR executives (table 5.8). Very few HR executives report that over 80 percent of their staff have the necessary skills. This disappointing rating suggests that the HR function in many companies is staffed with many individuals who lack the skills they need in order to perform well.

International Results of HR Skill Levels

The international results on skill set presence are shown in table 5.9. All the countries but China show the same result that we found in the United States. China shows a much lower percentage of professionals with the necessary skill set, not surprising given its low skill satisfaction scores in table 5.7. Together they provide strong evidence that HR professionals in China need to greatly improve their skills.

Strategic Focuses and HR Skill Satisfaction

The relationship between the strategic focuses and HR skill satisfaction as rated by HR executives is shown in table 5.10. All the correlations are positive and strong except for those with growth.

Organizations with strong strategic focuses have HR functions with higher satisfaction in their skill sets. It is easy to see why focuses on information, knowledge, sustainability, and innovation are associated with better HR skills. They often require HR functions that are able to

Table 5.9. HR professionals with necessary skills, by country					
Have Skills	Means				
	United States[1]	Canada[2]	Australia[3]	United Kingdom/ Europe[4]	China[5]
None	0.0	0.0	0.0	0.0	2.1
1%–20%	0.9	0.0	6.1	0.0	8.3
21%–40%	16.4	2.9	12.1	5.6	27.1
41%–60%	32.7	40.0	33.3	52.8	20.8
61%–80%	32.7	42.9	33.3	30.6	36.5
81%–99%	16.4	14.3	12.1	11.1	4.2
100%	0.9	0.0	3.0	0.0	1.0
Mean[a]	4.50[5]	4.69[5]	4.42	4.47	3.98[1,2]

[a]Response scale: 1 = none; 2 = 1–20 percent; 3 = 21–40 percent; 4 = 41–60 percent; 5 = 61–80 percent; 6 = 81–99 percent; 7 = 100 percent.

[1,2,3,4,5]Significant differences between countries ($p \leq .05$).

Table 5.10. Relationship of HR skills satisfaction to strategic focuses, United States					
Skills and Knowledge	Strategic Focuses				
	Growth	Information-Based Strategies	Knowledge-Based Strategies	Sustainability	Innovation
HR technical	.07	.34***	.36***	.18t	.33***
Interpersonal dynamics	.13	.38***	.49***	.28**	.33***
Business partner	.20*	.45***	.51***	.32***	.44***
Metrics	.08	.39***	.46***	.25**	.32***
Sustainability	.09	.21*	.35***	.52***	.28**
Social media	.22*	.36***	.41***	.27**	.32***
Globalization	.42***	.19t	.22*	.11	.29**
Risk management	.02	.19*	.18t	.25**	.27**
Organization culture	.24*	.42***	.54***	.24*	.43***
Workplace branding	.03	.31***	.43***	.36***	.30***

Significance level: t$p \leq .10$, *$p \leq .05$, **$p \leq .01$, ***$p \leq .001$.

do not only HR technical work but also to design systems and develop talent that supports organizational performance and knowledge development. The results for social media skills are interesting. Satisfaction with the skills of HR in this area is correlated with the three strategic focuses that are most likely to gain from having a social media capability: information, knowledge, and innovation.

Table 5.11. Relationship of HR skills satisfaction to management approaches, United States					
Skills and Knowledge	**Management Approaches**				
	Bureaucratic	**Low-Cost Operator**	**High Involvement**	**Global Competitor**	**Sustainable**
HR technical	−.17^t	−.18^t	.28**	.08	.17^t
Interpersonal dynamics	−.17^t	−.19*	.29**	.13	.27**
Business partner	−.25**	−.30**	.40***	.06	.32***
Metrics	−.19^t	−.09	.24*	.10	.33***
Sustainability	−.19*	−.16^t	.35***	−.06	.45***
Social media	−.18^t	−.20*	.35***	.05	.38***
Globalization	−.14	−.21*	.17^t	.27**	.20*
Risk management	−.08	−.10	.25**	−.01	.23*
Organization culture	−.34***	−.33***	.39***	.01	.29**
Workplace branding	−.40***	−.24*	.49***	−.10	.38***
Significance level: $^t p ≤ .10$, $*p ≤ .05$, $**p ≤ .01$, $***p ≤ .001$.					

Management Approach and HR Skill Satisfaction

The pattern of correlations between HR skills satisfaction and the five management approaches shown in table 5.11 is very interesting. The bureaucratic and low-cost-operator approaches are negatively related to satisfaction with all the skills, and in the case of culture, the relationship is significant. This most likely is due to the low importance these approaches place on human capital, which leads to their having HR functions with low skill levels.

The management approach that focuses the most on human capital, high involvement, has significant positive relationships with all but one type of HR skills satisfaction. This is not surprising since it places a major emphasis on talent and talent management and therefore needs skilled HR managers.

It is surprising that globalization and risk management are related to only a few of the management approaches. This may be due to their not being traditional HR skill areas and, as a result, not a focus of HR that is influenced by an organization's management approach an organization has.

Conclusion

Overall the results show some change in the use of the HR organizational design approaches studied: significant growth in service units and centers of excellence, which are related to HR being more of a strategic partner. There is a trend toward less use of HR practices that vary across business units and a greater emphasis on self-service HR practices. But we do not see greater career movement of individuals into and out of HR or information technology.

A number of important relationships between the characteristics of the HR organization and HR's role in strategy suggest what HR needs to do to become more of a strategic partner: establish centers of excellence, use joint task forces, and develop HR talent. In past surveys, HR organizations said they planned to use more teams and improve their efficiency, but they do not appear to have done either of these.

The results suggest that HR professionals suffer from a skills deficit that limits their role in business strategy development and implementation. It is notable that there is at best only moderate satisfaction with all HR skills: no rating by HR executives was higher than a mean of 4.1 on a 5-point scale, and that was on interpersonal skills. Most ratings in the countries studied fall around the neutral point. Of particular concern are the relatively low ratings given to business partner skills, since they are related to HR's playing a significant role in strategy; the low rating on metrics and organizational design are also particularly troubling. On the encouraging side, some business partner skills have shown significant improvement. Still, much work remains to be done on enhancing HR skills, as well as developing a common understanding about the level those skills need to be at in order to have an effective HR organization.

CHAPTER 6

Measuring Efficiency, Effectiveness, and Impact

- The most common HR measures reflect efficiency; there is moderate use of effectiveness and impact measures.

- Measurement use patterns show similar use of efficiency and effectiveness measures and some increase in impact measures compared to 2010 and 2013.

- Measuring efficiency, effectiveness, and impact is generally unrelated to HR's strategic role, with the exception of measuring the business impact of HR programs and processes.

- Unlike prior surveys, Chinese organizations' measurement of efficiency and effectiveness in 2016 is generally similar to that of other countries, and China surpasses other countries in measuring the quality of talent decisions and the pivotal impact of performance.

- Measurement of all three areas is generally positively associated with all strategic focuses except the growth focus, which has a slight negative association.

- For the first time, the sustainability strategic focus and management approach showed consistent positive associations with the use of all three types of measurement.

Two comments are frequently used when HR measurement is discussed: "What's measured gets managed," and "Not everything that counts can be counted, and not everything that can be counted actually counts." The first has led business and HR leaders to strive for more measurement in a belief that measures will produce increased attention and understanding of HR issues in organizations. The second caution is a key one: simply because something can be measured does not mean that it should be a major focus. It may not be important in terms of organizational performance.

A key decision for HR and business leaders is what to measure and how to use those measures in decision making. This chapter examines the focus of HR measures in terms of three key areas: efficiency, effectiveness and impact (Boudreau and Ramstad 2007; Cascio and Boudreau 2011; Boudreau and Cascio, 2017). Efficiency refers to the amount of resources that HR programs use, such as cost per hire. Effectiveness refers to the outcomes that HR activities produce, such as learning from training. Impact refers to the business or strategic value that HR activities create, such as higher sales. The next chapter examines the outcomes that result from using HR measures.

The emergence of big data applied to human capital is often cited as ushering in an era of increased reliance on analytics and increased prominence for HR (Bersin 2016). However, big data also represent the most recent evolution of a continuing and unresolved dilemma: the amount and variety of data available to organizations about their people exceeds the ability of leaders to digest, make sense of, and make decisions using such data.

It is common to recommend that HR measurement focus on business outcomes. For example, Rasmussen and Ulrich (2015) state, "HR Analytics needs to evolve and transcend HR, and will only become relevant when it takes an 'outside-in' approach, and is taken out of HR and integrated in existing end-to-end business analytics." This can be incorrectly interpreted to mean that only impact measures are truly strategic. In fact, just as with functions such as finance, marketing, and operations, a mix of all three types of measures can be useful, and indeed measuring all three is often required to fully understand how HR investments affect organizational performance. Each calls for somewhat different metrics and analytics. They can complement each other when they are used together.

Efficiency measures the resources that are devoted to HR and the functional processes delivered, such as cost per hire. Cost-benefit analysis most resembles efficiency and has often been referred to as the holy grail of HR measurement. It certainly has drawn the attention of many HR leaders and consultants. Effectiveness measures the immediate effects of HR processes, such as whether training produces learning and whether a recruitment program increases the number of applicants. Understanding the return on investment of HR programs is similar to effectiveness and is highly useful. Still, neither efficiency nor effectiveness reveals the ultimate business outcomes of HR investments, nor does it reveal the synergies among HR programs and how measures contribute to decisions about human capital. We refer to these ultimate outcomes, synergies, and decision effects as impact. A combination of efficiency, effectiveness, and impact measures is likely to be the most effective approach. This combination remains rare in most organizations but seems to be increasing.

Efficiency measures are basic to the HR function, and they connect readily to the existing accounting system. Increasing attention is being given to measuring effectiveness by focusing on such things as turnover, attitudes, and bench strength. However, organizations rarely consider impact (e.g., the relative effect of improving the quality of different talent pools on organizational effectiveness). HR measurement typically is not specifically directed to vital talent segments, where decisions are most important (see chapter 4). This is unfortunate because the evolution of HR measurement toward more comprehensive and analytically rigorous approaches that are based on a science for human capital is likely to be a requirement for HR to progress in such areas as strategic partnership, decisions support, and measurement and analytics.

Metrics and Analytics Use

Table 6.1 shows the pattern of HR's use of metrics and analytics for the U.S. sample. The results in the first four columns show the percentage of HR executives saying that they have these measures. These results suggest that most of the measurement and analytics elements remain relatively rare, with only three of them in 2016 rated as "Yes, have now" by more than 40 percent of organizations. Two of the three are in the efficiency category: the financial efficiency of HR operations and creating traditional HR data benchmarks; we include benchmarking in the efficiency category because the vast majority of such benchmarks reflect

Table 6.1. HR analytics and metrics use, United States									
Measures	**Yes, Have Now (%)**				**Means**				**2016 Correlation with HR Role in Strategy**
	2007	**2010**	**2013**	**2016**	**2007**[1]	**2010**[2]	**2013**[3]	**2016**[4]	
Efficiency									
Measure the financial efficiency of HR operations (e.g., cost per hire, time to fill, training costs).	50.5	53.8	48.9	47.4	3.1	3.1	3.1	3.1	.13
Collect metrics that measure the cost of providing HR programs and processes.	39.8	43.3	41.6	37.5	3.0	3.0	2.9	2.9	.08
Benchmark analytics and measures against data from outside organizations (e.g., Saratoga, Mercer, Hewitt).	48.5	54.9	48.5	44.7	3.0	3.0	3.0	2.9	−.02
Effectiveness									
Use HR dashboards or scorecards.	37.8	51.6	46.7	51.8	2.9	3.2	3.1	3.2	.03
Measure the specific effects of HR programs (e.g., learning from training, motivation from rewards, validity of tests).	19.2	32.4	17.5	27.2	2.4	2.6	2.3	2.5	.17[t]
Have the capability to conduct cost-benefit analyses (also called utility analyses) of HR programs.	18.4	26.4	25.0	25.4	2.3	2.5	2.3	2.4	.07
Impact									
Measure the business impact of HR programs and processes.	20.4	27.6	21.9	28.9	2.6	2.7	2.5	2.7	.26**
Measure the quality of the talent decisions made by non-HR leaders.	10.1	18.1	10.9	14.0	1.9	2.1	1.9	2.1	.08
Measure the business impact of high versus low performance in jobs.	12.1	18.1	10.9	17.5	2.0	2.1	1.9	2.2	.06

Response scale: 4 = yes, have now; 3 = being built; 2 = planning for; 1 = not currently being considered.

No significant differences ($p \le .05$) between years.

Significance level: [t]$p \le .10$, *$p \le .05$, **$p \le .01$, ***$p \le .001$.

costs and activity levels. Generally the percentage of organizations that report having the three efficiency measures is lower in 2016 than in all previous surveys.

Dashboards or scorecards are used interchangeably here to refer to reports that present an array of HR measures, usually reflecting both effectiveness and efficiency. They are the most frequently used type of measurement. It is the only item rated as "have now" by more than 50 percent of organizations. We label this type "effectiveness," because although dashboards and scorecards contain efficiency measures, they often also contain information on program outcomes or workforce behaviors such as skill levels, engagement, and turnover. The increasing use of scorecards likely reflects the emergence of vendor technology that can inexpensively integrate HR measures into such scorecards and the fact that standard scorecards are often a core feature of HR information and reporting systems. The two other measures of effectiveness, specific HR program effects and cost-benefit analysis, much rarer than efficiency measures and scorecards, are used by less than 30 percent of organizations.

Perhaps predictably, measures of impact are the least frequently used. Although 28.9 percent of organizations report having measures of the business impact of HR programs and processes, only 14 percent have measures of the business impact of performance differences in jobs and only 17.5 percent actually measure the quality of talent decisions. The finding on talent decisions reinforces our results in chapter 4, which show that while HR leaders believe they are moderately good at talent decisions, HR systems generally do not educate non-HR managers about their decision quality. Indeed, 28.9 percent may be an overestimate of the use of business impact measures. Our experience suggests that when HR executives are asked if they measure business impact, they often interpret it to mean the effects of specific programs on workforce attributes such as skills, competencies, and attitudes, rather than the effects of such programs on business outcomes such as sales, financial performance, and sustainable effectiveness.

Many have lamented the glacial pace of progress in people analytics (Green 2016), and our data reinforce the point that their use rate is low. The results in table 6.1 depict a generally stable level of the use of all three types of measures over the years. The 2013 survey showed some significant declines in some measures, but measurement use in the 2016 survey seems to have returned to the 2010 levels.

Measurement Use and HR's Role in Strategy

Is the use of measures important to HR's strategic role? The relationship between the use of HR metrics and HR's role in strategy is shown in the far-right column of table 6.1. Surprisingly, only one of the items is significantly correlated with HR's role in strategy: the impact item "measure the business impact of HR programs and processes." This is a significant change from all earlier surveys, where all the efficiency and effectiveness measures were positively related to HR's strategic role. The 2016 results continue a trend since 2007 in which the association with HR's strategic role has decreased for measures of the quality of non-HR leader talent decisions and understanding where performance differences are pivotal to strategic success.

Our data do not explain the causes for this change in 2016, but as we shall see in the next chapter, 2016 revealed a continuing positive association between the effectiveness of HR measures and HR's strategic role. It may be that simply using measures is no longer a differentiator and that attention is shifting to how they are used and their effects.

It is possible that in the period between the 2013 and 2016 surveys, the increased access to measures has reduced their novelty. Considering the nonsignificant correlation with HR's role in strategy for many measures, the increase in their use since 2013 is surprising. Perhaps organizational leaders have come to see HR measures as "table stakes" (necessary for minimum acceptable value), and thus the use of such measures no longer identifies HR organizations with a more strategic role.

The only item that relates to HR's strategic role is measuring the business impact of HR programs, which may suggest that strategic HR measurement increasingly means demonstrating the value of HR programs. This is supported by the frequent admonishments by HR consultants that HR must show its value to the business. However, showing the value of HR programs is hardly a complete approach to measurement. Ample evidence from other functional areas shows that a proper balance among the three types of measures is the best foundation for a strategic partnership. Unfortunately, the 2016 data suggest this may not be the relationship that HR leaders in most organizations experience.

We cannot say definitively that an increased use of measures will lead to higher HR strategy involvement, but there do seem to be significant opportunities for HR to boost its strategic involvement through greater use of efficiency and effectiveness measures. Such measures are fundamental to the development of a more sophisticated decision science, as the development of marketing and finance has shown (Boudreau and Ramstad 2007). We believe that impact metrics can be both a precursor and a result of HR strategic involvement, yet they remain in use by less than half of the organizations studied.

International Use

Table 6.2 shows the results for the use of HR metrics and analytics for the different national samples. All countries reflect the general pattern seen in the United States: efficiency measures are used more frequently than effectiveness and impact measures. This pattern occurs in the United States and United Kingdom/Europe primarily due to significantly more frequent use of efficiency measures and in Canada and Australia due to less frequent use of impact measures. It is least pronounced in China, where the results are much more similar across the three measurement types and where efficiency and effectiveness measures are used less frequently than in the United States.

China presents the most striking change from prior surveys. In the past, the China sample reported a generally lower use of measures across all categories. In 2016, however, the country is more similar to other countries in that the use of all measurement categories has increased. This is particularly true for the use of scorecards, which may reflect the emergence of ubiquitous and standard HR technology products that produce such scorecards. China actually surpasses many of the other countries

Table 6.2. HR analytics and metrics use, by country					
	Means				
Measures	United States[1]	Canada[2]	Australia[3]	United States/ Europe[4]	China[5]
Efficiency					
Measure the financial efficiency of HR operations (e.g., cost per hire, time to fill, training costs).	3.1[3,5]	3.1[5]	2.4[1]	2.8	2.5[1,2]
Collect metrics that measure the cost of providing HR programs and processes.	2.9[3,5]	2.5	2.2[1,4]	2.9[3]	2.4[1]
Benchmark analytics and measures against data from outside organizations (e.g., Saratoga, Mercer, Hewitt).	2.9[3,5]	3.1[3,5]	2.0[1,2,4]	3.2[3,5]	2.3[1,2,4]
Effectiveness					
Use HR dashboards or scorecards.	3.2	3.3	3.0	3.0	2.9
Measure the specific effects of HR programs (e.g., learning from training, motivation from rewards, validity of tests).	2.5	2.3	2.0	2.6	2.5
Have the capability to conduct cost-benefit analyses (also called utility analyses) of HR programs.	2.4[3]	2.1	1.7[1,5]	2.2	2.4[3]
Impact					
Measure the business impact of HR programs and processes.	2.7[3]	2.3	2.1[1,4]	2.8[3]	2.5
Measure the quality of the talent decisions made by non-HR leaders.	2.1[5]	1.7[5]	1.7[5]	2.0[5]	2.6[1,2,3,4]
Measure the business impact of high versus low performance in jobs.	2.2[3]	1.8[5]	1.6[1,5]	2.1	2.5[2,3]

Response scale: 4 = yes, have now; 3 = being built; 2 = planning for; 1 = not currently being considered.
[1,2,3,4,5]Significant differences between countries ($p \leq .05$).

in the frequency with which organizations measure the quality of talent decisions and the business impact of performance. This is striking, because in a separate analysis of the China sample, we found that the frequency of measurement across all items was significantly *negatively* associated with HR's role as a strategic business partner. It appears that Chinese HR leaders are increasing their measurement activity, even though it does not associate with a more frequent strategic role. These results are paradoxical; results in the next chapter will show that the *effectiveness* of HR measures is actually *positively* associated with HR's strategic role in the China sample, as it is in the U.S. sample.

Use and Strategic Focuses

Table 6.3 shows the relationship between the use of HR measurement in the three areas and the strategic focuses of organizations. The pattern shows that two of the strategic focuses (knowledge based and information based) are significantly associated with HR measurement in all three areas. This is different from 2013, when information-based strategic focus showed little association with measurement. The sustainability focus is associated more with the effectiveness and impact measures,

Table 6.3. Correlations of HR analytics and metrics use to strategic focuses, United States					
		Strategic Focuses			
Measures	Growth	Information-Based Strategies	Knowledge-Based Strategies	Sustainability	Innovation
Efficiency					
Measure the financial efficiency of HR operations (e.g., cost per hire, time to fill, training costs).	−.04	.21*	.42***	.18^t	.20*
Collect metrics that measure the cost of providing HR programs and processes.	−.04	.30***	.32***	.21*	.20*
Benchmark analytics and measures against data from outside organizations (e.g., Saratoga, Mercer, Hewitt).	.04	.27**	.29**	.16^t	.22*
Effectiveness					
Use HR dashboards or scorecards.	.10	.32***	.31***	.15	.26**
Measure the specific effects of HR programs (e.g., learning from training, motivation from rewards, validity of tests).	−.03	.38***	.46***	.34***	.41***
Have the capability to conduct cost-benefit analyses (also called utility analyses) of HR programs.	−.17^t	.32***	.40***	.36***	.25**
Impact					
Measure the business impact of HR programs and processes.	−.09	.33***	.37***	.29**	.29**
Measure the quality of the talent decisions made by non-HR leaders.	.01	.33***	.34***	.21*	.16^t
Measure the business impact of high versus low performance in jobs.	.04	.24**	.24*	.23*	.14
Response scale: 4 = yes, have now; 3 = being built; 2 = planning for; 1 = not currently being considered. Significance level: $^t p \le .10$, $^* p \le .05$, $^{**} p \le .01$, $^{***} p \le .001$.					

while the innovation focus is associated more with efficiency and effectiveness. The growth strategy is not associated with any measurement items, as is true for all the surveys since 2007.

The results for the knowledge-based and information-based strategies show that all three categories of HR measures are about equally correlated with an emphasis on these strategies, suggesting that a broadly balanced HR measurement approach characterizes these organizations. The fact that the growth strategy has been consistently uncorrelated with measurement use reinforces the observation that growth-focused strategic pursuit tends to have low correlations with decision science elements generally. It may be that growth-focused organizations are at an earlier stage of development or focused on traditional measures of financial growth.

The sustainability strategy shows an evolution across the 2010, 2013, and 2016 results. In the 2010 results, the sustainability focus showed nonsignificant correlations for all of the efficiency and most of the effectiveness measures, but relatively strong correlations for the use of cost-benefit analysis and all of the impact measures. This pattern was again present in the 2013 data, but all of the correlations were nonsignificant. In the 2016 data in table 6.3, the effectiveness and impact measures show strong correlations, with less pronounced correlations for efficiency. It may be that a sustainability focus typically carries with it a stronger focus on nonfinancial outcomes, leading to traditional efficiency measures being less emphasized. It may also be that a focus on nontraditional outcomes leads to a greater focus and accountability for the employment relationship as an outcome in itself, leading to greater use of impact measures that focus on the talent decisions of leaders.

Use and Management Approaches

Table 6.4 shows the correlations between measurement use and the degree to which organizations pursue different organizational and management approaches. The pattern is similar to what we have found since 2010. The bureaucratic and global competitor approaches are associated with few measurement categories, and the global competitor approach is negatively associated with the use of cost-benefit analysis. As in prior surveys, the low-cost-operator approach is negatively associated with all measurement categories and statistically significantly negatively associated with two effectiveness items and one efficiency item.

As in prior surveys, the high-involvement approach shows significant positive correlations with four HR measures: financial efficiency, providing services, HR program effects, and the business impact of HR programs. However, the particular items that correlated positively with

Measures	Management Approaches				
	Bureaucratic	Low-Cost Operator	High Involvement	Global Competitor	Sustainable
Efficiency					
Measure the financial efficiency of HR operations (e.g., cost per hire, time to fill, training costs).	−.09	−.25**	.28**	.10	.37***
Collect metrics that measure the cost of providing HR programs and processes.	−.03	−.13	.19*	.01	.42***
Benchmark analytics and measures against data from outside organizations (e.g., Saratoga, Mercer, Hewitt).	.02	−.15	.14	.09	.19*
Effectiveness					
Use HR dashboards or scorecards.	.13	−.02	.10	.10	.34***
Measure the specific effects of HR programs (e.g., learning from training, motivation from rewards, validity of tests).	.04	−.21*	.21*	.00	.29**
Have the capability to conduct cost-benefit analyses (also called utility analyses) of HR programs.	−.01	−.21*	.18†	−.21*	.31***
Impact					
Measure the business impact of HR programs and processes.	−.02	−.13	.23*	−.12	.35***
Measure the quality of the talent decisions made by non-HR leaders.	−.10	−.09	.15	−.13	.28**
Measure the business impact of high versus low performance in jobs.	−.02	−.12	.12	.10	.24*

Responses scored: 4 = yes, have now; 3 = being built; 2 = planning for; 1 = not currently being considered.
Significance level: †$p ≤ .10$, *$p ≤ .05$, **$p ≤ .01$, ***$p ≤ .001$.

high involvement are different from those that were correlated in the 2013 survey. This suggests that a high-involvement approach is generally positively associated with advanced HR practices. A significant difference between the 2013 and 2016 surveys is the relationship with the sustainability approach. In 2013, none of the measurement items were significantly related to this approach; in 2016 every one of the items is positively and significantly related. This pattern appears in other chapters as well, suggesting that the sustainability approach increasingly draws on advanced HR practices and is beginning to resemble the high-involvement approach, which has drawn on such practices for several waves of the survey.

Conclusion

There is significant variability in how much organizations use different types of HR measures. Efficiency measures are still used the most, effectiveness measures next, and impact measures the least. Only one measurement approach, scorecards, is used by over 50 percent of companies. In the U.S. sample, the trend since 2010 has been a decrease in the percentage using efficiency measures, a slight decrease in effectiveness measures, and an increase in impact measures. There has also been an increase in the use of scorecards, a pattern that holds across the national samples. In 2016, China showed a new pattern, with greater use of scorecards, talent decisions, and the value-of-talent variation. Clearly there is room for HR to do more measurement.

The evidence that greater measurement use is positively associated with HR's role as a strategic partner is decidedly weaker in the 2016 sample than in all previous samples. In 2016 only one measurement category, measuring the business impact of HR programs and processes, related significantly to HR's role in strategy. In the 2007 results, impact measures were significantly related to HR's role in strategy, but they were not significantly related in the 2010 and 2013 surveys. In 2010 and 2013, more traditional measures such as benchmarks and scorecards were more strongly related to HR's strategic role. The lack of significant association with HR's role in strategy in the 2016 sample may reflect the fact that using measures is no longer strategically distinctive. This trend also suggests that HR's role in strategy may be more associated with traditional measures that describe the cost savings or immediate effects of HR program investments rather than measures that track the eventual quality of talent decisions or impact on organizational outcomes.

Overall, the results present the tantalizing possibility of systematic variations in how HR measures are used and that the pattern of use significantly relates to organizations' strategies and management approaches. Despite the great deal of attention being given to big data and other developments in analytics, HR metrics and analytics remain underdeveloped and underused. Increasing attention to HR metrics and analytics is often recommended based on their potential for strategic improvement and added value. That said, it appears that the best way to increase HR's strategic role is to create and use traditional measures, such as the payoff from specific HR programs. Indeed, many of the examples where HR analytics has achieved visibility and respect reflect this approach (Green 2016). Cascio and Boudreau (2017) noted that not all human capital measurement standards must predict organizational performance and that there is value in establishing feasibility standards that most organizations can adopt and clearly distinguishing them from predictability standards, with evidence of an association with organizational performance.

It may be wise for HR to start in traditional areas and work toward more advanced measures as their constituents develop their understanding of HR metrics. Notably, the emphasis on sustainability management approaches that emerged in 2016 shows strong association with all types of measures, suggesting an organization's management approach can create a hospitable environment for HR measurement.

CHAPTER 7

The Results of HR Metrics and Analytics

- Strategic and functional HR metrics contributions received measurement effectiveness ratings at the midpoint of the scale, with some significant increases from earlier years.

- Using advanced data analysis and capitalizing on big data were the lowest rated for effectiveness, as in prior surveys.

- Measurement effectiveness is consistently and positively correlated with HR's role in strategy, as in prior surveys.

- China's measurement effectiveness was similar to that of other countries, but the Australian sample rated effectiveness generally lower than other countries.

- Measurement effectiveness is positively associated with a greater focus on information-based, knowledge-based, and innovation strategies and not associated with greater focus on growth, as in prior surveys. Unlike prior surveys, in 2016 the sustainability focus was positively associated with measurement effectiveness.

- Measurement effectiveness is higher the more that organizations pursue a high-involvement approach and lower the more that they pursue low-cost-operator and bureaucratic approaches, as in prior surveys. Unlike prior surveys, in 2016 the sustainable management approach was positively associated with measurement effectiveness.

The focus in this chapter is on the outcomes of HR metrics and analytics, which are also sometimes called human capital analytics (HCA). Evidence suggests that measurement effectiveness remains elusive. In a recent study, although 75 percent of surveyed companies believed that using HCA is important for business performance, only 8 percent viewed their organizational capabilities in this area as strong (Bersin, Agarwal, Pelster, and Schwartz 2015). A study of 255 European business and analytics professionals confirms that despite progress with operational reporting and strategic workforce planning, most organizations have yet to fully develop their analytical competencies (Kassim and Nagy 2017).

We first examine two broad areas of effectiveness: strategic contributions (such as contributing to decisions about strategy, identifying where talent makes the greatest strategic impact, connecting human capital practices to organizational performance, and supporting organizational change) and HR functional and operational contributions (such as improving HR department operations and evaluating and investing in HR practices).

Then we focus on four elements that contribute to the effectiveness of measures as catalysts for organizational change. These four elements comprise the LAMP framework, which identifies four vital features of measurement systems for driving strategic change (Boudreau and Ramstad, 2007; Cascio and Boudreau, 2011):

Logic: Frameworks that articulate the connections between talent and strategic success, as well as the principles and conditions that predict individual and organizational behavior

Analytics: Tools and techniques to transform data into rigorous and relevant insights such as statistical analysis and research design

Measures: The numbers and indexes calculated from data system

Process: Communication and knowledge transfer mechanisms through which the information becomes accepted and acted on by key organizational decision makers

Boudreau and Cascio (2017) suggested that these four elements represent the "push" factors, or conditions necessary for suitable HCA to be available. In the 2013 survey, we added an item referring to "capitalizing on big data," so we now have two waves of survey data on its impact.

HR Metrics and Analytics Effectiveness

Table 7.1 shows how HR leaders rated the effectiveness of HR analytics systems in contributing to outcomes related to HR strategic contributions, HR functional and operational contributions, and the four LAMP elements. Overall, the picture shows consistent average effectiveness ratings, hovering around 3.0, with a few less than 3.0. The 2016 effectiveness levels for both strategic and functional outcomes are higher than in 2010 and 2013. Although this is a relatively small change, this is the first time we have seen a statistically significant difference, which is promising. In 2010, none of these outcomes were rated effective or very effective by more than 40 percent of respondents; in 2016, four items achieved that level.

Two highly rated outcomes are related to strategic contributions: supporting organizational change efforts and contributing to decisions about business strategy and human capital management. These were also highly rated in 2010 and 2013. A third strategic outcome, identifying where talent has the greatest potential for strategic impact, showed a significant increase in the proportion of those who rated it as effective

Table 7.1. HR analytics and metrics effectiveness, United States

Outcomes	2016 Percentages					Means			Correlation with HR Role in Strategy
	Very Ineffective	Ineffective	Somewhat Effective	Effective	Very Effective	2010[1]	2013[2]	2016[3]	
Strategy contributions									
Contributing to decisions about business strategy and human capital management	2.7	7.2	35.1	46.8	8.1	3.1[3]	3.1[3]	3.5[1,2]	.32***
Identifying where talent has the greatest potential for strategic impact	2.7	21.6	27.9	41.4	6.3	2.8[3]	3.0[3]	3.3[1,2]	.28**
Connecting human capital practices to organizational performance	1.8	30.6	35.1	29.7	2.7	2.6[3]	2.7[3]	3.0[1,2]	.25**
Supporting organizational change efforts	3.6	9.0	23.4	52.3	11.7	3.2[3]	3.3[3]	3.6[1,2]	.32***
HR functional and operational contributions									
Assessing and improving HR department operations	1.8	14.4	26.1	47.7	9.9	3.1[3]	3.3	3.5[1]	.29**
Predicting the effects of HR programs before implementation	3.6	36.9	32.4	24.3	2.7	2.6[3]	2.6	2.9[1]	.18[t]
Pinpointing HR programs that should be discontinued	3.6	28.8	36.9	27.9	2.7	2.6[3]	2.7[3]	3.0[1,2]	.27**
Logic, analysis, measurement, and process (LAMP)									
Using logical principles that clearly connect talent to organization success	2.7	15.3	36.9	37.8	7.2	3.0[3]	3.0[3]	3.3[1,2]	.26**
Using advanced data analysis and statistics	12.6	27.0	36.0	19.8	4.5	2.6	2.5	2.8	.22*
Providing high-quality (complete, timely, accessible) talent measurements	4.5	26.1	31.5	33.3	4.5	2.7[3]	2.8	3.1[1]	.13
Motivating users to take appropriate action	3.6	23.4	43.2	27.0	2.7	2.9	2.8	3.0	.23*
Capitalizing on big data	18.2	35.5	26.4	18.2	1.8	—[a]	2.4	2.5	.16

[a] The item was not asked in that year.

[1,2,3] Significant differences ($p \le .05$) between years.

Significance level: [t] $p \le .10$, * $p \le .05$, ** $p \le .01$, *** $p \le .001$.

in 2016 as compared to 2010 and 2013. The other two highly rated items concern assessing and improving the HR department operations and using logical principles that clearly connect talent to organizational success. Again, these items showed statistically significant improvement compared to prior surveys. It is encouraging that some strategically related items are improving, but this is in the context of rather low effectiveness ratings overall. Most effectiveness ratings fall at or are slightly below the midpoint (3.0 = somewhat effective) of the 5-point scale, suggesting improvement is possible in all areas.

Among the four items reflecting the LAMP framework, the highest effectiveness ratings are for the logic element, high-quality measurements, and motivating users to take action. These two items also showed statistically significant improvement since 2010. Ratings for the elements of advanced data analysis and big data were lower and showed no increase. This pattern is similar to prior surveys.

The results concerning advanced data analysis contradict much of the anecdotal evidence we encountered. Most organizations report that their ability to generate measurements is well developed, and they have good data analysis capabilities. When measures are not used effectively, the difficulty is usually that those receiving the information lack the cognitive frameworks to make sense of the information (such as understanding how an engagement score or a turnover rate connects to business success) or fail to convey the information in ways that motivate and direct the right decisions and actions (Boudreau and Cascio 2017). Overall, the effectiveness ratings in table 7.1 are moderate or low for all four LAMP areas, leaving significant opportunity for improvement in the HR measures and analyses and on the part of managers using the data.

The ratings for the outcome of capitalizing on big data are the lowest in table 7.1 and had changed little since 2013. In 2013, we offered the possibility that this was due to the relatively recent emergence of big data as a significant objective for HR analytics. The continuing low rating after three years, however, suggests that HR has a lot of work to do in order for it to capitalize on big data.

Role in Strategy

All but two of the effectiveness ratings in table 7.1 are significantly associated with HR's role in strategy. The pattern of correlations is somewhat different from that in the 2010 and 2013 surveys. In 2016, the correlations are smaller and nonsignificant for the effectiveness of high-quality measurements and big data, and only marginally significant for predicting the effects of HR programs. This may reflect the evolution of HR measurement to something that leaders expect, and thus it is not as significant as a strategic differentiator for HR. In particular, providing high-quality measurements and using big data may be seen as "table stakes" and thus less likely to be associated with a strong strategic partnership.

It is notable that measurement effectiveness in three elements of the LAMP framework are positively related to HR's role in strategy (omitting high-quality measurement). This suggests that the four elements may work together to support or help advance HR's strategic role, as Boudreau and Ramstad (2007) and Cascio and Boudreau (2011) suggested.

Overall, the main conclusion is that many correlations with HR's role in strategy are statistically significant, though they seem to have moderated since 2013. Compared to the 2004 and 2007 results, these correlations are somewhat higher and more frequently statistically significant. Over time, the effectiveness level of HR measurement categories has increased, and their association with HR's strategic role remains positive.

We often encounter HR and business leaders who believe that the HR profession must improve its measurement capability and achieve functional effectiveness before focusing on its strategic effectiveness. The results reported here suggest that both strategy and HR functional measurement effectiveness contribute to a strong strategic role. Thus, they support the idea of developing measurement systems that are effective at measuring strategic outcomes, even if HR functional and operational outcomes are not yet perfect.

International Results

The international results for measurement effectiveness are shown in table 7.2. Overall, the results from other countries are quite similar to those for the United States in terms of the level of effectiveness and the relative effectiveness across the different measures. Canada, and particularly Australia, exhibit lower effectiveness ratings than other countries. In both the 2013 and 2016 surveys, Chinese HR executives consistently rate the effectiveness of their metrics slightly above the scale midpoint on almost all items. In the United States and other countries, the ratings are more varied, with some items receiving lower effectiveness ratings. However, the Chinese effectiveness ratings are largely in line with those of the other countries, with the exception of Australia.

Strategic Focuses

Table 7.3 shows the relationship between the effectiveness of HR metrics and analytics, and the different strategic focuses. Once again, the growth strategy focus shows less significant correlation with measurement effectiveness. However, unlike prior surveys, the growth focus is positively associated with two LAMP elements: using logical principles and using advanced data analysis and statistics, albeit at a moderate level. Consistent with the results in other chapters, a focus on growth seems to be less associated with advanced HR effectiveness—in this case, the effectiveness of HR measures.

In marked contrast to the correlations for growth are the correlations with the other focuses, all of which show significant positive correlations with virtually every element of measurement effectiveness. This was also true in the 2013 survey, but the correlations in 2016 are uniformly higher. It appears that for most strategic focuses, effective HR

Table 7.2. HR analytics and metrics effectiveness, by country					
	Means				
Outcomes	**United States[1]**	**Canada[2]**	**Australia[3]**	**United Kingdom/ Europe[4]**	**China[5]**
Strategy contributions					
Contributing to decisions about business strategy and human capital management	3.5[3]	3.5[3]	2.6[1,2,4,5]	3.4[3]	3.2[3]
Identifying where talent has the greatest potential for strategic impact	3.3[3]	3.0	2.4[1,4,5]	3.2[3]	3.1[3]
Connecting human capital practices to organizational performance	3.0[3]	2.8	2.3[1,4,5]	3.1[3]	3.1[3]
Supporting organizational change efforts	3.6[3,5]	3.5	2.9[1,4]	3.8[3,5]	3.1[1,4]
HR functional and operational contributions					
Assessing and improving HR department operations	3.5[3]	3.4	2.8[1,4]	3.5[3]	3.1
Predicting the effects of HR programs before implementation	2.9[3]	2.8	2.3[1]	2.7	2.8
Pinpointing HR programs that should be discontinued	3.0[3]	2.9	2.4[1,4]	3.1[3]	2.7
Logic, analysis, measurement, and process (LAMP)					
Using logical principles that clearly connect talent to organization success	3.3[3]	3.1[3]	2.4[1,2,4,5]	3.1[3]	3.1[3]
Using advanced data analysis and statistics	2.8	2.6	2.5	2.6	2.8
Providing high-quality (complete, timely, accessible) talent measurements	3.1[3]	2.8	2.2[1,4,5]	3.0[3]	3.1[3]
Motivating users to take appropriate action	3.0[3]	2.9	2.3[1,5]	2.8	3.1[3]
Capitalizing on big data	2.5	2.2[5]	1.9[5]	2.3	2.8[2,3]
Response scale: 1 = very ineffective; 2 = ineffective; 3 = neither; 4 = effective; 5 = very effective. [1,2,3,4,5]Significant differences between countries ($p \leq .05$).					

measurement plays an integral part. The correlations for the knowledge-based and information-based strategic focuses are particularly strong. These strategies may rely more on organizational integration and employee understanding and involvement, and because of this, such strategies put more of an emphasis on metrics and analytics. Certainly, knowledge-based strategies are explicitly built on human capital, and this may lead organizations that pursue knowledge-based strategies to develop more advanced HR practices and measures.

Table 7.3. Correlations of HR analytics and metrics effectiveness to strategic focuses, United States

Outcomes	Strategic Focuses				
	Growth	Information-Based Strategies	Knowledge-Based Strategies	Sustainability	Innovation
Strategy contributions					
Contributing to decisions about business strategy and human capital management	.09	.45***	.43***	.24*	.28**
Identifying where talent has the greatest potential for strategic impact	.19ᵗ	.47***	.53***	.23*	.32***
Connecting human capital practices to organizational performance	.13	.41***	.49***	.26**	.34***
Supporting organizational change efforts	.14	.42***	.45***	.23*	.34***
HR functional and operational contributions					
Assessing and improving HR department operations	.03	.32***	.30***	.17ᵗ	.14
Predicting the effects of HR programs before implementation	.08	.36***	.41***	.20*	.19*
Pinpointing HR programs that should be discontinued	.07	.26**	.21*	.19ᵗ	.23*
Logic, analysis, measurement, and process (LAMP)					
Using logical principles that clearly connect talent to organization success	.19*	.43***	.44***	.21*	.33***
Using advanced data analysis and statistics	.19*	.34***	.40***	.30***	.32***
Providing high-quality (complete, timely, accessible) talent measurements	.15	.31***	.35***	.24**	.25**
Motivating users to take appropriate action	.10	.33***	.33***	.29**	.23*
Capitalizing on big data	.10	.37***	.37***	.36***	.26**

Significance level: ᵗ$p \le .10$, *$p \le .05$, **$p \le .01$, ***$p \le .001$.

Management Approaches

The correlations of the five management approaches and the effectiveness of HR measures and analytics are shown in table 7.4. The high-involvement approach shows strong correlations with HR measurement effectiveness, as it did in 2010 and 2013. The global competitor focus does not show any significant associations with the effectiveness measures.

The sustainability approach has an interesting pattern over time. This approach showed many significant correlations with measurement effectiveness in 2010 but only a few in 2013. As table 7.4 shows, in 2016 the approach shows the most consistent and highest correlations of all. Effective measurement is particularly strongly associated with the sustainability approach. As noted earlier, our belief is that the sustainability approach has been maturing and is reaching a point where the benefits of advanced HR approaches are more apparent.

The other two strategic focuses, bureaucratic and low-cost operator, show an interesting pattern that parallels the results for HR decision science and measurement use. Specifically, both strategic focuses show negative correlations with most elements of measurement effectiveness,

Table 7.4. Correlations of HR analytics and metrics effectiveness to management approaches, United States					
	Management Approaches				
Outcomes	**Bureaucratic**	**Low-Cost Operator**	**High Involvement**	**Global Competitor**	**Sustainable**
Strategy contributions					
Contributing to decisions about business strategy and human capital management	−.17^t	−.14	.32***	.04	.40***
Identifying where talent has the greatest potential for strategic impact	−.12	−.20*	.30**	.10	.37***
Connecting human capital practices to organizational performance	−.15	−.25**	.34***	−.01	.46***
Supporting organizational change efforts	−.22*	−.20*	.24**	.09	.37***
HR functional and operational contributions					
Assessing and improving HR department operations	−.10	−.04	.16^t	−.02	.36***
Predicting the effects of HR programs before implementation	−.15	−.09	.19*	−.06	.41***
Pinpointing HR programs that should be discontinued	−.22*	.02	.10	.20*	.29**
Logic, analysis, measurement, and process (LAMP)					
Using logical principles that clearly connect talent to organization success	−.17^t	−.19*	.30***	.05	.49***
Using advanced data analysis and statistics	−.11	−.10	.26**	.00	.44***
Providing high-quality (complete, timely, accessible) talent measurements	−.04	−.24*	.17^t	−.07	.29**
Motivating users to take appropriate action	−.17^t	−.17^t	.36***	.03	.36***
Capitalizing on big data	−.03	−.03	.15	−.02	.38***
Significance level: ^t*p* ≤ .10, **p* ≤ .05, ***p* ≤ .01, ****p* ≤ .001.					

and some of these negative correlations are statistically significant. These results are consistent across our previous surveys and many areas of advanced HR in our 2016 survey.

It appears that when organizations emphasize a bureaucratic or low-cost-operator management approach, they are significantly less likely to find that measurement effectiveness contributes to strategic decisions, supports organizational change efforts, and improves HR department operations. They are also less likely to use the LAMP framework elements. The causal direction could go either way, but it seems most likely that use of the bureaucratic or the low-cost-operator approach leads directly to less attention to HR measurement and thus less effective HR measures. Considering the strong association between HR measurement effectiveness and HR's role in strategy (see table 7.1), this suggests that HR leaders wishing to pursue state-of-the-art measures and strategic roles might need to avoid organizations that emphasize bureaucratic or low-cost-operator approaches or accept that achieving them will require more effort in such organizations.

The strong relationship between the high-involvement and sustainability approaches with the HR measurement outcomes across virtually all items is important. It appears that the high-involvement and sustainably focused organizations make employees and the employment relationship a key element of competitive success, and that leads to investing in effective HR measurement.

Conclusion

The results for HR measurement effectiveness indicate moderate effectiveness and some significant improvement since our 2007 study. The outcomes of HR measurement continue to show consistently strong relationships with HR's strategic role, though less so for high-quality measures and using big data. This is an important area for HR and one where improvement is needed in order for HR to have a meaningful role in business strategy. Not only does measurement effectiveness relate to HR's strategic role, effectiveness in HR functional and operational areas relates to the strength of HR's strategic role.

Our results show a strong relationship between most LAMP elements and HR's strategic role, supporting the point that these elements are necessary for a strategically effective measurement system. Of course the causal direction cannot be proven from our data. It may be that as HR organizations become more strategically involved and relevant, organizations perceive and support more effective HR measures and create them. It seems plausible, however, that a significant causal effect may be that effective measures lead to a greater strategic contribution from HR.

The results for the effectiveness of HR measures and analytics in this chapter are in contrast to the findings from chapter 7 on the use of measures and strategy. In 2016, for the first time, the use of measures showed no significant correlation with HR's strategic role, yet in this chapter, the effectiveness of HR metrics and analytics generally does show that association. We speculate that this may reflect a maturation of the HR measurement and analytics discipline. With the increasing availability of HR data, measures, and scorecards, merely using HR measurements no longer appears to significantly differentiate the strategic role of HR. It is the effectiveness of those measures that appears to be more salient.

The results for strategic focuses suggest that organizations pursuing strategies focused on knowledge, information, sustainability, and innovation are likely to have measurement effectiveness across a wide array of outcomes, particularly for knowledge- and information-based strategic focuses. These results suggest that effective HR measurement may be more readily accepted and used in organizations that rely on broad-based talent understanding and involvement to achieve competitive advantage, innovation, or sustainability.

It appears that some management approaches such as the bureaucratic and low-cost-operator ones may actually discourage HR measurement excellence. Just the opposite appears to be true of the high involvement and sustainable management approaches. They are associated with higher HR measurement excellence, a finding that fits their focus on the importance of human capital.

Overall, the findings reinforce the conclusion from our prior surveys: the potential for HR metrics and analytics to contribute to HR's strategic value is significant, while the perceived effectiveness levels remain stubbornly moderate, though improving. Our results also suggest that leaders both inside and outside HR can find great value in pursuing HR measurement effectiveness at the strategic and functional levels. They further suggest doing it through a balanced approach of LAMP.

Recently Boudreau and Cascio (2017) drew attention to the importance of creating fertile ground for HR analytics so that the audience for them is motivated to "pull" for them, and HR is not simply "pushing" them onto a resistant or ambivalent audience. Boudreau and Cascio suggested these additional necessary factors:

- *Users must receive the analytics*. This goes to the timeliness of the analytics in the context of other organizational decision processes.

- *Users must attend to the analytics*. This refers to creating analytics that users believe will be useful to them and have the self-efficacy to use. Thus, it is important to distinguish among compliance, service quality, and decision support as outcomes of HC analytics. Analytics to verify compliance with rules serve a very different purpose than do analytics to evaluate the quality of the HR services delivered to clients, which in turn have a very different value proposition from analytics designed to support decisions or reduce mistakes. Users are often confused about these value propositions. Boudreau and Cascio have also written about the dilemmas in using HR analytics to provide standards for external constituents such as regulators, boards, or investor constituencies. One must carefully distinguish analytics that describe common practices from those that claim to predict organizational performance.

- *Users must believe the analytics*. Once decision makers receive and attend to the analytics, they must find them credible. Much research attention has been devoted to methods of making analytics' predictions valid and correct from a scientific standpoint, but relatively little research has examined how users perceive correctness. It is possible that users will not believe the results because those results reflect different situations or their logic is unfamiliar to them. One danger in providing users with analytics that suggest very high payoffs is that they may seem "too good to be true." Even if users believe the prediction, they may perceive that the results are so unreliable that they are not credible. As an alternative, break-even analysis can help leaders avoid being distracted by potentially large errors of estimation (see Cascio and Boudreau 2011), but relatively little research has looked at the effectiveness of such approaches.

- *Users must believe that the analytics suggest effects that are large and compelling enough to merit attention or action.* Users have limited resources and time and work to place those resources in areas with the greatest impact or value. It is important to focus analytics on things that are pivotal, meaning that the analytics are likely to improve decisions or correct mistakes that have large consequences to the user and the organization. Related to this is the time horizon of the analytics. Many aspects of human capital, such as promoting a culture of inquiry, take years to evolve. It is not uncommon for investors and analysts to suggest that while they believe in the results of HC analytics, the time delay in their effects makes the results less relevant to their decisions.

- *Users must see implications for their actions or decisions.* No matter how compelling the message, analytics do little to influence decisions and behaviors if users do not have the power, confidence, and understanding to act on them. Analytics that focus on improving the HR department are often not very relevant to leaders outside that department. Analytics that show broad effects of investments in high-performance work systems may seem irrelevant to leaders who have little authority to approve such programs. It may be that analytics have not advanced because they are not adequately tuned to the specific decisions that leaders make and presented in context. Artificial intelligence may allow analytics to be presented precisely when decision makers face the key decisions where those analytics are most relevant. In addition, it is possible that retooling analytics in the framework of accepted management models such as marketing, total quality management, supply chain, and engineering may allow users to see HC analytics more like other analytics, and to use their existing behavior patterns to engage with HC analytics.

CHAPTER 8

Information Technology in HR

- Human resource information systems (HRISs) are used for most HR processes, but they are not completely integrated.

- Although social networks, mobile technology, and cloud-based software-as-service are only moderately used, 2016 saw significantly more organizations using them in 2016 than in 2013.

- HRISs do not receive high effectiveness ratings (about 2 on a 5-point scale). The highest ratings are in traditional arenas of speed, costs, and service, a consistent pattern over fifteen years.

- HRIS effectiveness is most strongly associated with growth and knowledge and information-based strategies.

- The more activities an HRIS can do, the more effective it is perceived to be.

- Information technology use shows a positive relationship to HR's role in strategy.

- The most effective HRIS outcomes (efficiency, cost/head count reduction, speed) are positively related to HR's strategic role.

- HRIS outcomes related to business effectiveness (providing strategic information, integrating HR processes) are positively associated with HR's role in strategy but rated less effective than efficiency outcomes.

- Strategic HRIS outcomes (improving decisions, creating social/knowledge networks, strategic information, measuring HR impact) are not common but are increasing.

- HRISs are least extensively used to support social and knowledge networks.

- The more integrated and comprehensive HRISs are, the more likely they are to achieve high effectiveness ratings and be used to achieve more outcomes.

Information technology (IT) can accomplish HR record keeping, HR transactions, and many other administrative tasks quickly, efficiently, and accurately. Ideally, it can enable HR to save money and spend more time on strategic business support, but IT can do more than just serve as an administrative tool. It can be a way to deliver expert advice to managers and employees in areas such as selection, career development, talent management, and compensation. It can analyze data in ways that can guide and support evidence-driven HR practices and policies. It can also facilitate change efforts by assessing the capabilities of the workforce and providing information and training that support change. Finally, it can support the development and implementation of business strategy by providing important information about the capabilities and core competencies of the organization, as well as creating transparency with respect to organizational performance.

Amount of Use

Table 8.1 shows the state of IT-based HR processes from 1995 to 2016. In 2016, 56 percent of companies report using human resource information systems (HRISs for most or all of their HR processes, a moderately high level of use but no increase from 2013. The mean scores suggest there was not a significant increase in HRIS comprehensiveness and integration from 1995 to 2016, though 2016 was significantly higher than 2001. That there has been some increase is logical, considering the rapid evolution with respect to cloud-hosted systems and mobile technology. In many respects, an increase was almost required, given the increased popularity of business software and the fact that the major business software companies (e.g., SAP, Oracle, Workday) have HR applications. What is surprising is that the growth in the use of IT by companies has not led to a greater increase in comprehensiveness and integration.

International Results

The international results in table 8.2 show some significant differences in the state of HRISs. China and Australia have the lowest rate of use. This low rate is not surprising for China, since it lagged behind in the 2013 survey. The low rate in Australia is harder to explain because it was not lower in the past. It may be due to some changes in the 2016 sample, which tapped smaller Australian companies than in the past. As was true in our previous surveys, the United States had the highest rate.

Table 8.1. State of HRISs, United States								
	Percentages							
State of Information System	**1995[1]**	**1998[2]**	**2001[3]**	**2004[4]**	**2007[5]**	**2010[6]**	**2013[7]**	**2016[8]**
Little or no information technology present in the HR function	6.3	8.4	8.3	6.1	7.8	3.8	7.4	4.4
Some HR processes are information technology based	45.3	40.3	48.3	32.3	32.0	30.1	29.4	28.3
Most processes are information technology based but not fully integrated	40.6	42.9	35.9	48.5	51.5	49.7	55.9	55.8
Completely integrated HR information technology system	7.8	8.4	7.6	13.1	8.7	16.4	7.4	11.5
Mean[a]	3.50[6]	3.50[6]	3.41[6,8]	3.69	3.59	3.79[1,2,3]	3.63	3.74[3]

[a]Response scale: 1 = no information technology; 2 = little information technology; 3 = some processes integrated; 4 = most processes integrated; 5 = completely integrated.

[1,2,3,4,5,6,7,8] Significant differences ($p \leq .05$) between years.

Types of Use

Data on some of the many uses of IT are presented in table 8.3. In general, these show moderate to low use rates. That said, several items showed significant increases from 2013 to 2016. These include items that were added in 2013, such as use of social networks, mobile technology, and cloud-based software-as-service. In addition, the 2016 data suggest a significant increase in making advice available online.

Table 8.2. State of HRISs, by country					
	Percentages				
State of Information System	**United States[1]**	**Canada[2]**	**Australia[3]**	**United Kingdom/ Europe[4]**	**China[5]**
Little or no information technology present in the HR function	4.4	11.1	26.5	10.8	18.8
Some HR processes are information technology based	28.3	30.6	29.4	37.8	30.2
Most processes are information technology based but not fully integrated	55.8	55.6	44.1	43.2	44.8
Completely integrated HR information technology system	11.5	2.8	0.0	8.1	6.3
Mean[a]	3.74[3,5]	3.50	3.18[1]	3.43	3.35[1]

[a]Response scale: 1 = no information technology; 2 = little information technology; 3 = some processes integrated; 4 = most processes integrated; 5 = completely integrated.

[1,2,3,4,5]Significant differences between countries ($p \leq .05$).

Table 8.3. Use of information technology, United States								
	Means							**Correlation with HR Role in Strategy**
	1998[1]	**2001[2]**	**2004[3]**	**2007[4]**	**2010[5]**	**2013[6]**	**2016[7]**	
Information Technology	—	—	—	—	—	2.6[7]	2.8[6]	.24*
Transactional HR work is outsourced.	2.3	2.3	2.5[7]	2.4	2.3	2.2	2.0[3]	.09
Some transactional activities that used to be done by HR are done by employees on a self-service basis.	2.3[3,4,5,6,7]	2.5[3,4,5,6]	2.9[1,2]	3.0[1,2]	2.9[1,2]	3.1[1,2]	2.9[1]	.19*
HR information and advice are available online for managers and employees.	—	—	2.5[7]	2.7	2.6[7]	2.5[7]	3.0[3,5,6]	.20*
Uses social networks for HR activities such as recruiting, performance management, and work assignments.	—	—	—	—	—	2.7[7]	3.0[6]	.25**
Uses mobile technology to support HR activities such as recruiting, self-service, and communication.	—	—	—	—	—	2.3[7]	2.7[6]	.18[t]
Uses software-as-a-service model (subscription based, hosted in the cloud).	—	—	—	—	—	2.5[7]	3.0[6]	.05

Note: Empty cells indicate that the item was not asked in that year.

Response scale: 1 = little or no extent; 2 = some extent; 3 = moderate extent; 4 = great extent; 5 = very great extent.

[1,2,3,4,5,6,7]Significant differences ($p \leq .05$) between years.

Significance level: [t]$p \leq .10$, *$p \leq .05$, **$p \leq .01$, ***$p \leq .001$.

Overall, these uses of IT are rated as used to a moderate extent or lower. This suggests that the growth in the use of IT and the growing popularity of the cloud and big data for HR have just begun. It may be that these uses are being written and talked about more than they are occurring.

Increasing the moderate to low level of HRIS uses offers an opportunity to increase the strategic contribution of HR, because HRIS uses are positively related to HR's role in strategy. This positive relationship is particularly strong for self-service transactions, online advice, and using social networks. Although cloud-based software-as-service has increased significantly since 2013, it is not related to HR's role in strategy, suggesting that it may be a basic expectation but not a strategic differentiator. Overall, it appears that the selective use of information technology is yet another way that can help HR play a more significant role in strategy.

Table 8.4 presents data on HR technology use and budget for questions that we asked for the first time in 2016. Only 23 percent of organizations report that more than 60 percent of HR work is done with technology, and only 17 percent report that more than 61 percent of HR work is done by employees and managers outside HR and IT. Yet over 45 percent of organizations report that more than 41 percent of HR budgets are for cloud-based applications, confirming that organizations are moving to the cloud, but most HR work is not done there.

The mobile, social, and analytical uses of HR technology are shown in table 8.5. Less than 50 percent of U.S. organizations reported using mobile devices, enterprise social media platforms, and deep analytics for HR to more than a moderate extent.

Overall, HR technology is present in most organizations but is not yet the dominant way that HR work is done. Advanced uses of HR technology also only rarely penetrate deeply into the work of HR. The growth of cloud-based services, mobile apps, social media, and analytics may increase the use of advanced applications and more social and user-focused approaches soon, but they do not appear to have done so yet.

Table 8.4. Use of HR technology, United States						
	Percentage Use					
About what percentage of ...	**0%–20%**	**21%–40%**	**41%–60%**	**61%–80%**	**81%–100%**	**Means**
the work of the HR function is conducted using HR technology?	6.2	37.2	33.6	19.5	3.5	2.77
HR work that uses technology is conducted using a single integrated software suite, such as Workday, Success Factors, or Oracle HCM?	26.5	19.5	13.3	23.9	16.8	2.85
the HR transactions using HR technology are performed by employees and managers rather than by HR or IT staff?	27.4	32.7	23.0	12.4	4.4	2.34
the HR technology budget is for applications that are housed in the cloud?	27.4	27.4	10.6	23.0	11.5	2.64

IT System Effectiveness

Beginning in 2001 we asked questions about both the general effectiveness of HRISs and their effectiveness in key areas (table 8.6). We have added new questions to every survey since then because of the growing importance of HRIS.

Table 8.5. Characterization of HR technology, United States	Percentage					
To what extent does each of the following statements characterize your HR technology?	Little or No Extent	Some Extent	Moderate Extent	Great Extent	Very Great Extent	Means
It is enabled for mobile devices (usable over cell phones or tablets).	31.6	21.1	27.2	13.2	7.0	2.43
It makes an enterprise social media platform available to all employees.	35.1	25.4	17.5	13.2	8.8	2.35
It provides tools that permit deeper analysis of human capital issues.	23.9	30.1	28.3	10.6	7.1	2.47

Table 8.6. HRIS outcomes, United States	Means						Correlation with HR Role in Strategy 2016
HRIS Outcomes	2001[1]	2004[2]	2007[3]	2010[4]	2013[5]	2016[6]	
Overall effectiveness[a]	**2.6**	**2.8**	**2.7**	**2.7**	**2.6**	**2.9**	**.30*****
Employee satisfaction	**2.4[6]**	**2.7**	**2.6**	**2.7**	**2.5**	**2.8[1]**	**.15**
Efficiency	**2.9**	**3.0**	**2.8**	**2.8**	**2.7**	**3.0**	**.30*****
Improve HR services	3.0	3.0	2.9	3.0	2.9	3.2	.29**
Reduce HR transaction costs	2.9	3.0	2.8	3.0	2.8	3.1	.29**
Speed up HR processes	3.1	3.2	3.0	3.0	2.9	3.2	.20*
Reduce the number of employees in HR	2.4	2.6	2.4	2.3	2.4	2.4	.27**
Business outcomes	**2.2[6]**	**2.3**	**2.5**	**2.5**	**2.5**	**2.7[1]**	**.28***
Provide new strategic information	2.1[4,5,6]	2.3[6]	2.5	2.5[1]	2.5[1]	2.7[1,2]	.24*
Integrate HR processes (e.g., training, compensation)	2.4	2.4	2.5	2.4	2.5	2.7	.26**
Measure HR's impact on the business	—	**2.1**	**2.3**	**2.3**	**2.2**	**2.3**	**.21***
Improve human capital decisions of managers outside HR	—	—	**2.4**	**2.3**	**2.3**	**2.5**	**.26***
Be effective	—	—	**2.9**	**3.0**	**2.8**	**3.0**	**.29***
Create knowledge networks	—	—	—	**1.9**	**1.9**	**2.0**	**.16[1]**
Offer a positive user experience	—	—	—	—	**2.5[6]**	**2.8[5]**	**.12**
Represent a state-of-the-art solution	—	—	—	—	**2.2**	**2.5**	**.15**
Use the most advanced technology	—	—	—	—	**2.1[6]**	**2.4[5]**	**.14**
Analyze and optimize social networks	—	—	—	—	—	**1.8**	**.08**

Note: Empty cells indicate that the item was not asked in that year. Bold numbers are scale means.

[a]Includes items from Employee Satisfaction, Efficiency, and Business Effectiveness scales only.

Response scale: 1 = little or no extent; 2 = some extent; 3 = moderate extent; 4 = great extent; 5 = very great extent.

[1,2,3,4,5,6] Significant difference ($p \le .05$) between years.

Significance level: [1]$p \le .10$, *$p \le .05$, **$p \le .01$, ***$p \le .001$.

In every survey since 2001, including for 2016, HRIS effectiveness ratings are not high. The highest ratings are in the areas of speed, cost, and service, but even there, the highest-rated item received a rating just above the middle of the 5-point scale. It is hardly surprising that the highest ratings came in the area of efficiency (costs, speed, and service level), since that is where IT systems should achieve quick payoffs. Nevertheless, our longitudinal data confirm that these important, albeit traditional, HRIS outcomes are consistently achieved.

In contrast, the ratings concerned with business outcomes are among the lowest. HR executives do not see their HRISs strongly affecting organizational performance, strategic decision making, HR's impact on the business, or human capital decision making. Overall it is clear that HRISs are not yet doing a good job of providing the information that HR executives need to be strategic business partners. Even in 2016, the ratings on these business outcome measures do not rise above 3.0 on a 5-point scale. Still, the 2016 results are consistently higher than the 2013, even if only moderately so. This is encouraging, and there are good reasons to believe that HRIS can have a big impact in these areas. The failure of HRISs to have an immediate large impact may be in part due to the newness of some of the systems and the fact that organizations are just beginning to learn how to use HRISs as strategic tools.

We added a "create knowledge networks" item in 2010 and "analyze and optimize social networks" in 2016. Both received very low effectiveness ratings in 2016. HRIS systems do not yet appear to contribute widely to networks that help employees share knowledge and facilitate getting work done.

The three items added in 2013 on user experience, state-of-art solutions, and using the most advanced technology show results in 2016 that are very similar to the data for the other items. The scores are relatively low but increasing.

The relationships between the effectiveness of HRISs and HR's role in strategy are also shown in table 8.6. Most are statistically significant, although the correlations are relatively low. The pattern suggests that the strongest relationships are for improving HR efficiency and for strategic outcomes, including providing strategic information, measuring business impact, and improving managerial decisions. These positive correlations suggest that HRIS systems can lead to a more important role for HR in strategy and that extending HRIS effects beyond simply achieving HR efficiency is an opportunity for improvement. Outcomes such as positive user experience, advanced technology, and improving knowledge and social networks are not related to HR's role in strategy. It may be that organizational leaders are not yet experienced enough with these outcomes for them to distinguish HR as a strategic contributor.

Only time will tell what impact HRISs will have on HR and organizations. As Boudreau and Ramstad (2003) have noted, a decision science for HR remains elusive, yet it is essential for guiding decision makers through the increasingly daunting amount of information available in HRIS systems. They note that having such a decision science is one reason that data systems in finance, marketing, supply chains, and other areas have been so influential. As the HR profession develops a deeper and more precise decision science, HRISs may become more effective in the HR arena.

Strategic Focuses and Management Approach

In table 8.7, we see a number of significant relationships between HRIS effectiveness and the strategic focuses. All of the strategic focuses show

Table 8.7. Relationship of HRIS outcomes to strategic focuses, United States					
	Strategic Focuses				
HRIS Outcomes	Growth	Information-Based Strategies	Knowledge-Based Strategies	Sustainability	Innovation
Overall effectiveness[a]	**.25****	**.23***	**.30****	**.18**^{t}	**.16**^{t}
Employee satisfaction	**.26****	**.14**	**.19***	**−.04**	**.09**
Efficiency	**.19***	**.22***	**.29****	**.20***	**.17**^{t}
Improve HR services	.22*	.11	.18^t	.12	.05
Reduce HR transaction costs	.13	.19*	.28**	.20*	.19*
Speed up HR processes	.21*	.16^t	.17^t	.11	.13
Reduce the number of employees in HR	.12	.30***	.35***	.23*	.21*
Business outcomes	**.28****	**.22***	**.30****	**.20***	**.13**
Provide new strategic information	.22*	.11	.17^t	.16^t	.06
Integrate HR processes (e.g., training, compensation)	.28**	.27**	.35***	.20*	.17^t
Measure HR's impact on the business	**.04**	**.30*****	**.24***	**.24***	**.13**
Improve human capital decisions of managers outside HR	**.23***	**.37*****	**.30*****	**.21***	**.22***
Be effective	**.20***	**.17**^{t}	**.23***	**.05**	**.04**
Create knowledge networks	**.16**^{t}	**.40*****	**.41*****	**.33*****	**.21***
Offer a positive user experience	**.20***	**.19***	**.24****	**.11**	**.10**
Represent a state-of-the-art solution	**.26****	**.12**	**.19***	**.11**	**.01**
Use the most advanced technology	**.23***	**.14**	**.18**^{t}	**.11**	**.00**
Analyze and optimize social networks	**.23***	**.30*****	**.47*****	**.22***	**.17**^{t}
Note: Bold items are scale means.					
[a]Includes items from Employee Satisfaction, Efficiency, and Business Effectiveness scales only.					
Response scale: 1 = little or no extent; 2 = some extent; 3 = moderate extent; 4 = great extent; 5 = very great extent.					
Significance level: $^t p \le .10$, *$p \le .05$, **$p \le .01$, ***$p \le .001$.					

some significant positive relationships, with the most frequent ones involving growth and knowledge- and information-based strategies. These results are not surprising since all of these can be aided by an effective HRIS. The stronger the strategic focus is, the more likely it is that many of the HRIS outcomes are greater.

Some significant correlations appear between the management approach items and the HRIS effectiveness items. The global competitor approach scores higher on networks and state-of-the-art solutions. Given the need to manage a dispersed workforce, they most likely put more emphasis on building an effective HRIS.

Effectiveness and Use

Table 8.8 shows the relationship of various HRIS system effects and outcomes to the comprehensiveness and integration of HRIS (see table 8.1). The correlations suggest a strong positive relationship, and this is consistent with findings in all surveys since 2001. Significantly, though less strongly, related is the social network item. This may reflect the fact that

Table 8.8. Relationship of HRIS outcomes to use, United States	
HRIS Outcomes	**HRIS Amount of Use**
Overall effectiveness[a]	**.52***
Employee satisfaction	**.36***
Efficiency	**.52***
Improve HR services	.53***
Reduce HR transaction costs	.48***
Speed up HR processes	.47***
Reduce the number of employees in HR	.32***
Business outcomes	**.48***
Provide new strategic information	.35***
Integrate HR processes (e.g., training, compensation)	.49***
Measure HR's impact on the business	**.37***
Improve human capital decisions of managers outside HR	**.43***
Be effective	**.57***
Create knowledge networks	**.34***
Offer a positive user experience	**.47***
Represent a state-of-the-art solution	**.49***
Use the most advanced technology	**.46***
Analyze and optimize social networks	**.25****

Note: Bold numbers are based on scale means.

[a]Includes items from Employee Satisfaction, Efficiency, and Business Effectiveness scales only.

Significance level: $^{\dagger}p \leq .10$, $^{*}p \leq .05$, $^{**}p \leq .01$, $^{***}p \leq .001$.

social networks can be created without a comprehensive and integrated HRIS system and that most systems are not yet designed to facilitate social networks.

The strong relationships between HRIS outcomes and their comprehensiveness and integration undoubtedly reflect the power of integrated systems. They can enhance analyses related to business effectiveness and strategy, assess the practicality of a business strategy by determining whether the organization has the capability to execute it, and determine the impacts of HR programs and more effectively develop and place employees. The more integrated and comprehensive the HRIS is, the more likely it is to be rated as effective and used for more outcomes.

Conclusion

The use and effectiveness of IT and HRISs are increasing, but change is slow. Moreover, the most common outcomes are in traditional arenas of cost efficiency and service provision and those related to decision support and emerging social and knowledge networks. There is a slow but sure movement toward companies having integrated HRISs that improve decision making and organizational performance; nevertheless, there is a long way to go.

HRISs are not rated as more effective in 2016 than they were in 2013 and not rated as very effective in an absolute sense. There are many possible reasons for this result. In the past we have suggested that such systems are relatively new and that companies and managers are just beginning to learn how to use them effectively. That explanation seems less plausible in 2016, because such systems now have a relatively long history. HR technology is advancing rapidly now, but many companies may be experiencing difficulties dealing with a technology that is not well developed. Expectations about what HRIS can and should deliver are rising, and as a result, great improvement is needed just to maintain an existing satisfaction level.

The evidence is quite clear that HRISs are rated most effective when an organization has a strong strategic focus. They are particularly likely to be perceived as successful when companies with strong knowledge- and information-based strategies use them. Perhaps the strongest finding is that the more comprehensive and integrated the HRIS is, the more effective it is perceived to be. Thus, in the future, HR should focus on improving the comprehensiveness and integration in HRISs.

CHAPTER 9

The Effectiveness of HR

- HR is rated most effective at delivering HR services and being an employee advocate. Both show increases over the past twenty years.

- HR's rating as an effective business partner is equal to its effectiveness in delivering HR services and being an employee advocate for the first time in 2016, and it showed significant increases since the 1990s.

- HR is rated as least effective at analyzing HR and business metrics, managing outsourcing, operating shared services, and helping develop business strategies, though analyzing metrics showed a significant increase in 2016.

- Providing HR services is rated as important, but preparing talent for the future, being a business partner, providing change consulting, and improving human capital decisions were rated even more important.

- Managing outsourcing is rated least important, as in the past, and actually declined in importance compared to 2004.

- HR effectiveness in every area is significantly and positively related to HR's role in strategy.

- U.S. HR leaders' effectiveness ratings have increased over the past decade.

- Chinese and Australian HR executives generally rate HR effectiveness lower than do those in the United States, Canada, and the United Kingdom/Europe, particularly in working with the corporate board and being an employee advocate.

- Chinese HR executives attach low importance to making contributions to the business and strategy.

The effectiveness of an HR organization must be based on an assessment of its performance in a number of areas. Traditionally, the most obvious area is service delivery, but good service delivery is just the foundation; it is not enough. To be an effective contributor to organizational effectiveness, HR must also contribute to effective employment relationships, organizational strategy and change, strategic talent management decisions, and organizational design. This chapter examines HR effectiveness in these areas, how it has changed, and how it relates to HR's role in strategy and the strategic and management focuses of the organization.

HR Effectiveness

HR executives were asked to judge the overall effectiveness of their HR organizations and their effectiveness in performing twelve activities. Our analysis suggested the twelve items fall into three groups: HR services, corporate roles, and business and strategy (table 9.1).

The 2016 effectiveness ratings in most cases are slightly higher than in previous years. This is particularly true for providing HR services, being an employee advocate, operating HR centers of excellence, and being a business partner. HR's performance seems to have generally improved in the opinion of HR executives.

The effectiveness ratings in all surveys, including 2016, are highest for items related to HR services. The highest-rated items are providing HR services and being an employee advocate. This is consistent with other

Table 9.1. Effectiveness of the HR organization, United States									
	Means								Correlation with HR Role in Strategy to 2013 Means
Activities	**1995**[1]	**1998**[2]	**2001**[3]	**2004**[4]	**2007**[5]	**2010**[6]	**2013**[7]	**2016**[8]	
Overall effectiveness (all items)	—	—	—	**6.8**	**6.4**	**6.4**	**6.4**	**6.8**	.50***
HR services	—	—	—	**7.0**	**6.7**	**6.9**	**6.6**	**7.1**	.43***
Providing HR services	7.1[6,8]	7.0[4,6,8]	7.3	7.8[1,2]	7.4	7.7[1,2]	7.4	7.7[1,2]	.39***
Being an employee advocate	—	6.8[8]	7.2	7.4	7.3	7.1[8]	7.4	7.8[2,6]	.33***
Analyzing HR and business metrics	—	—	—	5.9	5.3[8]	5.9	5.3	6.1[5]	.29**
Preparing talent for the future	—	—	—	—	—	—	6.4	6.6	.38***
Corporate roles	—	—	—	**6.9**	**6.5**	**6.2**	**6.3**	**6.6**	.47***
Managing outsourcing	—	—	—	7.3[5,6,7,8]	6.1[4]	5.9[4]	6.1[4]	6.2[4]	.30**
Operating HR centers of excellence	—	5.5[4,5,6,7,8]	5.6[4,5,8]	6.8[2,3]	6.7[2,3]	6.3[2]	6.4[2]	6.9[2,3]	.44***
Operating HR shared service units	—	5.7[4,6]	6.0	6.9[2]	6.3	6.6[2]	6.4	6.4	.39***
Working with the corporate board	—	—	—	7.1[6]	6.8	6.2[4]	6.7	7.0	.36***
Business and strategy	—	—	—	**6.5**	**6.1**	**6.4**	**6.1**[8]	**6.8**[7]	.52***
Providing change consulting services	5.8	5.5[4,8]	5.7	6.5[2]	5.9	6.1	5.8	6.5[2]	.37***
Being a business partner	6.3[8]	6.5[8]	6.4[8]	7.1	6.8	6.9	6.8	7.3[1,2,3]	.52***
Helping to develop business strategies	—	6.2	5.8	6.0	5.8	5.9	5.6	6.4	.50***
Improving decisions about human capital	—	—	—	6.7	6.1[8]	6.4	6.3	6.9[5]	.47***

Note: Empty cells indicate that the item was not asked in that year. Bold numbers are scale means.

Response scale: 1 = not meeting needs; 10 = all needs met.

[1,2,3,4,5,6,7,8] Significant difference ($p \le .05$) between years.

Significance level: [1]$p \le .10$, *$p \le .05$, **$p \le .01$, ***$p \le .001$.

studies, which have found that HR tends to be rated particularly high when it comes to traditional HR services (Csoka and Hackett 1998).

The ratings of HR's performance in its corporate roles are mixed. It gets low ratings on managing outsourcing. Its ratings for work with the board are higher, but as we discussed in chapter 2, HR has a limited role with respect to boards, so these high ratings may reflect a narrow set of more traditional activities. Many have suggested that HR may be satisfied with traditional HR contributions to the board, because HR leaders and board members are unaware of the more extensive role that HR might play (Boudreau 2016).

HR receives some of its lowest effectiveness ratings in the business and strategy area. The ratings by both HR executives in this survey and managers in past surveys are lowest on developing business strategy. However, being a business partner is rated relatively high and showed significant increases in 2016 compared to prior years. This finding supports the point made in chapter 1 that there is a difference between being a business partner and having an active role in strategy development. When managers and HR executives consider what a successful business partnership is, they do not seem to see it as synonymous with playing an active role in developing and implementing business strategies.

To better understand the key drivers of the overall effectiveness ratings, we did a regression analysis. The highest-weighted item predicting the overall effectiveness rating was the rating of HR's performance in delivering services, followed by change consulting services. When we ran these analyses on the 2010 data that we gathered from managers outside HR, we got a different result. For the non-HR managers, the best predictors were being a business partner and developing business strategies (Lawler and Boudreau 2012). HR executives seem to emphasize HR's effectiveness as a service deliverer, while non-HR managers emphasize HR's effectiveness as a business partner. One clear implication is that in order to be seen by others as effective, HR needs to perform better as a strategic partner, currently a relatively low performance area for it.

The absolute levels of the effectiveness ratings suggest that HR still has room to improve. The ratings are on a 10-point scale, so even the highest average rating of 7.8, for being an employee advocate, falls significantly short of the top of the scale. There are particularly low ratings for analyzing HR and business metrics and the low (though improving) rating for developing business strategies and change consulting. Clearly there is still plenty of room for HR to improve its effectiveness, particularly in activities related to strategy, decision support, and analytics. It is also notable that the effectiveness ratings for strategy and decision support are the most strongly correlated with HR's role in strategy, suggesting that progress in these areas may have a strong impact.

International Results

The international data show some significant differences in HR organization effectiveness ratings, most of which concern China (table 9.2). In all three effectiveness areas (HR services, corporate roles, and business and strategy) and overall effectiveness, the results are much lower for China compared to the United States, Canada, and the United Kingdom/Europe. Overall, as it was in 2013, the difference between China and the other countries is larger here than anywhere else, and this is the most

Table 9.2. Effectiveness of the HR organization, by country					
	Means				
Activities	United States[1]	Canada[2]	Australia[3]	United Kingdom/ Europe[4]	China[5]
Overall effectiveness (all items)	**6.8[3,5]**	**6.8**	**5.6[1]**	**6.5**	**5.8[1]**
HR services	**7.1[3,5]**	**6.8**	**5.7[1]**	**6.7**	**6.2[1]**
Providing HR services	7.7[5]	7.7[5]	6.9	7.4	6.7[1,2]
Being an employee advocate	7.8[3,5]	7.7[3,5]	6.2[1,2]	6.8	5.9[1,2]
Analyzing HR and business metrics	6.1	5.4	5.2	5.5	6.0
Preparing talent for the future	6.6[3]	6.4[3]	4.6[1,2,4,5]	6.9[3]	6.3[3]
Corporate roles	**6.6[3,5]**	**5.9**	**5.1[1]**	**6.5**	**5.5[1]**
Managing outsourcing	6.2[3]	5.5	4.6[1]	5.5	5.4
Operating HR centers of excellence	6.9[3,5]	6.5	5.5[1]	6.9[5]	5.3[1,4]
Operating HR shared service units	6.4	6.7	5.5	6.5	5.6
Working with the corporate board	7.0[3,5]	6.7	5.1[1,4]	7.4[3,5]	5.8[1,4]
Business and strategy	**6.8[5]**	**6.9[5]**	**6.1**	**6.4**	**5.8[1,2]**
Providing change consulting services	6.5[5]	6.7[5]	6.2	6.3	5.3[1,2]
Being a business partner	7.3[5]	7.4[5]	6.7	7.0	6.0[1,2]
Helping to develop business strategies	6.4	6.3	5.5	6.2	5.5
Improving decisions about human capital	6.9	6.9	5.9	6.2	6.2

Note: Bold numbers are scale means.

Response scale: 1 = not meeting needs; 10 = all needs met.

[1,2,3,4,5] Significant differences between countries ($p \leq .05$).

important area since it is concerned with the effectiveness of the function. Notably, the Australian sample in 2016 also scored relatively low on effectiveness, often lower than all other countries, including China. This change from 2013 may be because the 2016 Australian sample included more smaller organizations.

Role in Strategy

Table 9.1 shows the correlations between the role that HR plays in strategy and its effectiveness. All of these correlations are high. As noted earlier, the strongest positive relationship to HR's role in strategy is with the effectiveness of HR in business and strategy, particularly being a business partner and helping to develop business strategies. The implication is clear: if HR wants to play a more important role in strategy formulation, it needs to be more effective when it comes to the business and strategy activities listed in table 9.1.

Effectiveness in providing HR services is significantly related to HR's strategic role. It is impossible to tell from the data whether the correlations with service effectiveness mean that providing good services is prerequisite to playing a strategic role or simply that when HR plays a stronger strategic role, it also delivers services more effectively. We believe that it most likely means that delivering high-quality services is a prerequisite for HR to be a strategic contributor, because ineffective service delivery reduces credibility and prevents HR from being a business partner.

The Importance of HR Activities

We did not survey HR leaders about the importance of HR activities in 2016, so table 9.3 shows the importance ratings for the U.S. sample in 2013. The highest importance ratings concerned improving decisions about human capital and being a business partner, a pattern that is similar to the one found in 2007 and 2010. The lowest ratings in 2013 were given to the corporate role items.

In 2013, HR executives rated providing HR services very highly. In our 2010 study, non-HR managers also rated it the highest (Lawler and Boudreau 2012). Business leaders valued HR's contribution to service delivery more highly than they did its developing business strategies, so HR must not lose sight of the importance of delivering basic HR services. HR leaders may need to do some selling to the non-HR community with respect to what they can contribute to business strategy. The relatively high importance rating for all the performance areas except managing outsourcing highlights again the challenge HR faces: providing services as well as contributing to corporate strategy and business effectiveness.

The 2013 correlations between HR's role in strategy and HR activity importance ratings suggest that the importance placed on HR services was less highly correlated with HR's role in strategy than the importance placed on its corporate roles (particularly operating centers of excellence and shared service units) and role in business and strategy (particularly providing change consulting and improving human capital decisions). This may mean that attention to HR services is more of a basic expectation than a strategic contributor.

The Gap between Importance and Effectiveness

Table 9.4 shows the results of subtracting the effectiveness ratings from the importance ratings for 2007, 2010, and 2013. Thus, the larger the number, the greater the gap was between importance and effectiveness in that year and the greater potential opportunity for improved impact.

The results are relatively similar for 2007, 2010, and 2013. For all years, the largest gaps were in the business and strategy area and the smallest ones in being an employee advocate and managing outsourcing. The

Table 9.3. Importance of HR activities					
	Means				**Correlation with HR Role in Strategy to 2013 Means**
Activities	**2004[1]**	**2007[2]**	**2010[3]**	**2013[4]**	
Overall Importance (all items)	**8.1**	**8.0**	**7.9**	**8.0**	**.23***
HR services	**8.2**	**8.0**	**8.2**	**8.4**	**.13**
Providing HR services	9.0	8.5	8.7	8.5	.04
Being an employee advocate	7.9	7.5	7.9	7.8	.05
Analyzing HR and business metrics	7.9	8.2	8.2	8.3	.14
Preparing talent for the future	—	—	—	9.2	.12
Corporate roles	**7.6**	**7.3**	**7.2**	**7.4**	**.25***
Managing outsourcing	7.6[2,3,4]	6.6[1]	6.5[1]	6.2[1]	.18[1]
Operating HR centers of excellence	7.7	7.9	7.9	7.9	.27**
Operating HR shared service units	7.6	7.4	7.6	7.8	.20*
Working with the corporate board	8.0[3]	7.2	7.2[1]	7.8	.06
Business and strategy	**8.4**	**8.6**	**8.3**	**8.4**	**.21***
Providing change consulting services	8.2	8.3	7.9	8.0	.26**
Being a business partner	9.0	9.1	8.8	9.0	.13
Helping to develop business strategies	8.0	8.4[4]	7.9	7.7[2]	.09
Improving decisions about human capital	8.3	8.8	8.6	8.8	.22*

Note: Empty cells indicate that the item was not asked in that year. Bold numbers are scale means.

Response scale: 1 = not important; 10 = very important.

[1,2,3,4]Significant difference ($p \le .05$) between years.

Significance level: [1]$p \le .10$, *$p \le .05$, **$p \le .01$, ***$p \le .001$.

Table 9.4. HR importance and effectiveness rating differences			
	Mean Differences		
Activities	2007[1]	2010[2]	2013[3]
Mean importance-effectiveness difference (all items)	**1.6**	**1.5**	**1.7**
HR services	**1.3[3]**	**1.3[3]**	**1.8[1,2]**
Providing HR services	1.0	1.0	1.1
Being an employee advocate	0.1	0.8	0.4
Analyzing HR and business metrics	2.9	2.3	2.9
Preparing talent for the future	—	—	2.8
Corporate roles	**0.8**	**1.1**	**1.2**
Managing outsourcing	0.5	0.5	0.3
Operating HR centers of excellence	1.2	1.6	1.5
Operating HR shared service units	1.1	1.1	1.4
Working with the corporate board	0.5	1.0	1.1
Business and strategy	**2.5**	**2.0**	**2.3**
Providing change consulting services	2.3	1.9	2.3
Being a business partner	2.3	1.9	2.2
Helping to develop business strategies	2.6	2.1	2.1
Improving decisions about human capital	2.8	2.2	2.5

Note: Empty cells indicate that the item was not asked in that year. Bold numbers are scale means.

Importance response scale: 1 = not important; 10 = very important.

Effectiveness response scale: 1 = not meeting needs; 10 = all needs met.

[1,2,3]Significant difference ($p \leq .05$) between years.

largest gaps with the 2013 importance ratings were in analyzing metrics, preparing talent for the future, and improving human capital decisions. These emerged as significant opportunities for improved HR impact.

Conclusion

HR executives have shown a consistent pattern of effectiveness ratings from 1995 to 2016. It is notable that the average of all of our effectiveness items (6.8 on a 10-point scale) is the same in 2016 as it was in 2004. HR is rated as most effective in delivering HR services and being an employee advocate. In 2016 we saw an encouraging and significant increase in the effectiveness of HR in being a business partner. The ratings also suggest important areas where the function falls short. One is developing business strategies, an important area where the effectiveness of HR is not rated as highly. This seems to go hand-in-hand with the low effectiveness ratings for analyzing business and HR metrics, because increasingly contributions to business strategy are expected to be evidence based and supported with data.

HR executives placed high importance on HR's role as a business partner and on improving decisions about human capital. Yet these are areas of relatively low effectiveness for HR and thus offer a tremendous opportunity for HR improvement. These areas also are related to HR's strategic role. Thus, by making improvements in these areas, HR is likely to become much more of a strategic contributor and more effective.

CHAPTER 10

Determinants of HR Effectiveness

- HR effectiveness is associated with many changeable HR organizational design features and roles.

- HR effectiveness is strongly and consistently related to how it is organized and the role it takes in an organization.

- HR effectiveness patterns show that HR needs to do administration well, but the best opportunities are to improve strategic contributions and business connections.

- The most significant predictors of HR effectiveness are the use of information technology and organizing into service units, as well as focusing on organizational design and development.

- HR effectiveness is higher when the HRIS is effective and integrated within the company.

- The use of HR metrics and analytics is strongly associated with HR effectiveness.

What determines the effectiveness of an HR organization? In this chapter, we address that question by calculating an index of overall HR effectiveness. Then we examine the relationship between that HR effectiveness index and the HR strategies, practices, organizing structure, and activities we have described in previous chapters. The results suggest a pattern of opportunities for more effective HR in the future with a higher impact.

Time Spent

The pattern of time spent on various HR roles relates significantly to HR effectiveness. Our results for 2016, in table 10.1, show a strong negative relationship between effectiveness and the amount of time HR executives report that their function spends maintaining records, auditing, and controlling. In contrast, there is a strong positive relationship between HR effectiveness and the amount of time spent as a strategic business partner. These results are consistent with what we have found in every survey since 2004. Yet as we saw in chapter 2, our 2016 data repeated the pattern that the relative amount of time HR actually spends on these roles has not changed over the years.

The strong positive correlation between time spent on being a business partner and HR effectiveness is consistent with the positive correlation between HR effectiveness and the role HR plays in strategy, as reported in chapter 9. The more that HR is involved in business strategy, the more effective it is seen to be. Our findings paint a consistent picture: the most

Table 10.1. Relationship of HR time spent to HR effectiveness

HR Roles[a]	HR Effectiveness[b]				
	2004	2007	2010	2013	2016
Maintaining records: Collect, track, and maintain data on employees	−.47***	−.33**	−.42***	−.37***	−.50***
Auditing/controlling: Ensure compliance with internal operations, regulations, and legal and union requirements	−.04	−.18	−.30***	−.38***	−.19[t]
HR service provider: Assist with implementation and administration of HR practices	−.05	.05	−.24**	−.06	−.08
Development of HR systems and practices: Develop new HR systems and practices	.24[t]	.02	.12	.15	.11
Strategic business partner: Member of the management team; involved with strategic HR planning, organizational design, and strategic change	.30*	.27*	.54***	.40***	.45***

[a]Based on percentage of time spent on HR roles as rated by HR executives.

[b]Based on total score for all twelve effectiveness items as rated by HR executives.

Significance level: $^tp \le .10$, $^*p \le .05$, $^{**}p \le .01$, $^{***}p \le .001$.

Table 10.2. Relationship of business strategy activities to HR effectiveness

Activities[a]	HR Effectiveness[b]				
	2004	2007	2010	2013	2016
Help identify or design strategy options	.32*	.31**	.45***	.47***	.55***
Help decide among the best strategy options	.45***	.35**	.53***	.48***	.53***
Help plan the implementation of strategy	.31*	.35**	.55***	.58***	.51***
Help identify new business opportunities	.27*	.28*	.47***	.40***	.52***
Assess the organization's readiness to implement strategies	.30*	.32**	.59***	.53***	.52***
Help design the organization structure to implement strategy	.42***	.35**	.62***	.58***	.49***
Assess possible merger, acquisition, or divestiture strategies	.23[t]	.17	.55***	.44***	.37***
Work with the corporate board on business strategy	.32*	.19	.51***	.41***	.50***

[a]Based on response scale: 1 = little or no extent; 2 = some extent; 3 = moderate extent; 4 = great extent; 5 = very great extent.

[b]Based on total score for all twelve effectiveness items as rated by HR executives.

Significance level: $^tp \le .10$, $^*p \le .05$, $^{**}p \le .01$, $^{***}p \le .001$.

effective HR organizations spend less time on record keeping and controlling activities and more time on human capital and business strategy.

Business Strategy Activities

HR's role in the business strategy process is significantly related to HR effectiveness (see table 10.2). Indeed, when compared to the 2004 and 2007 results, the relationships in 2010, 2013, and, 2016 are stronger and more consistent, with all of the correlations being positive, statistically significant, and larger. In these recent years, it appears that all eight of the strategy activities are similarly related to HR effectiveness. None are consistently more strongly related to effectiveness than the others. The biggest difference between 2004 and 2016 is that the absolute level of the correlations is generally higher in 2016 than in 2004. Over the past decade, the strategy activities of HR have become more significant determinants of its effectiveness.

HR Strategy Features

The extent to which the HR function has advanced HR strategy features is strongly related to HR executives' ratings of HR effectiveness. Table 10.3 shows that all the relationships between the HR strategy features and HR effectiveness are highly statistically significant in every survey since 2004. While in 2004 there was a somewhat weaker association between effectiveness and analytics support for business decision making, that correlation became one of the highest in the later surveys, and this was particularly true in 2016. This suggests an increasing understanding of the value of a decision science paradigm for HR. It means that HR's mandate extends beyond compliance and service delivery to include an increasing emphasis on the quality of decision support (Boudreau and Ramstad 2007; Boudreau and Jesuthasan 2011).

The two new questions about HR strategy features in the 2016 survey show a strong correlation with HR effectiveness. The stronger association was with HR's involvement in decisions about alternative work

Table 10.3. Relationship of HR strategy and activities to HR effectiveness					
HR Strategy and Activities	**HR Effectiveness[a]**				
	2004	**2007**	**2010**	**2013**	**2016**
Data-based talent strategy	.50***	.44***	.50***	.49***	.56***
A human capital strategy that is integrated with business strategy	.48***	.51***	.54***	.53***	.65***
Provides analytical support for business decision making	.38**	.67***	.58***	.65***	.67***
Provides HR data to support change management	.46***	.61***	.60***	.71***	.70***
Drives change management	.48***	.59***	.65***	.63***	.60***
Makes rigorous data-based decisions about human capital management	.47***	.62***	.60***	.62***	.73***
HR is involved in decisions about whether and where to use project-based, freelance, and platform gigs in order to get work done	—	—	—	—	.61***
Provides direction and services for workers who are not covered by a traditional employment relationship (e.g., contract, gig, platform workers)	—	—	—	—	.37***
Note: Empty cells indicate that the item was not asked in that year.					
[a]Based on total score for all twelve effectiveness items as rated by HR executives.					
Significance level: $^{t}p \leq .10$, $^{*}p \leq .05$, $^{**}p \leq .01$, $^{***}p \leq .001$.					

arrangements such as freelancers, platforms, and gigs. There was also a significant positive association with the extent to which HR provides direction and services to workers outside the traditional employment relationship. The latter question had a somewhat smaller association with HR effectiveness than the other items. It seems likely that its pattern may resemble the item on support for business decision making, where the correlation may increase in the future as the importance of such workers increases (Boudreau, Jesuthasan, and Creelman 2015).

Taken together, the results in tables 10.2 and 10.3 indicate that HR is more effective when it plays a major role in business strategy development and implementation, as well as having a well-developed and comprehensive HR strategy that is aligned with the business strategy. This conclusion has consistently emerged in every survey since 2004.

HR Organization

The effectiveness of the HR organization is clearly related to how it is organized and managed. Effectiveness is positively associated with some HR organizational features and negatively associated with others. As can be seen in table 10.4, the results from all surveys since 2001 are similar. The use of shared service units and information technology is strongly and positively related to effectiveness. Indeed, these associations are even stronger than in earlier years, suggesting an evolving opportunity for HR to distinguish itself by improving in these areas. Developing HR talent is generally positively related to effectiveness, with the exception of the 2004 survey, which now appears to have been an anomaly.

It is notable that the decentralization of HR is not positively correlated with HR effectiveness in any survey since 2001. In fact, in 2013 and

Table 10.4. Relationship of HR organization to HR effectiveness						
	HR Effectiveness[c]					
HR Organization	**2001**	**2004**	**2007**	**2010**	**2013**	**2016**
HR service units[a]	.44***	.43***	.36***	.54***	.59***	.56***
Decentralization[a]	−.01	−.09	−.17	.00	−.22*	−.28**
Information technology[b]	—	—	—	—	.53***	.57***
HR talent development[a]	.32***	−.04	.30**	.51***	.45***	.48***

Note: Empty cells indicate that the scale was not asked in that year.

[a]See table 5.1 for items in scale.

[b]See table 8.3 for items in scale.

[c]Based on total score for all twelve effectiveness items as rated by HR executives.

Significance level: ˈ$p \le .10$, *$p \le .05$, **$p \le .01$, ***$p \le .001$.

2016, decentralization was actually significantly and negatively associated with HR effectiveness. Much has been written advocating locating HR centrally for efficiency and control, and similarly strong positions are often taken in favor of decentralizing it for responsiveness, being close to the customer, and customizing practices. Our results suggest a more nuanced conclusion. The strong positive association of service units with effectiveness suggests that HR organizations need responsive shared service units, with some central coordination. Our measure of decentralization was the extent to which HR has decentralized HR generalists who support business units, which is negatively associated with HR effectiveness. It appears that pushing HR generalists away from the functional hub of HR may actually be counterproductive.

Activity Changes

The relationship between reported HR activity changes in the last five to seven years and HR effectiveness is shown in table 10.5 (not asked in 2016). The results for 2001 and 2004 show no strong relationship. In 2007, HR effectiveness was strongly related to increasing time on design and organizational development and on metrics and analytics. The results for 2010 show five significant relationships, but the results for 2013 show only three such relationships. Design and organizational development, and metrics show the significant relationships in 2007, 2010, and 2013, suggesting that spending more time on them has created more effective HR organizations.

Table 10.5. Relationship of HR activity changes to HR effectiveness					
	HR Effectiveness[b]				
HR Activities[a]	2001	2004	2007	2010	2013
Design and organizational development	.20*	.21	.37***	.35***	.36***
Compensation and benefits	.30**	−.08	.11	.23**	.11
Employee development	.13	.17	.22^t	.38***	.12
Recruitment and selection	.08	.13	.08	.25**	.08
HR metrics and analytics	—	.12	.26*	.34***	.22*
HR information systems	.11	−.14	−.01	.15^t	−.14
Union relations	−.05	.18	−.12	−.01	−.08
Social networks	—	—	—	—	.23*

Note: Empty cells indicate that the items were not asked in that year.
[a]See table 7.1 in Lawler and Boudreau (2015) for items in scales.
[b]Based on total score for all twelve effectiveness items as rated by HR executives.
Significance level: $^t p \leq .10$, $^* p \leq .05$, $^{**} p \leq .01$, $^{***} p \leq .001$.

Table 10.6. Relationship of information system use to HR effectiveness						
	Mean HR Effectiveness					
Information System	**2001***	**2004***	**2007***	**2010***	**2013***	**2016***
Completely integrated HR IT system	6.6	7.7	7.5	7.4	7.2	8.1
Most processes are IT based but not fully integrated	6.5	6.9	6.6	6.5	6.6	7.0
Some HR processes are IT based	6.0	6.5	5.9	5.4	6.1	6.1
Little IT present in the HR function	4.6	6.4	6.0	6.0	4.9	5.7
No IT present	5.1	No respondents	4.7	No respondents	No respondents	No respondents

ᵃBased on total score for all twelve effectiveness items as rated by HR executives.

*Significant correlation between HR effectiveness and information system use levels ($p \leq .05$).

In 2007, 2010, and 2013, the relationship between increased attention to metrics and HR effectiveness is significant. As we saw earlier, the effectiveness of HR measurement and analytics is related to HR having a strategic role as well. This suggests that metrics have reached the point where increased attention to them makes a significant difference in the impact of the HR function, likely because of an increasing technical capability to develop effective HRISs and meaningful metrics that tie closely to functional and organizational performance effectiveness.

Information Technology

The results from all surveys since 2001 show a positive relationship between the comprehensiveness of HR information systems and HR effectiveness (table 10.6).

Table 10.7 goes deeper, examining a detailed set of HRIS outcomes and their relationship to HR effectiveness. The results show strong positive correlations with virtually all HRIS outcomes and effectiveness, and this is consistent in every survey since 2004. The changes in the correlations over time offer insight into the evolving role of HR and HRISs. In 2004, efficiency-related outcomes generated the highest correlation, but these correlations steadily decreased in later years. The same pattern is seen for the outcome of increasing employee satisfaction, with the correlation dropping from .55 in 2004 to .25 in 2016. In contrast, some items show increasing associations with HR effectiveness, including improving non-HR managers' human capital decisions and creating knowledge networks. It is also notable that "analyze and optimize social networks" achieved a correlation among the highest of the HRIS outcomes.

These findings suggest that HR systems drive effectiveness less through their technical elegance and contributions to the efficiency of

Table 10.7. Relationship of HRIS outcomes to HR effectiveness					
	HR Effectiveness[b]				
HRIS Outcomes[a]	2004	2007	2010	2013	2016
Overall effectiveness	**.61***	**.47***	**.49***	**.40***	**.37***
Employee satisfaction	**.55***	**.40***	**.34***	**.44***	**.25***
Efficiency	**.63***	**.46***	**.48***	**.36***	**.39***
Improve HR services	.56***	.45***	.40***	.42***	.31**
Reduce HR transaction costs	.49***	.44***	.45***	.34***	.39***
Speed up HR processes	.40**	.37***	.42***	.37***	.28**
Reduce the number of employees in HR	.55***	.39***	.36***	.10	.39***
Business effectiveness	**.40**	**.42***	**.47***	**.36***	**.31**
Provide new strategic information	.23[t]	.28*	.41***	.40***	.20*
Integrate HR processes (e.g., training, compensation)	.49***	.47***	.43***	.26**	.36***
Measure HR's impact on the business	**.49***	**.41***	**.41***	**.35***	**.44***
Improve human capital decisions of managers outside HR	—	**.37***	**.38***	**.33***	**.47***
Be effective	**.44***	**.39***	**.33***	**.39***	**.22***
Create knowledge networks	—	—	**.40***	**.34***	**.48***
Offer a positive user experience	—	—	—	**.36***	**.28***
Represent a state-of-the-art solution	—	—	—	**.23***	**.27***
Use the most advanced technology	—	—	—	**.20***	**.18[t]**
Analyze and optimize social networks	—	—	—	—	**.39***

Note: Empty cells indicate that the items were not asked in that year. Bold numbers are based on scale means.

[a]Includes items from Employee Satisfaction, Efficiency, and Business Effectiveness scales only.

[b]Based on total score for all twelve effectiveness items as rated by HR executives.

Significance level: $^t p \leq .10$, $^* p \leq .05$, $^{**} p \leq .01$, $^{***} p \leq .001$.

the HR function and increasingly through their contribution to decisions and knowledge/social networks. Leaders traditionally design, justify, and evaluate HRIS investments based on cost savings and user satisfaction, but our results suggest that HR leaders would do well to extend these criteria to include decision support and knowledge/social networks.

Metrics and Analytics Use

The use of HR metrics and analytics for efficiency, effectiveness, and impact are all significantly related to HR effectiveness. As seen in table 10.8, this is true in all surveys since 2004 . This supports the position that like other disciplines, such as finance and marketing, attention to all three areas is an important determinant of HR effectiveness.

As with the HRIS items, the pattern of correlations over time suggests an evolving role for HR metrics and analytics use. Some correlations with HR effectiveness have decreased from 2004 to 2016, including "measuring the financial efficiency of HR operations," "measuring the cost of HR program," "cost-benefit analysis of HR program," and "using HR dashboards or scorecards." Other correlations with HR effectiveness increased from 2004 to 2016, including "measuring the specific effects of HR program," and the impact items of measuring the "business impact of HR programs," "quality of non-HR leaders' talent decisions," and "business impact of high versus low job performance." This suggests a potential shift, where using metrics for efficiency and effectiveness is less associated with HR functional effectiveness, and using metrics for impact and decision support is more associated with effectiveness. HR leaders and their constituents may be gaining greater value and becoming more adept at impact and decision support.

Table 10.8. Relationship of HR analytics and metrics use to HR effectiveness					
	HR Effectiveness[b]				
Measures[a]	2004	2007	2010	2013	2016
Efficiency					
Measure the financial efficiency of HR operations (e.g., cost per hire, time to fill, training costs).	.53***	.42***	.39***	.40***	.30**
Collect metrics that measure the cost of HR programs and processes.	.45***	.49***	.35***	.41***	.33***
Benchmark analytics and measures against data from outside organizations (e.g., Saratoga, Mercer, Hewitt).	.17	.22^t	.38***	.26**	.24*
Effectiveness					
Use HR dashboards or scorecards.	.37**	.29*	.48***	.41***	.22*
Measure the specific effects of HR programs (e.g., learning from training, motivation from rewards, validity of tests).	—	.32**	.28**	.21*	.44***
Have the capability to conduct cost-benefit analyses (also called utility analyses) of HR programs.	.53***	.19^t	.28***	.30***	.46***
Impact					
Measure the business impact of HR programs and processes.	.44***	.24*	.36***	.31***	.58***
Measure the quality of the talent decisions made by non-HR leaders.	—	.33**	.18*	.16^t	.41***
Measure the business impact of high versus low performance in jobs.	—	.24*	.34***	.24*	.43***
Note: Empty cells indicate that the item was not asked in that year.					
[a]Response scale: 1 = not currently being considered; 2 = planning for; 3 = being built; 4 = yes, have now.					
[b]Based on total score for all twelve effectiveness items as rated by HR executives.					
Significance level: $^t p \leq .10$, $^* p \leq .05$, $^{**} p \leq .01$, $^{***} p \leq .001$.					

Metrics and Analytics Effectiveness

Table 10.9 examines how overall HR effectiveness relates to the effectiveness of metrics and analytics. The results for 2016 are very similar to those for all surveys since 2004. They show that overall HR effectiveness is strongly related to the effectiveness of virtually all of the outcomes of HR metrics and analytics. This is also true for all the elements of the LAMP framework.

It is somewhat surprising that there is relatively little difference in the size of the correlations in table 10.9. This suggests that having effective HR analytics and metrics in almost any area is a way to improve the effectiveness of the HR function, possibly because it helps to make the HR organization more strategic. It is also possible that even for metrics that are not used directly to advance strategic decisions (such as those focusing on HR department operations), their existence signals rigor and effectiveness. Perhaps at this point in the evolution of the HR

Table 10.9. Relationship of HR analytics and metrics effectiveness to HR effectiveness					
	HR Effectiveness[b]				
Effectiveness[a]	2004	2007	2010	2013	2016
Strategy contributions					
Contributing to decisions about business strategy and human capital management	.52***	.55***	.58***	.53***	.51***
Identifying where talent has the greatest potential for strategic impact	.47***	.49***	.51***	.52***	.48***
Connecting human capital practices to organizational performance	.42***	.57***	.40***	.44***	.56***
Supporting organizational change efforts	.47***	.56***	.45***	.65***	.51***
HR functional and operational contributions					
Assessing and improving the HR department operations	.61***	.63***	.50***	.55***	.41***
Predicting the effects of HR programs before implementation	—	.50***	.43***	.50***	.45***
Pinpointing HR programs that should be discontinued	.52***	.52***	.46***	.54***	.40***
Logic, analysis, measurement, and process (LAMP)					
Using logical principles that clearly connect talent to organization success	—	.55***	.53***	.44***	.53***
Using advanced data analysis and statistics	—	.54***	.52***	.40***	.47***
Providing high-quality (complete, timely, accessible) talent measurements	—	.49***	.51***	.46***	.52***
Motivating users to take appropriate action	—	.52***	.45***	.54***	.39***
Capitalizing on big data	—	—	—	.44***	.44***

Note: Empty cells indicate that the item was not asked in that year.

[a]Response scale: 1 = very ineffective; 2 = ineffective; 3 = neither; 4 = effective; 5 = very effective.

[b]Based on total score for all twelve effectiveness items as rated by HR executives.

Significance level: $^{\dagger}p \le .10$, $^{*}p \le .05$, $^{**}p \le .01$, $^{***}p \le .001$.

profession, demonstrating the effective use of metrics and analytics in virtually any HR area is a significant contributor to its effectiveness.

The pattern of correlations over time suggests some evolution. Specifically, all of the correlations of metrics effectiveness related to HR functional and operational contributions decreased from 2004 to 2016. In contrast, all of the correlations of metrics effectiveness related to strategy contributions either held steady at high levels or increased from 2004 to 2016. It may be that there is a shift in which metrics used to improve the HR function remain vital but less distinctive in improving effectiveness than using metrics used to improve HR's strategic contribution.

The best conclusion concerning the use of metrics and analytics is that the effective use of them is clearly tied to the effectiveness of the HR function and that the HR function needs to make increasing use of them. It is particularly important that HR develop greater effectiveness in metrics and analytics areas considering the relatively low effectiveness ratings the metrics and analytics items received from HR executives (see table 7.1), where the typical response was "somewhat effective" to all of these items.

Decision Science

The sophistication of managers' decisions about human capital and the ability of HR to improve those decisions with evidence and logic are clearly and strongly related to HR effectiveness. This result holds true in every survey since 2004. As can be seen in table 10.10, all of the decision

Table 10.10. Relationship of decision science sophistication to HR effectiveness					
	HR Effectiveness[a]				
Decision Making	2004	2007	2010	2013	2016
We excel at competing for and with talent where it matters most to our strategic success.	—	.47***	.58***	.41***	.43***
Business leaders' decisions that depend on or affect human capital (e.g., layoffs, rewards) are as rigorous, logical, and strategically relevant as their decisions about resources such as money, technology, and customers.	.44***	.51***	.57***	.38***	.59***
HR leaders have a good understanding about where and why human capital makes the biggest difference in their business.	.52***	.58***	.61***	.57***	.66***
Business leaders have a good understanding about where and why human capital makes the biggest difference in their business.	.44***	.60***	.46***	.45***	.62***
HR systems educate business leaders about their talent decisions.	—	.46***	.55***	.42***	.61***
HR adds value by ensuring compliance with rules, laws, and guidelines.	—	.20[t]	.34***	.25**	.31**
HR adds value by delivering high-quality professional practices and services.	—	.56***	.72***	.63***	.70***
HR adds value by improving talent decisions inside and outside the HR function.	—	.56***	.64***	.62***	.64***

Note: Empty cells indicate that the item was not asked in that year.

[a]Based on total score for all twelve effectiveness items as rated by HR executives.

Response scale: 1 = little or no extent; 2 = some extent; 3 = moderate extent; 4 = great extent; 5 = very great extent.

Significance level: $^{t}p \le .10$, $^{*}p \le .05$, $^{**}p \le .01$, $^{***}p \le .001$.

science items are significantly correlated with HR effectiveness. Notably, we saw the same pattern in 2010 when we asked non-HR managers.

The pattern of decision science correlations over time suggests a similar evolution to the items on HRIS and metrics/analytics. To be sure, the extent to which HR adds value through high-quality professional practices shows an increasing association with HR effectiveness. Adding value by ensuring compliance has also increased its correlation with effectiveness, but it remains the lowest correlation in all years, and it is notably lower than the other correlations in the 2016 survey. HR effectiveness correlations have increased over time to the extent to which business leaders make rigorous decisions about human capital and understand where human capital has a pivotal impact on their business. This is consistent with the increasing association between HR effectiveness and the extent to which HR systems educate business leaders about their talent decisions. It appears that we may be seeing a shift from compliance to decision support and professional services in driving HR effectiveness. Notably, the extent to which HR delivers on these items was rated only about 3.0 on a 5-point scale and educating business leaders was rated less than 3.0 (see chapter 4 and table 4.1). There is significant opportunity for improvement impact.

Sustainability

The relationship between HR's role in company sustainability programs and HR effectiveness is shown in table 10.11. The correlations are positive and high. It is clear that effective HR functions are more likely to be involved in sustainability than are ineffective ones.

It is impossible to tell whether being an effective HR function leads to its being involved in sustainability or the reverse. Our guess is that it

Table 10.11. Relationship of HR role in sustainability activities to HR effectiveness		
	HR Effectiveness[b]	
Sustainability Activities[a]	2013	2016
Sustainability performance and competences are explicitly built into HR processes such as selection, rewards, and development.	37***	.43***
HR is involved in the design of sustainability initiatives and programs.	.39***	.38***
HR provides support and expertise in organization design issues that impact sustainability.	.57***	.59***
HR's role is:[c]	.52***	.35***

[a]Response scale: 1 = strongly disagree; 2 = somewhat disagree; 3 = neither disagree nor agree; 4 = somewhat agree; 5 = strongly agree.

[b]Based on total score for all twelve effectiveness items as rated by HR executives.

[c]Response scale: 1 = no role; 2 = minor role; 3 = active support; 4 = major support; 5 = leader.

Significance level: $^{t}p \le .10$, $^{*}p \le .05$, $^{**}p \le .01$, $^{***}p \le .001$.

might be a mutually reinforcing causal relationship that creates a virtuous spiral. When an HR function is effective, it has the credibility and resources to help create effective sustainability activities. As a result, it is seen as more effective and can do even more to create effective sustainability programs and HR activities.

Skill Satisfaction

Table 10.12 shows the relationships between HR effectiveness and the satisfaction of HR managers with the HR and business skills of HR professionals. There are very strong correlations for all the skills. This is consistent in all surveys since 2004. The strong relationship for all of these skills once again confirms the importance of HR professionals having skills beyond just HR technical skills. From 2013 to 2016, the correlation with HR effectiveness increased markedly for HR technical skills, but also for skills in sustainability, social media, and risk management. The emergence of these areas as strongly associated with HR effectiveness may signal that leaders inside and outside the HR profession see an increasingly important contribution for HR in these areas. As we noted in previous chapters, HR executives rated interpersonal, business partner, and metrics skills as only moderately present and effective in HR. This means that there is a great opportunity to enhance HR effectiveness by the skills of HR professionals.

Table 10.12. Relationship of HR skill satisfaction to HR effectiveness					
	HR Effectiveness[b]				
HR Skills[a]	**2004**	**2007**	**2010**	**2013**	**2016**
HR technical skills[c]	.32*	.43***	.52***	.48***	.61***
Interpersonal dynamics	.62***	.66***	.65***	.68***	.70***
Business partner skills	.65***	.76***	.64***	.72***	.80***
Metrics skills[d]	.56***	.69***	.54***	.62***	.58***
Sustainability	—	—	—	.45***	.56***
Social media	—	—	—	.38***	.59***
Globalization	—	—	—	.41***	.43***
Risk management	—	—	—	.39***	.51***
Organization culture	—	—	—	—	.68***
Workplace branding	—	—	—	—	.51***

Note: Empty cells indicate that the item was not asked in that year.

[a]Response scale: 1 = very dissatisfied; 2 = dissatisfied; 3 = neutral; 4 = satisfied; 5 = very satisfied.

[b]Based on total score for all twelve effectiveness items as rated by HR executives.

[c]Scale for HR technical skills recalculated for pre-2013 surveys.

[d]Scale for metrics skills recalculated for pre-2016 surveys.

Significance level: $^{\dagger}p \leq .10$, $^{*}p \leq .05$, $^{**}p \leq .01$, $^{***}p \leq .001$.

Importance of HR Practices and Activities

In order to determine the relative importance of the many practices, structures, and skills that are associated with HR effectiveness, we performed a final analysis: running a regression analysis using key items from tables 10.1 to 10.12. The following items (in the order of predictive power) were the best predictors of HR effectiveness.

1. Satisfaction with business partner skills

2. Provides analytics support for business decision making

3. HRIS that improves HR operations

4. Increased activity in organizational design and development

Once again, our data suggest that HR needs to perform its administrative activities well and to be an effective business and strategic partner. In terms of relative importance, the data suggest that HR's business and strategic performance are the most important practices and activities.

Conclusion

Our results show a number of strong relationships between the effectiveness of the HR function and the way it is organized, managed, and staffed. Among the most important findings are the following:

- Spending time on maintaining records is negatively related to HR effectiveness; being a strategic partner is positively related.

- Strategic activities such as helping plan the implementation of strategy and choosing strategy options are strongly related to HR effectiveness.

- Using information technology and service units as delivery mechanisms for HR services is strongly related to HR effectiveness.

- Increased focus on organizational design and development is related to HR effectiveness.

- Having a completely integrated HRIS leads to the highest level of HR effectiveness.

- The effectiveness of the HRIS system is strongly related to the overall effectiveness of the HR organization.

- Having a wide array of effective HR metrics and analytics is strongly related to HR effectiveness. There is an increasing association of HR effectiveness with metrics related to decision support and business strategy.

- The decision science sophistication of business leaders is strongly related to the effectiveness of the HR function. Over time there is an increasing association of effectiveness with educating and improving the decisions of leaders outside the HR function.

- There is a clear relationship between the skills of HR managers and the effectiveness of the HR function.

Overall, the findings tell an important story. HR effectiveness is associated with a wide array of HR activities, structures, systems, and skills that are within the control of HR. HR can do a lot to make HR more effective. It certainly needs to be sure its administrative processes work well, but its best opportunities for improvement appear to be in the business partner role and in strategy.

CHAPTER 11

Determinants of Organizational Performance

- How HR is organized, managed, and staffed is related to overall organizational performance, and many of the relationships have increased over time.

- The strongest contribution to organizational effectiveness is an integrated human capital and business strategy.

- Other strong associations with organizational effectiveness are when HR is helping to decide among strategy options and assessing organizational strategic readiness.

- Having a more comprehensive and integrated HRIS is associated with organizational performance, as is HRIS effectiveness.

- The use of analytics and metrics for efficiency, effectiveness, and impact is related to organizational performance, as is HRIS effectiveness in making strategy contributions and enhancing the logic, analytics, metrics, and processes that motivate user action.

- Decision science sophistication is strongly associated with organizational performance, particularly in competing for the most pivotal talent.

- HR skills are strongly related to organizational performance, particularly skills in business partnering, workplace branding, and organizational culture, and the relationship has increased over time.

- Higher-performing organizations have HR functions that are active in sustainability.

How does the design, operation, role, and effectiveness of HR influence organizational performance? At first glance, one might think that the same HR practices that influence the effectiveness of the HR function in organizations (the focus of chapter 10) also influence overall organizational effectiveness. Yet HR features can have a different relationship to organizational performance than on HR effectiveness. In our sample, the relationship between HR executives' ratings of organizational performance and their rating of HR effectiveness is only moderate ($r = .31, p \leq .001$). This is actually not surprising because HR effectiveness is just one of many determinants of organizational performance. Furthermore, some HR practices and activities do not have a direct impact on the bottom line of organizations, and as a result, some activities that influence HR effectiveness may not affect organizational performance. Finally, some HR features may affect organizational

Table 11.1. Relationship of time spent and organizational performance			
HR Time Spent[a]	**Organizational Performance**[b]		
	2010	**2013**	**2016**
Maintaining records: Collect, track, and maintain data on employees	–.12	.01	–.17[t]
Auditing/controlling: Ensure compliance with internal operations, regulations, and legal and union requirements	–.13	.00	–.19[t]
HR service provider: Assist with the implementation and administration of HR practices	–.23*	–.05	.01
Development of HR systems and practices: Develop new HR systems and practices	.16[t]	.08	–.10
Strategic business partner: Member of the management team; involved with strategic HR planning, organizational design, and strategic change	.27**	–.01	.25**

[a]Based on percentage of time spent on HR roles as rated by HR executives.

[b]Response scale: 1 = much below average; 2 = somewhat below average; 3 = about average; 4 = somewhat above average; 5 = much above average.

Significance level: [t]$p \le .10$, *$p \le .05$, **$p \le .01$, ***$p \le .001$.

performance directly while having only a limited impact on the function itself. Because of this, it is important to examine how HR features affect organizational performance, in addition to how they affect HR functional effectiveness (chapter 10).

Time Spent

The results in table 11.1 show that time spent on maintaining records, auditing, controlling, and HR service provision was negatively related to organizational performance in 2010 and negatively or not related in 2013 and 2016. Of these, only the HR service provider correlation for 2010 was statistically significant. Development of HR systems and being a strategic business partner were both positively related to organizational performance in 2010 but not significantly related in 2013 or 2016. The largest and most significant correlation for organizational performance in 2010 and 2016 is with being a strategic business partner. This reinforces the importance of HR being involved in strategic decisions of corporations and playing a role in organizational design and strategic thinking.

The pattern of correlations for 2010 and 2016 in table 11.1 is similar to that in table 10.1 which presents data on HR effectiveness. In both cases, effectiveness is associated with spending more time on being a strategic contributor and less time on traditional HR compliance and service activities.

Business Strategy

HR's involvement in specific business strategy activities shows positive and significant relationships with organizational performance, for virtually all items. As can be seen in table 11.2, the strength of these associations has increased from earlier years. In 2010 and 2013, the correlations for all business strategy activities were positive but low. In 2016, they are much higher and significant. Given the overall positive pattern, it is reasonable to suggest that having HR involved in most business strategy activities will be positively associated with organizational performance. This finding is particularly compelling in that HR's business strategy activities are only one of many factors affecting organizational performance. Yet the 2016 relationships show a consistent and significant positive effect.

HR Strategy Features

The results for the HR strategy features in table 11.3 show strong positive relationships between virtually all of the features of the HR strategy and organizational performance. This pattern also existed in 2010 and 2013, but in the 2016 results, the associations are stronger, and more of the strategy features show a significant relationship. By far the strongest correlation with any single feature is with human capital strategies that are integrated with the business strategy. This was true in both 2010 and 2016. This feature was also significantly associated with organizational performance in 2013, but the highest correlation then was with data-based human capital decisions. Notably, for the first time in 2016, all of the strategy features are significantly related to organizational performance. In addition, the new strategy item in 2016, reflecting decisions about freelance and gig workers, is significantly related to organizational performance.

Overall, the results indicate that a well-designed HR strategy with features that use data, integrate with business strategies, drive decisions, and address all types of workers has a positive impact on organizational performance. The associations with organizational performance are not as strong as with HR effectiveness, but this is hardly surprising given the many factors that determine organizational performance.

HR Organizational Design

Organizational performance is not strongly related to the design features of HR organizational design. As can be seen in table 11.4, although all the correlations are positive, only one association reached statistical significance in any of our surveys. HR talent development reached statistical significance in 2010. That design feature also reached marginal significance ($p < .10$) in 2013 and 2016 and has always been the strongest association of all the features we included. The fact that HR talent development is correlated with organizational performance points to the value of having a well-staffed, well-run HR organization.

Table 11.2. Relationship of business strategy activities to organizational performance

Activities[a]	Organizational Performance[b]		
	2010	2013	2016
Help identify or design strategy options	.15	.02	.29**
Help decide among the best strategy options	.14	.04	.32***
Help plan the implementation of strategy	.11	.20*	.20*
Help identify new business opportunities	.12	.05	.12
Assess the organization's readiness to implement strategies	.13	.12	.35***
Help design the organization structure to implement strategy	.12	.11	.26**
Assess possible merger, acquisition, or divestiture strategies	.18[t]	.14[t]	.21*
Work with the corporate board on business strategy	.09	.10	.21*

[a]Response scale: 1 = little or no extent; 2 = some extent; 3 = moderate extent; 4 = great extent; 5 = very great extent.

[b]Response scale: 1 = much below average; 2 = somewhat below average; 3 = about average;
　　　　　4 = somewhat above average; 5 = much above average.

Significance level: $^t p ≤ .10$, $^* p ≤ .05$, $^{**} p ≤ .01$, $^{***} p ≤ .001$.

Table 11.3. Relationship of HR strategy to organizational performance

HR Strategy[a]	Organizational Performance[b]		
	2010	2013	2016
Data-based talent strategy	.22*	.21*	.22*
A human capital strategy that is integrated with business strategy	.33***	.19*	.40***
Provides analytical support for business decision making	.24**	.16[t]	.26**
Provides HR data to support change management	.23*	.20*	.22*
Drives change management	.20*	.12	.23*
Makes rigorous data-based decisions about human capital management	.18[t]	.28***	.23*
HR is involved in decisions about whether and where to use project-based, freelance, and platform gigs in order to get work done	—	—	.21*

Note: Empty cells indicate that the item was not asked in that year.

[a]Response scale: 1 = little or no extent; 2 = some extent; 3 = moderate extent; 4 = great extent; 5 = very great extent.

[b]Response scale: 1 = much below average; 2 = somewhat below average; 3 = about average; 4 = somewhat above average;
　　　　　5 = much above average.

Significance level: $^t p ≤ .10$, $^* p ≤ .05$, $^{**} p ≤ .01$, $^{***} p ≤ .001$.

Table 11.4. Relationship of HR organizational design to organizational performance

HR Organization[a,b]	Organizational Performance[b]		
	2010	2013	2016
HR service units	.11	.09	.11
Decentralization	.06	.13	−.02
HR talent development	.18*	.14[t]	.18[t]

[a]See table 5.1 for items in scale.

[b]Response scale: 1 = much below average; 2 = somewhat below average; 3 = about average;
　　　　　4 = somewhat above average; 5 = much above average.

Significance level: $^t p ≤ .10$, $^* p ≤ .05$, $^{**} p ≤ .01$, $^{***} p ≤ .001$.

Activity Changes

Multiple changes in HR activity levels are significantly related to organizational performance. As can be seen in table 11.5, three activity level changes had particularly strong relationships in 2013. Employee development, recruitment and selection, and HR metrics show relatively strong statistically significant relationships with organizational performance. In 2010, all of these relationships were strong, as was the relationship with organizational design and development. This indicates that shifting more time and effort into these areas has been a high-payoff activity for these organizations. Particularly interesting are the relationships with the amount of activity change having to do with talent management. They indicate that increasing the focus on talent management is potentially a high-payoff activity for many organizations.

Comprehensiveness, Integration, and Effectiveness of HR Information Technology

The comprehensiveness and integration of HR's information technology shows a strong positive relationship with organizational performance in 2010, 2013, and 2016. As can be seen in table 11.6, the level of organizational performance reported by HR leaders whose information systems are completely integrated is significantly higher than for those with less IT use and integration. The relationship is not as strong as is the one for HR effectiveness, but it is strong enough to establish the importance of having IT-based HR systems.

Table 11.7 shows the relationship between HRIS outcomes and organizational performance. The results for 2016 generally show positive

Table 11.5. Relationship of HR activity changes to organizational performance		
	Organizational Performance[b]	
HR Activities[a]	**2010**	**2013**
Design and organizational development	.30***	.13
Compensation and benefits	.18*	.11
Employee development	.34***	.29***
Recruitment and selection	.35***	.19*
HR metrics and analytics	.13	.24**
HR information systems	.11	.07
Union relations	.05	.08
Social networks	—[c]	.16[t]

[a] Not asked in 2016.

[b] Response scale: 1 = much below average; 2 = somewhat below average; 3 = about average; 4 = somewhat above average; 5 = much above average.

[c] The item was not asked in that year.

Significance level: [t] $p \le .10$, *$p \le .05$, **$p \le .01$, ***$p \le .001$.

Table 11.6. Relationship of HR information technology integration to organizational performance

Information System	Organizational Performance[a]		
	2010	2013*	2016*
Completely integrated HR IT system	4.3	4.2	3.8
Most processes are IT based but not fully integrated	3.8	4.0	4.1
Some HR processes are IT based	3.7	3.7	3.4
Little IT present in the HR function	3.8	3.5	2.8
No IT present	No responses	No responses	No responses

[a]Response scale: 1 = much below average; 2 = somewhat below average; 3 = about average; 4 = somewhat above average; 5 = much above average.

*Significant correlation between organizational performance and information system use levels ($p \le .05$).

Table 11.7. Relationship of HRIS outcomes to organizational performance

HRIS Outcomes[a]	Organizational Performance[b]		
	2010	2013	2016
Overall effectiveness[c]	**.21***	**.13**	**.30***
Employee satisfaction	**.13**	**.18***	**.25****
Efficiency	**.22***	**.17***	**.31***
Improve HR services	.19*	.19*	.31***
Reduce HR transaction costs	.18*	.14	.31***
Speed up HR processes	.25**	.18*	.30***
Reduce the number of employees in HR	.17^t	.07	.15
Business effectiveness	**.18***	**.07**	**.23***
Provide new strategic information	.17^t	.14	.17^t
Integrate HR processes (e.g., training, compensation)	.16^t	.02	.23*
Measure HR's impact on the business	**.32***	**.07**	**.16^t**
Improve human capital decisions of managers outside HR	**.20***	**.06**	**.16^t**
Be effective	**.13**	**.12**	**.27****
Create knowledge networks	**.22***	**.05**	**.10**
Offer a positive user experience	**—**	**.15^t**	**.30***
Represent a state-of-the-art solution	**—**	**.08**	**.23***
Use the most advance technology	**—**	**.12**	**.23***
Analyze and optimize social networks	**—**	**—**	**.11**

Note: Empty cells indicate that the item was not asked in that year. Bold numbers are scale means.

[a]Response scale: 1 = little or no extent; 2 = some extent; 3 = moderate extent; 4 = great extent; 5 = very great extent.

[b]Response scale: 1 = much below average; 2 = somewhat below average; 3 = about average; 4 = somewhat above average; 5 = much above average.

[c]Includes items from Employee Satisfaction, Efficiency, and Business Effectiveness scales only.

Significance level: $^t p \le .10$, $*p \le .05$, $**p \le .01$, $***p \le .001$.

relationships with most HRIS outcomes, and stronger and more numerous significant positive relationships than in past surveys. The most consistently positive associations are with efficiency-related outcomes. It appears that traditional uses of HRIS continue to offer organizational value. System features such as integrated HR processes, state-of-the-art solutions, and advanced technology also reached significance in 2016, as did providing a positive user experience. The last may reflect an increasing emphasis on HR having a customer orientation and designing systems that create a positive workforce experience. The trend over time of an increase in the number and strength of HRIS outcomes associated with organizational performance provides further evidence that using information technology properly can have a positive impact on HR's organizational performance.

Metrics and Analytics Use and Effectiveness

The use of HR metrics to support efficiency, effectiveness and impact shows many significant positive relationships with organizational performance (table 11.8). Interestingly, the statistically significant relationships for 2010 and 2013 were all with effectiveness and impact areas and much smaller relationships with efficiency. In 2016, all of the efficiency items have significant positive relationships, and most of them are stronger than the effectiveness and impact items. Some of the highest correlations with organizational performance are with measuring the effectiveness of HR programs and processes. Overall, it appears that

Table 11.8. Relationship of HR analytics and metrics use to organizational performance			
	Organizational Performance[b]		
Measures[a]	2010	2013	2016
Efficiency			
Measure the financial efficiency of HR operations (e.g., cost per hire, time to fill, training costs).	.13	.14[t]	.31***
Collect metrics that measure the cost of HR programs and processes.	.14	.14[t]	.20*
Benchmark analytics and measures against data from outside organizations (e.g., Saratoga, Mercer, Hewitt).	.09	.06	.27**
Effectiveness			
Use HR dashboards or scorecards.	.13	.20*	.21*
Measure the specific effects of HR programs (e.g., learning from training, motivation from rewards, validity of tests).	.20*	.20*	.28**
Have the capability to conduct cost-benefit analyses (also called utility analyses) of HR programs.	.23*	.19*	.10
Impact			
Measure the business impact of HR programs and processes.	.34***	.02	.20*
Measure the quality of the talent decisions made by non-HR leaders.	.04	.23**	.13
Measure the business impact of high versus low performance in jobs.	.24**	.08	.00

[a]Response scale: 1 = not currently being considered; 2 = planning for; 3 = being built; 4 = yes, have now.

[b]Response scale: 1 = much below average; 2 = somewhat below average; 3 = about average; 4 = somewhat above average; 5 = much above average.

Significance level: $^t p \leq .10$, $^* p \leq .05$, $^{**} p \leq .01$, $^{***} p \leq .001$.

Table 11.9. Relationship of HR metrics and analytical effectiveness to organizational performance

Effectiveness[a]	Organizational Performance[b]		
	2010	2013	2016
Strategy contributions			
Contributing to decisions about business strategy and human capital management	.19*	.07	.33***
Identifying where talent has the greatest potential for strategic impact	.38***	.18*	.20*
Connecting human capital practices to organizational performance	.19*	.11	.37***
Supporting organizational change efforts	.10	.09	.24*
HR functional and operational contributions			
Assessing and improving the HR department operations	.16[t]	.09	.13
Predicting the effects of HR programs before implementation	.16[t]	.09	.27**
Pinpointing HR programs that should be discontinued	.19*	.10	−.02
Logic, analysis, measurement, and process (LAMP)			
Using logical principles that clearly connect talent to organizational success	.26**	.23**	.27**
Using advanced data analysis and statistics	.23*	.28***	.19*
Providing high-quality (complete, timely, accessible) talent measurements	.32***	.05	.23*
Motivating users to take appropriate action	.30***	.07	.20*
Capitalizing on big data	—[c]	.12	.17[t]

[a]Response scale: 1 = very ineffective; 2 = ineffective; 3 = somewhat effective; 4 = effective; 5 = very effective.

[b]Response scale: 1 = much below average; 2 = somewhat below average; 3 = about average; 4 = somewhat above average; 5 = much above average.

[c]The item was not asked in that year.

Significance level: [t]$p \leq .10$, *$p \leq .05$, **$p \leq .01$, ***$p \leq .001$.

the degree to which HR is able to operate programs and make decisions that influence the way organizations develop and manage talent and HR programs is related to organizational performance.

Our 2016 results suggest that organizational performance is more strongly associated with more traditional HR metrics focused on functional efficiency, benchmarks, and HR program effects than with measures that track non-HR leader decisions and the pivotal impact of job performance. This is in contrast to the frequent calls for HR measurements to engage users and drive decisions outside the HR function. It is also interesting that this pattern was somewhat different from the effects on HR functional effectiveness (see table 10.8), where tracking decision quality and the impact of pivotal talent had some of the strongest positive associations. It may be that metrics used for decision support and to understand the impact of pivotal performance are emerging first as important elements of the HR function and that their impact on organizational performance awaits a broader understanding of their use by non-HR leaders.

The effectiveness of HR metrics and analytics is significantly related to organizational performance, as shown in table 11.9. Although some individual items were not as strong as in our 2010 survey, the pattern over time is generally that metrics and analytics effectiveness is more broadly and strongly associated with organizational performance. Three of the four strategy contributions measures, one of the functional and operational measures, and all of the LAMP items are significantly related to organizational performance in 2010, 2013, or 2016. Others are related in multiple years.

As Boudreau and Ramstad (2007) suggested, our results show a fairly consistent pattern that all of the LAMP items are positively related to organizational effectiveness, suggesting that they build on and reinforce each other. Among the strategy contributions, there is a consistent and significant correlation between identifying where talent has the greatest potential for strategic impact and organizational effectiveness. This once again reinforces the point that more informed decision making about talent is an HR function that contributes to organizational performance. For example, using the logical principles that connect talent to organizational success is significantly related to organizational performance. Similarly, providing high-quality talent measurements is significantly related in 2010 and 2016.

Decision Science Sophistication

The decision science sophistication results are shown in table 11.10. In all of our survey years, virtually all of these items are positively and significantly associated with organizational performance. In prior years, the significant correlations were approximately the same. In 2016, one

Table 11.10. Relationship of decision science sophistication to organizational performance			
	Organizational Performance[b]		
Decision Making[a]	2010	2013	2016
We excel at competing for and with talent where it matters most to our strategic success.	.32***	.27**	.50***
Business leaders' decisions that depend on or affect human capital (e.g., layoffs, rewards) are as rigorous, logical, and strategically relevant as their decisions about resources such as money, technology, and customers.	.27**	.22*	.33***
HR leaders have a good understanding about where and why human capital makes the biggest difference in their business.	.33***	.26**	.22*
Business leaders have a good understanding about where and why human capital makes the biggest difference in their business.	.24*	.31***	.34***
HR systems educate business leaders about their talent decisions.	.27**	.18*	.33***
HR adds value by ensuring compliance with rules, laws, and guidelines.	.27**	.23*	.22*
HR adds value by delivering high-quality professional practices and services.	.30***	.14	.16
HR adds value by improving talent decisions inside and outside the HR function.	.29**	.07	.21*

[a]Response scale: 1 = little or no extent; 2 = some extent; 3 = moderate extent; 4 = great extent; 5 = very great extent.
[b]Response scale: 1 = much below average; 2 = somewhat below average; 3 = about average; 4 = somewhat above average; 5 = much above average.
Significance level: [1]p ≤ .10, *p ≤ .05, **p ≤ .01, ***p ≤ .001.

item, about competing for talent where it matters most to organizational success, had a much higher correlation, .50. This may reflect the improving economy in the United States, with the greater challenges it has created with respect to attracting and retaining well-qualified talent. The items reflecting how HR enhances human capital decisions and understanding among non-HR leaders show increasing relationships with organizational performance. Another trend over time is that organizational performance is less strongly associated with HR's adding value by delivering high-quality practices and services, which may reflect the fact that such services are minimum expectations, and not significant differentiators.

As with all of the results in this chapter, these findings are correlational. So, there is the possibility that because an organization is performing well, it is seen as making good decisions. Perhaps the best explanation for why this relationship exists is based on a kind of virtuous spiral in which good decisions drive good performance, which in turn encourages managers to focus on making good talent management decisions (Lawler 2008). Overall the data strongly support having managers both within and outside the HR function who understand how and why good talent management leads to high organizational performance.

Sustainability

Both the role of HR in sustainability and its sustainability activities are significantly related to organizational performance. This was true in both 2013 and 2016, but the relationship are much weaker in 2016. The overall relationship still shows that when HR is involved in sustainability, both HR functions and their organizations perform better. This raises the question of what causes this relationship. This most likely is that well-functioning organizations choose to have their HR function involved in sustainability rather than that HR's involvement makes the organizations more effective.

HR Skills

Satisfaction with virtually all HR skills is significantly related to organizational performance in 2016, the only exceptions being skills in globalization and risk management, as can be seen in table 11.11. While none of the skill items reached statistical significance in 2013, the results from 2010 and 2016 suggest consistent, positive relationships. The four skills measured in 2010 (HR technical skills, interpersonal dynamics, business partner, and metrics) showed statistically significant relationships in both 2010 and 2016. In 2016, the two new items that were added, organizational culture and workplace branding, emerged as having the strongest positive relationships with organizational performance.

Table 11.11. Relationship of HR skill satisfaction to organizational performance			
	Organizational Performance[b]		
HR Skills[a]	2010	2013	2016
HR technical skills[c]	.19*	.13	.20*
Interpersonal dynamics	.29***	.10	.24*
Business partner skills	.23*	.01	.31***
Metrics skills[d]	.18[t]	.14	.26**
Sustainability	—	.04	.22*
Social media	—	.00	.28**
Globalization	—	−.02	.13
Risk management	—	.07	.17[t]
Organizational culture	—	—	.35***
Workplace branding	—	—	.35***

Note: Empty cells indicate that the item was not asked in that year.

[a]Response scale: 1 = very dissatisfied; 2 = dissatisfied; 3 = neutral; 4 = satisfied; 5 = very satisfied.

[b]Response scale: 1 = much below average; 2 = somewhat below average; 3 = about average; 4 = somewhat above average; 5 = much above average.

[c]Scale for HR technical skills recalculated for 2010 survey.

[d]Scale for metrics skills recalculated for pre-2016 surveys.

Significance level: $^t p \leq .10$, $^* p \leq .05$, $^{**} p \leq .01$, $^{***} p \leq .001$.

Overall, the pattern is clear: better HR skills go with better organizational performance. The overall positive relationship between HR skills and organizational performance in 2016 argues for investing in the development of HR professionals. We think it is very important to make this investment. Without it, an HR function cannot be expected to deliver the outcomes that have been shown to lead to organizational effectiveness. Moreover, these skills will increasingly reside not only within the HR function itself, but throughout the organization, as the CHREATE project demonstrated (Boudreau 2016).

Conclusion

Our results show a number of strong relationships between organizational performance and HR's organizational design, effectiveness, activities, and role. As expected, many of the relationships with organizational performance are not as strong as with the effectiveness of the HR function, but the trend appears to show increasing relationships with organizational performance. Among the most important are the following:

- The amount of time spent on strategic issues is positively related to organizational performance.

- A number of HR strategy activities are related to organizational performance. The strongest relationship is with having a human capital strategy that is integrated with the business strategy.

- The amount of HR talent development that is done by an organization is positively related to its performance, as is the skill level in HR.

- Increasing HR's focus on talent is associated with high organizational performance.

- Having an integrated HRIS system is associated with high organizational performance.

- Employing metrics and analytics that measure the impact and quality of HR programs, processes, and talent decisions is associated with organizational performance.

- High-performance organizations have a high level of decision science sophistication with respect to talent and its impact on organizational performance.

- High-performance organizations have HR functions that are active in sustainability.

Overall, the results tell an important story about how HR can contribute to organizational performance. Talent management is clearly an area where HR can have a positive impact on organizational performance by improving its data, analytics, and decision making. HR also can make important contributions to organizational performance by developing its role as a strategic contributor. It is also notable that many of the HR features most strongly related to organizational performance are in areas where the extent of those features is moderate or low. Thus, the encouraging relationships with organizational performance that emerged in this chapter suggest that HR can improve its impact by increasing those features.

CHAPTER 12

How HR Has Changed

Our study provides unique data that answer numerous important questions about how HR is changing. Other studies have asked about the importance of HR taking a new direction, adding new skills, adopting new practices, and offering new services. They have also asked HR managers to report on the amount and kind of change they think has occurred. This is the only study that has examined change by measuring the activities and effectiveness of HR functions over time.

Reports of change are almost always less valid than are comparisons among data collected at two or more times. The former are influenced by memory and other factors. The problem with reports of change is demonstrated in our study by the responses to our question concerning how HR time is spent. HR executives responding to each of our seven surveys from 1995 to 2013 report significant shifts in the way HR time is being spent. However, when we examine actual changes in activity levels using reports of current practice from different time periods, the percentages have not shifted (see chapter 2). Thus, if we had relied on self-reported change, we would have concluded after every survey that HR had reduced the time spent on maintaining records and auditing operations by over 12 percentage points and had increased the time spent as a strategic business partner by over 13 percentage points. Yet the actual reports of time spent on strategic partnership, maintaining records, and auditing are virtually unchanged since 1995. HR has spent about 25 percent of its time as a strategic partner. In fact, the impression of progress is the result of a bad memory that is most likely the result of wishful thinking.

In our surveys from 1995 to 2013 we asked how the focus of HR activities had changed over the previous five to seven years (not asked in 2016). The results in table 12.1 show a consistent pattern of reported change. The only one that has not gotten greater attention is unions, which is not surprising given the decline of union activity in the United States. This result suggests change is occurring, but a word of caution is in order: it may be the result of the same memory problem that seems to have led to the reports of increased time spent as a strategic partner.

There is no question that the business environment has changed dramatically in the past twenty years, but the HR function in most organizations does not look very different than it did twenty years ago. There is widespread agreement and much writing about the need for HR to change and how it needs to change to be more strategic and more of a business

Table 12.1. Change in focus on HR activities, United States

HR Activities	Means						
	1995[1]	1998[2]	2001[3]	2004[4]	2007[5]	2010[6]	2013[7]
Design and organizational development	—	3.8	3.9	3.9	3.9[6]	3.7[5]	3.8
Compensation and benefits	3.9[6,7]	3.7[4]	3.8	4.0[2,6,7]	3.8[6]	3.5[1,4,5]	3.6[1,4]
Executive compensation	—	—	—	—	—	3.8	3.9
Employee development	—	—	3.6	3.8	3.8	3.6	3.7
Recruitment and selection	3.4[2,3,4,5,7]	3.9[1]	3.8[1,5]	3.8[1]	4.1[1,3,6]	3.6[5]	3.9[1]
HR metrics and analytics	—	—	—	3.8	3.9	3.8	3.9
HR information systems	4.1	4.1[6]	4.0	4.0	3.9	3.8[2]	3.8
Union relations	3.1	2.9	2.7	3.0	2.8	2.9	2.8
Developing social networks	—	—	—	—	—	—	3.6

Note: Empty cells indicate that the item was not asked in that year.

Response scale: 1 = greatly decreased; 3 = stayed the same; 5 = greatly increased.

[1,2,3,4,5,6,7] Significant differences ($p \leq .05$) between years.

partner; offer higher-quality HR information systems (HRIS) and human capital management systems; and be more of a leader on issues such as globalization, sustainability, workplace personalization, and organizational agility (Boudreau 2016; Boudreau and Ziskin 2011; Lawler and Worley 2011; Worley, Williams, and Lawler 2014; Lawler 2017).

Despite the many changes that have occurred, our data, and the tables throughout this book, show little change from 1995 to 2016 with respect to how HR is organized and how it operates in large corporations. We can point to some areas where change has occurred, but most of the changes took place in the late 1990s and have leveled off or even reversed since then. In this chapter, we provide a summary of what has and has not changed and seek to reconcile our evidence of slow or nonexistent change in HR with the widespread view that the profession needs to and is changing.

What Has and Has Not Changed

Our analysis of the results of our 1995 to 2016 surveys establishes that some significant changes have occurred in how HR functions are organized and how they deliver services. The most significant changes are the way the HR function is organized, where HR activities and information are located, and HR's role in employee advocacy and shaping a labor market strategy. These changes may well set the stage for a greater strategic partnership, but they are largely focused on how the HR function itself is organized and managed and how it defines its relationships with its clients. The most important changes are these:

- HR is more likely to be either a full partner or have input in shaping business strategy.

- HR is more likely to use service teams to support and serve business units.

- HR is more likely to have corporate centers of excellence.

- Companies are more likely to have similar HR practices in different business units.

- HR is paying increased attention to recruitment and selection, as well as organizational design and development.

- More companies' HR processes are information technology based.

- Employees are increasingly making use of HRISs on a self-service basis.

- There is greater satisfaction with the interpersonal dynamics and business understanding skills of HR professionals.

- Boards request HR help in providing information about workforce capability.

- HR decision support contributions are increasingly associated with HR's strategic role.

- The strategic elements of HR's decision support and metrics and analytics use are increasingly associated with HR and organizational effectiveness.

- HR is increasingly effective in helping to shape a viable employment relationship for the future, providing HR services, operating centers of excellence, and being an employee advocate.

Most of these changes occurred in the late 1990s. Since then, the major changes have been in information technology.

In comparing our earlier results to those of 2016, it is clear that a number of things have not changed very much, if at all. Many of these elements reflect HR's role in shaping strategy and building effective HR skills. Among them are the following:

- The general lack of change in HR, despite the consistent and positive relationship between many HR features with HR's strategic role, effectiveness, and organizational performance

- The time HR spends as a strategic partner and the estimated time it spends as a strategic partner

- The desire of HR executives to be business and strategic partners

- The tendency of HR advice to boards to be about executive compensation and succession rather than change, governance, risk, strategy, or sustainability

- The quality of human capital decisions that business leaders make

- The relatively low levels of business leaders' use of sound principles for human capital decisions compared to their use with respect to more tangible assets

- The infrequent use of HR systems to educate business leaders about the quality of their talent decisions

- The implementation of HR metrics and analytics systems and their effectiveness

- The moderate use of efficiency and effectiveness measures and the less frequent use of measuring HR impact on decisions and strategy

- The use of fully integrated HR information technology systems

- A rating by less than a quarter of respondents who think that more than 80 percent of HR professionals have the skills they need to be effective

- An HR skill satisfaction level that averages below "neither satisfied nor dissatisfied" for all HR skills except those in traditional areas of HR technical skills and interpersonal dynamics

- The business partner skills of the HR professionals rated as moderate to low

- The highest effectiveness of HR being in areas such as providing HR services and being an employee advocate, and the lowest effectiveness being in areas related to business strategy

Overall, when we analyze our data from 1995 to 2016, we find that more things have stayed the same than have changed. Although many of the changes we found are significant and important, the amount of change in them is surprisingly small. Frankly, given the tremendous amount of attention paid to the importance of HR being a business and strategic partner and adding value in new ways, we expected much more change. In fact, we have expected more change than we have seen in every wave of our study since it began. This "stubborn traditionalism" (Boudreau and Ramstad 2007; Boudreau and Lawler 2014) is also apparent in the continuing flow of articles about frustration among non-HR executives with HR's unrealized potential.

Much about HR has remained the same despite the enormous amount of change that is going on around it. This raises a critical question: Are there particular organizational and environmental conditions that are associated with HR being more of a business and strategic partner? The answer is yes, and looking at them can help us understand what it takes to change how HR operates in organizations.

Strategic Focuses

Our 2016 study found a strong relationship between what is happening in the HR function and an organization's strategic focuses. In particular, three of the five focuses—information, knowledge, and innovation—were positively related to most of the strategic and advanced features of HR functions. This is a bit different from the survey in 2010, which showed a positive relationship with them and a positive association also with the sustainability focus. In the 2013 and 2016 results, sustainability sometimes emerged as positively associated with strategic and advanced HR elements, though less so than in 2010. Generally it appears that an emphasis on information, knowledge, and innovation creates a much more favorable situation for the HR function because it places a premium on acquiring, developing, deploying, and retaining talent.

Overall, our results clearly show that strategy focuses influence the way the HR function operates and its success as a business partner. When there are strong focuses on information knowledge and innovation, HR performs more high-valued-added activities and is more strategic, and the HR function is more positively regarded.

Our strategy results raise the issue of the direction of causality. One possibility is that an organization's strategy causes HR to take on a particular role. The alternative is that a more strategic HR role causes organizations to adopt strategies that rely more on knowledge and talent quality. Our guess is that the most common causal direction is from strategy to the nature of HR, not the reverse. One implication is that how an HR organization operates in a company may be largely determined by the company's business strategy. Perhaps HR is more the victim than the guilty party in cases where it is not a business or strategic partner. Certainly every senior HR leader we have worked with has said that it is easier to find an organization that understands and supports strategic HR than to try to change an organization that does not.

Management Approach

Of the five management approaches we asked about, two of them had a strong and consistent positive relationship with the nature of the HR function in organizations. The high-involvement and sustainable approaches were associated with HR being more involved in business strategy activities, employee development, working with the board, and with advanced levels of decision science, decision support, and HR metrics and analytics. This is not surprising. These approaches, more than the others, require a clear focus on human capital and an organization that understands how talent and organizational design decisions affect strategic success.

The bureaucratic and the low-cost-operator approaches had negative relationships to most of the HR items. This is not surprising. These management approaches do not look to talent as a source of competitive advantage, so it is not surprising that they do not invest in building effective HR organizations.

The results for the global competitor approach tend to fall in the middle. It does have a positive relationship to the importance of HR, but the relationship is not as strong as it is for the high-involvement and sustainable approaches. This may reflect the fact that global competitors focus on many approaches to strategic success, including low cost. They may also use elements of the bureaucratic management approach in order to coordinate their global operations and operate their international units. In contrast, the high-involvement approach explicitly focuses on talent involvement as a key to performance, and the sustainable approach specifically emphasizes the quality of the employment relationship as a key performance indicator, in addition to its contribution to organizational success.

As with the results for strategic focuses, there is the question of what comes first: the management approach or an HR function that is a strong business and strategic participant. As with the strategic focuses, our best guess is that it is more often the high-involvement and the sustainable approaches that lead to the strong HR role, but there are probably organizations where HR has had a major influence when the organization adopts the high-involvement approach and the sustainable approach.

Boudreau and Lawler (2014) note that some common management approaches are not friendly to the advancement HR, which may explain why the profession has been so slow to change. They add that HR leaders who want to advance their profession need to consider whether it is better to battle the headwind of working in low-cost or bureaucratic organizations or to move to organizations that have or are willing to adopt sustainable and innovation-focused approaches.

HR as a Strategic Contributor

The data concerning the strategic role of the HR function are clearly consistent with the argument that HR can and should be more of a strategic contributor. Yet the data also show that HR is not a strategic contributor in most organizations and that it is making little progress in becoming one. It appears to have some influence when it comes to how staffing relates to strategy and in influencing organizational structure and its relationship to implementing strategy. But our results suggest that HR plays a less prominent role when it comes to the development of strategy, consideration of strategic options, and other strategy areas, including acquisitions and mergers.

A number of HR capabilities and practices are significantly associated with a stronger strategic role for HR, including these:

- Having an HR strategy that is integrated with the business strategy
- The use of information technology by HR
- Focusing on HR talent development
- Using HR service teams that provide expertise and support the business
- Having HR activities that focus on organizational design, organizational development, change management, employee development, and metrics
- Using computer systems for training and development
- Having an effective HRIS system
- Having effective HR metrics and analytics
- Having business leaders who make rigorous, logical human capital decisions
- Having an HR staff with technical, organizational dynamics, business partner, and metrics skills
- Having effective decision support
- Having an HR function that effectively provides services
- Strong HR involvement and support of sustainability initiatives

Overall, being a strategic contributor demands that high levels of business knowledge and skill be present in HR. It also requires HRISs that have the right metrics and analytics, and organizational designs and practices that link HR managers to business units. And it needs to provide HR services effectively and efficiently.

HR Effectiveness

The factors leading to HR effectiveness are a combination of approaches that promote efficiency in routine transactional processing and allow

HR professionals to focus on expanding their knowledge base, providing expertise, and partnering with others. In chapter 10, we addressed whether organizational needs are being met across our twelve elements of HR effectiveness, which provide an actionable agenda for HR functions. It is marked by an important characteristic: most of the practices are rated between 6 and 7 on a 10-point scale of met needs. The traditional elements of "providing HR services" and "being an employee advocate" have been rated higher than 7 prior to 2016. The year 2016 saw an increase in the effectiveness of "being a business partner" to 7.3, which may be a promising signal of progress. Still, for the most part, these measures have shown little change since 1995, which strongly suggests that one of the reasons that HR is not increasing its effectiveness is that it has not done the things that it needs to do in order to be and to be perceived as more effective.

The results so far have shown that in virtually every major area, there is a positive association between key advanced HR activities and functional characteristics and the strength of HR's role as a strategic partner. Despite the clear path this shows, the time spent on strategic partnership has not changed, and the nature of HR's role in strategy remains largely the traditional support role rather than a shaping or major partner role.

Organizational Effectiveness

In a similar vein, our results in chapter 11 show that many HR practices are significantly related to organizational performance. The results confirm our prior findings that organizational performance is higher when HR professionals focus on talent, use metrics and analytics to address HR effectiveness and impact, and develop their skills and knowledge. Indeed regarding HRIS and metrics and analytics, it appears that effectiveness and use related to more strategic and emerging issues (such as social and knowledge networks) are increasingly related to organizational effectiveness compared to those related to more traditional and functional HR issues.

In our 2013 survey, the responses to new questions revealed that HR's role in sustainability is also positively related to organizational performance. In 2016 the new questions related to HR's role in managing new work relationships were also positively related to organizational performance.

What HR needs to do to improve its effectiveness is clear and unsurprising. What is surprising is that it continues to do business as usual in a rapidly changing world. This has been a consistent finding since the 1995 survey and is the most striking result of our research on HR.

Obstacles to Change

There are a number of possible explanations for why HR has not changed more. One is that HR executives do not believe that HR needs to change. But based on the results of our surveys and many others, this does not seem to be true. Although in all of our surveys, HR executives have said they need to change and that it is important that they act as more of a business partner, little change has happened. They seem to be just saying what is professionally and politically correct and giving lip-service to the idea of being a business partner.

A second possible reason for the failure of HR to change is that in most organizations, there is no great demand for this change. HR's existing role and activities are well institutionalized and have created a kind of codependency relationship. The individuals in the HR function are satisfied with their current role and are comfortable delivering traditional HR services, and the recipients of these services are satisfied with HR primarily being an administrative function that does what they consider onerous HR work for them. This situation leads to an institutionalized devaluation of the HR function because of its low level of contribution to the business and to unwillingness to let it change because it serves many organization members well enough as it is (Boudreau and Lawler 2014). However, our results showing an increase in the use of centralized HR services, HRIS, and the movement of HR activities into the hands of employees and their managers may signal the end of highly attentive and personal HR services.

The managers outside HR whom we surveyed in 2010 acknowledged the importance of HR being a strategic partner, but they also focused on the importance of HR's contributing to talent management (Lawler and Boudreau 2012). Ironically, it is possible that their focus on talent may be operating against upgrading the strategic role of HR. It may focus a disproportionate amount of professional HR time on delivering services related to recruiting, orienting, developing, and retaining employees, leaving HR little time and few resources to spend on upgrading the competencies and systems needed in order for it to be a contributor to strategy development and implementation.

Recruiting, developing, and retaining a highly mobile and competitive workforce can often impose high demands on HR time and energy and can lock HR professionals into activity patterns that are difficult to change. Certainly a common refrain we hear from HR leaders is that they rarely have time to think about big picture issues or to develop in areas beyond their specific functional responsibilities. We have found that the attention being paid to almost all HR activities has increased since we began our surveys, suggesting that although there is agreement that some HR activities add greater value than others, HR functions are still required to spend an increasing amount of time on activities that may have low strategic value. Though our results suggest that more integrated and comprehensive HRISs are associated with greater effectiveness, it does not appear that such systems have yet met their promise of allowing HR leaders to shift their activities in a more strategic direction, and provide more decision support. It may be that such systems must still be sold to a market of HR leaders that still largely focus on a more traditional role.

The skills of the professionals in the HR function offer an additional reason for the limited change in their function. Just how difficult it is to change the HR function becomes apparent when we look at the kinds of skills that members of the HR function must have in order to be rated highly and to perform the roles of strategic contributor and business partner. HR professionals need skills ranging from relatively routine administrative processing skills to organizational dynamics and business skills. Although business and organizational dynamics skills are the most highly related to HR's effectiveness, our results suggest that the HR function must be effective in its core administrative functions if it wants to be respected. Interestingly, in our surveys, HR does not score very high in administrative skills, especially with respect to managing contractors and managing HRISs. The latter is particularly concerning since it is the future of HR operations and strategy.

Business and strategic contributor effectiveness requires knowledge and skills in areas such as change management, strategic planning, and organizational design. It also requires a knowledge of decision science for human capital that provides logical and unique strategic insights using human capital principles. HR professionals have traditionally had little experience with these areas, which involve complex judgments. Such expertise is both hard to acquire and in short supply. Becoming expert in business partnering demands the acquisition of explicit knowledge and tacit knowledge that comes from experience. Applying this expertise demands the ability to influence line management and to be part of effective teaming relationships with others who have deep business knowledge.

The results of our surveys show that HR professionals are seen as having increased some of their interpersonal dynamics skills and their business understanding skills since 1995. However, they are still perceived to fall short in most business skills and in metrics and analytical skills as well. HR leaders also often lack cross-functional business experience. Understanding HR strategy is at best a ticket to a seat at the table.

Expertise in business strategy is required to set the table and add value once there. Thus, HR is in a bit of a catch-22: it must get to the table in order to gain the knowledge and skills it needs to get there!

In a related study at the Center for Effective Organizations, John Boudreau and Ian Ziskin surveyed several hundred HR professionals in eleven leading organizations on the current and ideal role of HR leaders in the talent applications of emerging trends such as gamification, big data, segmentation, and sustainability (Boudreau and Ziskin 2011). Across the board, that research showed that the ideal role was akin to being a leader or key contributor, but the current role was much less involved, often rated as "occasional input." Participants commented that while leaders inside and outside HR recognized the importance of getting ahead of such trends, the day-to-day demands of traditional HR made it virtually impossible to systematically evolve to leadership roles.

Conclusion

HR wants to be a strategic partner, and the door is open because of the growing recognition that talent is a key determinant of an organization's effectiveness. But HR has not gotten through the door in many organizations, much less taken a seat at the table. The good news is that our results consistently identify a pattern of HR activities, skills, and relationships that are associated with HR effectiveness and a stronger strategic role. Difficult as it may be to make them happen, the changes that are required are easy to identify.

CHAPTER 13

What the Future of HR
Should Be

What should the future be for the HR function? What does HR need to do to become a strategic contributor? When we reported on our 1998 results (Lawler and Mohrman 2000, p. 71), we wrote, "Change has just begun. The next decade will probably see dramatic change in the human resource function in most companies. The opportunity exists for human resource management to become a true strategic partner, and to help decide how organizations will be managed, what human resource systems will look like, and how human resource services will be created and delivered."

Our 2016 results suggest that many of the changes we predicted have not yet taken place. Yes, there has been some change, but it is not the kind of game-changing change that we thought would happen. Nevertheless, we have not altered our view that HR needs transformational change. If anything, that need is much greater now than it was in 1998. The world of work has undergone tremendous change since 1998 (Lawler 2017). Today organizations in the United States and the rest of the developed world have an ever higher percentage of their employees doing knowledge work. Information technology has changed how work is done and what work is done. The economy has become more global. Environmental sustainability has become an increasingly important global issue. Human capital has become increasingly important as a source of competitive advantage, as has intellectual capital (Lawler and Worley 2011). Furthermore, the rate of change is likely to increase (Worley, Williams, and Lawler 2014).

The slow progress of the HR profession was one motivator for the development of CHREATE (Global Consortium to Reimagine HR, Employment Alternatives, Talent, and the Enterprise) in 2013. It involved over seventy chief HR officers (CHROs) and other thought leaders in a three-year project to disruptively accelerate the HR profession. They noted the paradox that while HR is often well regarded for its traditional contributions, it has evolved too slowly and must disruptively accelerate to address a host of future issues to remain relevant and have impact (Boudreau, 2014). The group identified the key forces for the future set out in table 13.1 (Boudreau 2016).

Our results show that when organizations focus on developing their competencies, capabilities, and knowledge assets, especially in combination with a strong focus on the strategy of the firm, HR is a strong strategic and business contributor and the HR function is markedly different

Table 13.1. Five forces, effects, and the business responses that define HR's future		
Five Forces	**Effect of Force**	**Business Response**
Exponential pattern of technology change	Technological breakthroughs produce exponential disruptions in markets and business. The rapid adoption of robots, autonomous vehicles, commoditized sensors, artificial intelligence, and global collaboration renew the re-thinking of work.	Business will be productive with flexible, distributed, and transient workforces who adapt to rapid cycles of business reinvention. Employees will need to successfully engage with automation transitions, constant legacy job loss, and rapid skills obsolescence.
Social and organizational reconfiguration	Increased democratization of work will shift away from the hierarchy toward more power-balanced organizations and communities, built upon relationships that are less employment based and more project based. Talent will increasingly "join" and engage based on aligned purpose.	Businesses will source and engage talent in diverse work arrangements that go beyond traditional full-time employment to include part-time, freelance, outsourced, and crowdsourced workers. Results will be increasingly achieved through purpose-built networks vs. hierarchies.
A truly connected world	The world will be increasingly connected through mobile personal devices and the cloud, empowering work to be done from anywhere. New media will enable global and real-time communication that accelerates ideation, product development, and go-to-market strategies.	Work will be managed through newly defined talent systems that support a distributed and global workforce. High-trust cultures and purpose-built networks, empowered with big data, will create a new level of innovation that develops and releases products in very short cycles.
All inclusive, global talent market	Work will be seamlessly distributed around the globe with 24/7 operations enabled by new corporate and social policies. Extreme longevity will allow mature talent to work longer, and female and non-white ethnicities will become talent majorities.	Organizations will increasingly segment and direct work to the best talent, whether inside or outside the organization, through diverse work relationships. Differentiated leadership and engagement approaches will address varied cultural preferences in policies, practices, work designs, pay, and benefits.
Human-machine collaboration	Advances in analytics, algorithms, and automation will continue to improve productivity and decision making. Smarter computing will increasingly automate mundane tasks previously performed by humans.	Organizations will successfully migrate tasks from people to machines and/or robots and find the optimal human-machine balance through big data. Organizations will create and maintain external partnerships to augment capabilities they do not own and use them to manage workforce transitions humanely and without hurting reputation.

Source: Boudreau, J. (2015). Reimagining HR: The paradox of a profession at the tipping point. *People + Strategy*, 38:4. ©HR People + Strategy. Reprinted with permission.

than it has been. Thus, there is good reason to believe that if organizations increasingly pursue strategic focuses and management approaches that draw on deep and widespread human capital excellence, HR must change quite dramatically.

HR as a High-Value Contributor

We pointed out in chapter 1 that HR potentially can have three roles. The first is to execute the processes and activities required to provide services such as compensation, administration, staffing, development, and deployment. The second is to respond to business plans developed by others, helping business units and general managers realize their plans. In this role, HR provides advice and services concerning how to develop, design, and install HR practices in areas such as employee relations, talent management, organizational development, change management, and connecting HR practices with business operations. The third role is helping to develop and implement the strategic direction of an organization. It requires acquiring, developing, and accessing an organization's human capital and creating the organizational capabilities required to support its strategic direction. It also requires shaping strategy by providing a unique perspective through the lens of the talent market, talent management, and human behavior. This requires HR leaders who understand business strategy and how it relates to organizational capabilities and core competencies and how those connect to pivotal talent and organizational design decisions. In this role, HR leaders need to use their knowledge to help organizations set their strategic direction and develop their design and business plans in ways that are consistent with a talent decision science.

What do CEOs want from HR in the future? One CHREATE project involved interviews with leading CEOs conducted by their CHROs. When presented with the five forces listed in table 13.1, these CEOs acknowledged the strong contributions of HR, but they also described new ways that the HR profession must add value (Boudreau 2016). They included being:

- A chief operating officer of organizational culture

- A leader of a board committee on culture and innovation

- A definer of the new workforce (people, organization, talent, structure) that delivers business strategy, considers emerging employment and work styles, drives purpose and engagement, reflects permeable and changing organizational boundaries, and is much more diverse

- A profession that can get in between organizations where partnerships are formed and bring science to cross barriers between companies, with suppliers and customers

- A profession that uses the cloud, through a world of apps and personal devices, to bring personalized experiences based on big data and artificial intelligence, like Amazon or Google.

HR Administration

HR administrative services are increasingly becoming a commodity. Historically, they were delivered by an in-house HR function, often in a labor-intensive and costly manner. Three alternative approaches are emerging as ways to acquire and operate the technology and skills needed to deliver HR services.

The first is to use web-based custom systems that are designed and operated by the user organization. This model is currently being used by IT companies such as Google, IBM, Cisco, HP, and Microsoft. Some of these systems are impressive and allow individuals outside of the HR function to "serve themselves" by performing important HR tasks and accessing their own information. More powerful personal devices such as phones and tablets promise a future of HR apps that will make such activities easier and more user friendly. Video authoring tools promise a future in which individuals may be able to easily record and post their knowledge to a library in the cloud, enabling virtual social learning. However, it is highly unlikely that most companies will ever develop the kind of custom systems that large technology companies have developed because it is expensive and time-consuming.

A second approach is to acquire software and systems from vendors using one of two approaches. The first is to buy an integrated web-based system from a major enterprise resource planning (ERP) vendor (e.g., Oracle, SAP, Workday). The second is to acquire individual HR applications for specific tasks like compensation administration, staffing, and training from different software vendors. While using separate best-in-class applications for each function may improve performance within each function, our results suggest great value in integration. The best use of HR data often is integration across multiple HR processes, but this can be costly and time-consuming. Integrated total HR systems may provide the remedy because they are already integrated.

We may see the evolution of a core set of data standards against which multiple software vendors can develop their applications (Cascio and Boudreau 2012). We found that a new item in our 2016 survey, which asked about software as a service hosted in the cloud, achieved a higher-rated effectiveness level than all levels of outsourcing, suggesting that a more modular and cloud-based model may be the most effective.

The third model is to use business process outsourcing. The results of our 2016 survey suggest that outsourcing may not be growing quickly and may even be declining. They also suggest that it is seen as most effective when it is done on a "very limited" or "moderate" level, not at a "substantial" level.

Our findings in 2016 show a continuing trend for more HR administration to be done by employees on a self-service basis and that employee self-service is associated with a stronger HR role in strategy, perhaps because it frees up time for HR to be involved in strategic activities. In our 2013 survey, we added new items on the use of social networks, mobile technology, and software as service. Each was rated as being used less than a moderate extent, but greater use of each of them was associated with increases in HR's strategic role. Their use seems to have increased somewhat since then. Thus, there is some evidence that self-service, social networks, mobile technology, and software as service may be enablers of other actions that HR can take to become more of a strategic contributor.

Overall, we believe that information technology and systems can be a key delivery vehicle for HR services and contribute to a fuller strategic role for HR. They have the potential to free up HR to do more strategic work and to collect important talent management and organizational effectiveness data. In addition, the value of such systems in conveying HR knowledge and decision frameworks to managers and employees represents an untapped opportunity for improving an organization's talent management decisions.

Business Partner

What about HR activities that involve responding to the business plans others have developed and implemented? Can this role be outsourced? Can or should these activities be put on the web?

HRISs can collect, aggregate, and analyze ever increasing amounts of data about the human resources of an organization and they can do it at ever lower costs and higher speeds. HR data can contribute to change management, business plan development and implementation, and business operations by making human capital information readily available and obtaining feedback and suggestions about HR process improvement and effectiveness. These are enablers that can enhance human judgment in problem solving and decision making but can never replace it.

As for outsourcing the business partner role, consultants can provide insight into the HR implications of business plans and organizational change. However, the work of tailoring HR programs and practices to specific strategies and business plans and implementing them always needs internal skilled HR professionals to provide the services, information, and knowledge that are necessary for them to be effective business partners.

Performing the business partner role entails solving problems and making decisions that are value laden, highly uncertain, and context specific. Because of this, they require understanding the business, its strategy, the nature of the workforce, and the required competencies. It entails the application of tacit, experience-based knowledge of employee relations, as well as knowledge of the HR discipline and the ability to combine

HR knowledge with the perspectives of other disciplines, such as business management, marketing, information technology, and technology.

The key question for us is not whether HR professionals should perform the business partner role but whether current HR professionals are the ones who can and should do it. The results of our study suggest that the comfort level and effectiveness of today's HR professionals remain highest in the traditional HR areas, such as HR operations, interpersonal relationships, compliance, implementing (not shaping) strategy, and giving corporate boards advice on HR issues such as executive compensation and succession. To become better at helping their organizations to implement business plans, HR professionals need to develop capabilities in areas such as organizational design, change management, vendor and contract management, decision support, finance, and strategy analysis.

Strategic Contributor

Perhaps the most intriguing results of our study are those that have implications for the strategic contributor role. As organizations face a more complex and rapidly changing sustainability-conscious environment, there is an increasing need for HR leaders to not only respond to business strategies but to shape them based on talent and organizational competencies and capabilities. In addition, the rapid rate of change, the need to develop new strategies and quickly translate them into talent strategies, and the likelihood that the availability of talent will be a key strategic differentiator have combined to increase the importance of HR as an effective strategic contributor.

The role of strategic contributor requires individuals who understand how business strategies and plans connect to talent management and organizational design. They also need to know how to shape business strategies to fit emerging human capital opportunities and threats. Some of this work can be outsourced to HR strategy consultants, but we believe that most organizations need an internal group with good HR knowledge who can manage consultants and shape organizational strategies. Ideally, HR's strategic role ultimately needs to be led by a senior executive in the organization, not a consultant.

The importance of the HR strategic role and the need to fill it with somebody who understands business may be one reason that our research finds that almost a quarter of all chief HR executives come from the business function rather than the HR function. In essence, some companies seem to have decided that the HR strategic partner role is too important to be entrusted to someone whose background is exclusively in HR. This is not completely surprising given that our results show that satisfaction with the skills of HR managers is highest when it comes to

HR technical and interpersonal skills. not for business partner, metrics, and decision support skills.

As tempting as it is to staff the top HR role with a business executive, it is dangerous if this person has little HR knowledge. Just as with other functions such as IT, operations, legal, supply chain, and finance, this role requires strong knowledge of the function, and not solely business and strategy. In the case of HR, it requires the capacity to understand the principles and practices that underlie labor markets and human behavior at work, just as knowledge about portfolio theory or customer behavior is a prerequisite to be the chief financial officer and knowledge of customer behavior is to be a chief marketing officer (Boudreau and Ramstad 2007). Indeed, effective strategic partnership may require that HR leaders retool their current logic frameworks to better apply the principles of disciplines such as marketing, finance, and operations directly to such HR functions as staffing, rewards, and talent management (Boudreau 2010).

The arrival of big data on the HR scene can strengthen HR's position as a strategic contributor. Big data can potentially help HR professionals make significant contributions to strategy formulation by providing both cost and organizational effectiveness data with respect to HR practices. They can provide information on how to develop certain key competencies and about the existing levels of organizational effectiveness and organizational capabilities. These are all critical to the strategy planning process. They can codify and teach decision frameworks and principles that contribute importantly to strategic decisions (Boudreau and Ramstad 2007). They also can enable HR executives to translate what they know about an organization and its capabilities into change programs, thus allowing the organization to develop the capabilities to implement new strategic plans and new directions (Lawler and Worley 2006).

Our results suggest that for decades, the skills, resources, and time to deliver on a powerful strategic role remain stubbornly lacking in the HR function of most organizations. There is a real possibility that organizations will grow impatient with the HR profession's failure to develop strategic HR leaders and will increasingly decide to populate HR leadership positions with individuals who possess the business, analytical, and change skills necessary to formulate human capital strategy—even if those individuals are not well versed in HR. This is far from the best approach. What is needed is HR leaders who have both skills sets.

Talent Management for the HR Profession

Quite possibly the biggest change that needs to occur has to do with how talent is managed in the HR function itself. In many respects, talent management in HR is a case of the shoemakers' children lacking shoes. Our results suggest that HR often does not have the right talent, and too often it has talent that is inferior to that in other key parts of the organization even though HR professionals need to have a comparable set of skills and knowledge.

HR professionals need the following abilities:

- To understand and be able to formulate a business model for the HR function and contribute to the firm's business model

- To understand business operations and be able to craft HR management approaches that reflect their organization's competitive situation

- To understand organizational design, work design, and change management principles and approaches so they can play a leadership role when they are considered

- To understand different models of staffing, compensation, and other HR talent management practices so that they can effectively implement HR systems that support the organization's business plans

- To educate and develop business leaders so they can make human capital decisions that are as logical, rigorous, and strategic as are their decisions about finance, technology, and customers

- To identify the pivot points in the business that drive strategic and organizational effectiveness and connect human capital decisions to those points

There are some reasons to think that at least at the senior levels, the talent level in HR is improving. More CEOs now recognize the importance of having a talented HR executive and have acted on this recognition. Organizations have been particularly willing to promote women to senior HR management positions. Many highly talented female business leaders have become HR executives because it is their best career opportunity. This has created a gender diversity in HR that offers significant opportunities for the HR profession to provide a unique perspective at the executive and board levels of organizations. Because organizations must consider more diverse employee populations and customers, this is an important change.

The skills and knowledge that HR professionals need are not easily acquired. They are likely to exist only in organizations that take HR talent management seriously and have an integrated approach to talent management. This has important implications for HR's performance management and staffing practices at all levels of the HR function. At the entry level, for example, HR needs to significantly increase the quality of those it hires. Today few of the best students in the leading business schools pursue HR careers because of low starting salaries and a perception that HR is not a good place to start a career. As a result, there often is a scarcity of highly talented business school students with an academic concentration in HR. Because of that, organizations should consider hiring non-HR majors who are very talented and interested in HR. Indeed, the ground may be shifting; some business school students have been very articulate about the wisdom of their decision to pursue an HR career (Breitfelder and Dowling 2008). However, at least until it does shift, HR needs to hire more non-HR majors.

Once HR professionals are hired, it is important that they spend time working outside HR. Our data suggest that this does not happen very often and that most organizations have no plans to increase it. This is a problem because without experience in non-HR jobs, HR professionals miss important opportunities to gain an understanding of the business as a whole and miss the chance to build personal credibility by doing a non-HR job well.

It may be even more important to have non-HR managers and professionals rotate into HR than it is for HR professionals to rotate out. At this point, very few U.S. corporations have CEOs and senior executives other than the head of HR who have worked in HR. Increasing the number of senior managers who have HR experience has important benefits. One is that it can improve their performance when they make human capital decisions. Another is that it makes top organizational talent available to the HR function and brings to HR the perspective of non-HR executives regarding its role and effectiveness.

Our results show that business leaders are held to higher standards regarding their use of sound principles in areas such as finance and marketing than they are in human capital and talent management. Considering the acknowledged importance of talent to competitiveness, it would seem prudent to give senior leaders deep experience in HR so they can build their understanding of this important area.

The value of shared and valid principles about human capital and talent management has important implications for the development of future HR executives. HR professionals should be trained and should develop and use research-based knowledge about labor markets, human behavior, and organizational effectiveness. They need to move beyond just being good to work with and knowledgeable about people and employee relations. They need to know and act on the large amount of research that has been done on talent management, organizational design, and a host of other organizational effectiveness issues. Making decisions on instinct or "knowing people" is not enough. Evidence-based decision making is needed, along with an understanding of how to transform organizations through evidence-based change.

The future competency set of HR executives may well draw on disciplines outside the traditional business areas. The CHREATE consortium envisioned a future HR profession relying on disciplines such as architecture, engineering, storytelling, and political science. The consortium described the following roles to illustrate the need for disruptive acceleration in the definition of HR capabilities and the talent pipeline (Boudreau, 2016):

- The *organizational engineer*, an expert in these new ways of working. She is a facilitator of virtual team effectiveness, a developer of all types of leadership, and an expert at talent transitions. She is an expert at talent, task optimization, and organizational principles such as agility, networks, power, and trust.

- The *virtual culture architect*, a culture expert, advocate, and brand builder. He connects current and potential workers' purpose to the organization's mission and goals. He is adept at principles of values, norms, and beliefs, articulated through virtual and personal means.

- The *global talent scout, convener, and coach*, who understands new talent platforms and optimizes the relationships between workers, work, and the organization, using whatever platform is best (e.g., free agent, contractor, regular employee). She is a talent contract manager, talent platform manager, and career/life coach.

- The *data, talent, and technology integrator*, an expert at manipulating big data, understanding and modeling trends, and using code to adjust algorithms, as well as design work to optimally combine technology, automation and human contributions.

- The *social policy and community activist*, a social responsibility leader. She produces synergy between the social goals of the organization, such as economic returns, social purpose, ethics, sustainability, and worker health. She influences beyond the organization, shaping policies, regulations, and laws that support the new world of work through talented community engagement.

HR Organizational Design

How should the HR function be managed and structured? Should it be a large function, employing approximately one out of every one hundred employees and organized primarily using a service delivery paradigm focused on activities such as compensation, training, and staffing? There is good reason to believe that it should not. HR needs to use a deeper and more strategic perspective on how it adds value to justify its cost. Strategic influence, business decision support, organizational agility, and sustainability need to define the HR value proposition; providing low-cost, high-quality services is necessary but not sufficient (Worley et al. 2014).

One possible approach to the design of the HR function is to centralize operations and infrastructure within a chief operating officer function for HR. Such a function would span both the business partner and the administrative components of the HR function, providing specialized support in areas such as compensation, talent development, and performance management. This structure would free the CHRO of many of the ongoing tasks associated with running the HR department and allow him or her to focus on the strategic role of human capital in the organization, as well as on being a member of the executive team.

An increasingly common feature of HR function design, particularly in companies with multiple business units, is to place an HR executive in each business unit. This role involves contributing to business unit plans and tailoring HR practices to the workforce needs of the unit. These executives are also expected to be liaisons to the corporate HR staff and services on behalf of their business units. This liaison role is likely to be increasingly important in the future. Instead of locating many of the HR services in the business unit, many multidivision corporations are creating shared service units and corporate centers of excellence for the business units to draw on. They also are outsourcing HR transactional services and require business units to use them. In both approaches, the role of the business unit HR executive is to translate business strategies into necessary HR responses and coordinate the centralized HR services for the business unit. In this design, there is an increasing use of "double-hatting" HR executives to ensure connections between HR functional expertise and business unit goals. For example, the head of learning and development may double-hat as the business partner for a major organizational division or product line where learning and development are particularly pivotal.

In some organizations, the HR organization appears to be becoming a type of front-back organization where the business unit HR leaders are the front, customer-focused part (Galbraith 2014). The back is the vendors, shared services units, and centers of excellence that are available to the business units. Our results show that the front-back approach to HR function design has increased in popularity since 1994, and there is reason to believe that some versions of it will be the most popular approaches in the future. Nevertheless, it is worth considering an alternative organization for the HR function since it does not directly position HR to make it a maximum contribution to organizational effectiveness.

Potentially, HR can be in three businesses (administration, business partner, and strategic contributor) that are related but require different competencies and capabilities. One comparison here is to sales and marketing; another is to accounting and finance. They both do work that is related but requires different competencies and capabilities; therefore, they are split and operate at different levels of an organization's hierarchy. Applying this logic to HR would mean creating an HR function that does administration and business partnering with respect to strategy implementation and HR service delivery to the organization. Another function would be created that has overall responsibility for organizational effectiveness.

The organizational effectiveness corporate function would combine business strategy and planning, human capital management, organizational development, and organizational design. It would be headed by a chief organization effectiveness officer (COEO) and would have responsibility for strategy formulation, implementation, and talent management. In this approach, the COEO would report to the CEO, and the CHRO would report to the COEO.

Having an organizational effectiveness function is a good fit for many knowledge work organizations because it integrates expertise in business strategy and talent management. It is unlike the typical organizational design of most large organizations because it recognizes and creates a function charged with managing the fit between talent and strategy. All too often, this fit is not considered because no one, except perhaps the CEO, is responsible for the fit. It is a particularly good design for organizations that need to be agile because they face a rapidly changing environment.

The CHREATE consortium suggested a disruptively accelerated approach to the design and function of the HR discipline in organizations that includes the following (Sage-Gavin and Foster-Cheek 2015):

- *Trend forecasting and change leadership.* Business and HR leaders will anticipate trends and then lead change so organizations can thrive in the new world of work. One critical skill will be the ability to analyze diverse sources of data and develop insights, providing "sense making" with strategic recommendations that can guide CEOs, boards, and organizations. HR must shift its mind-set from change management to change leadership and foster truly agile leadership.

- *Talent sourcing and community building.* Talent management will move beyond our current view of company boundaries to encompass an extended workforce, including those who will come together to deliver work outside a regular employment relationship, such as e-lancers, contractors, and partners. Sourcing and recruiting must evolve to develop relationships over an extended period of time, leveraging global talent pools and using crowdsourcing or technology-enabled channels. HR leaders have the opportunity to serve as connectors, orchestrators, and brokers of a constantly evolving talent marketplace, bringing unique and innovative solutions to best match the demand and supply of skills and capabilities.

- *Performance engineering.* Diverse forms of employment and new ways of collaborating will challenge traditional approaches to how organizations have inspired and rewarded people to deliver results. Business practices will need to truly optimize talent and create less hierarchical, nonemployment relationships. Organizations will need to apply a market segmentation approach to develop highly personalized deals for individuals that are still considered fair and equitable across a global framework.

- *Culture and community activism.* HR will continue to shift away from legacy, company-centric views of the world toward views that consider an ecosystem of stakeholders including customers, vendors, and current and future "employees," be they freelancers, partners, or shareholders. Company brand and reputation management strategies will shift from being externally focused to engaging employees and the larger talent ecosystem as companies realize that employees are the best brand ambassadors. While corporate social responsibility will remain critically important, employees will want to bring their whole selves to work in a very different way. They will want to share their knowledge and skills beyond simply building houses or serving the less advantaged in limited volunteer engagements. They will want their personal contributions outside and at work to serve a greater good, and they will want to constantly experience personal growth. They will want to craft employment to leverage their strengths, while also enabling them to have an impact on social capital priorities they consider important.

- *Service delivery and contracting.* The influence of technology will increasingly present options for work to be deconstructed and delivered by diverse talent pools anywhere and anytime. This will change the landscape of human capital contracting and service delivery as we contend with new practices, regulations, and governance. Private and public partnerships will emerge to shape new global ways of working, with transparency and equity as key themes.

The Impact of Evolving Work Arrangements "Beyond Employment"

One of the most significant defining future issues will be the continued evolution of work arrangements different from traditional full-time employment. Cascio and Boudreau (2017b) note that such arrangements can include:

- Independent contractor
- Outsourcing and temporary help agency
- Part-time employment
- Professional employment organizations
- Freelance platforms
- Crowdsourcing
- Volunteers
- Borrowing employees from another organization
- Loaning employees to another organization

Boudreau, Jesuthasan, and Creelman (2015) suggested that these new work arrangements have the potential to change the meaning of virtually every element of HR, because HR and most organizations overwhelmingly still define their work systems as if regular employment is the exclusive work approach.

Boudreau (2015) noted several ways that HR must evolve in light of new work arrangements. In a world beyond employment, *planning* is transformed from employee supply and demand to worker optimization. The focus becomes the work, not employee head counts or FTEs. Organizations have permeable boundaries where fundamental concepts such as head count, worker availability, movement between jobs, and worker separation must take on very different meanings. The key planning issue may be where to allow your boundary to open and where to keep it closed.

The new world of work requires a process of seamlessly engaging multiple systems (procurement, contracting, partnering, recruiting) to attract workers for engagements that may not be full time. No company could afford to have a "job" exclusively devoted to developing YouTube advertisements during the Super Bowl, but that project can be sourced to crowdsourcing or freelance platforms.

Today's selection systems focus on assessing skills and cultural fit to make sure the employee has potential for a career beyond his or her first job. But companies today are selecting talent based on short-term benefits (for both sides). For example, when Siemens created an innovative hearing aid for children, it didn't hire employees to devise its marketing campaign; instead, it borrowed employees from the Walt Disney Company through an alliance, and they came up with packaging that included a comic book and a children's story about coping with hearing loss.

Employee development systems now focus on experiences gained by moving through jobs and hierarchical levels. But a "career" today is not necessarily a progression through positions; instead, it's often an accumulation of projects and task credits. What does it mean to get "promoted" in such a fluid system? Should we take mentoring to the cloud? A company called Everwise does just that. The mentorship platform has amassed a database of sixty thousand relationships, pairing experienced professionals with protégés across organizations. When work and workers can move across organizational boundaries, it's a recipe for extreme employment-at-will with little long-run exchange. But if organizations make permeability a central part of their reward structure, they can create rewards that entice workers to move out and in. For example, organizations can offer a big bonus if a worker returns after an outside stint where he or she acquired valuable skills. There is already talk of "tours of duty" across organizations, with more portable rewards and flexible systems that track skills and achievements.

Employee "turnover" is the end of the employment relationship and perhaps the most frequently measured HR outcome. In a new world beyond employment, the whole notion of employee separation could be obsolete. The end of a project by a contractor or freelancer is hardly a separation when that worker could easily be available in the future. This makes employee separation less of "the end" of a talent life cycle and more of an integral element in an ongoing series of engagements between work and workers (Lawler 2017).

As we noted in chapter 1, we added new items in the 2016 survey to tap the degree to which organizations employ elements of the new work arrangements. These new work arrangements remain relatively rare, with flexibility in location, individualized rewards, and project design most frequent, and use of platforms and task-based rewards the least frequent.

Should CEOs expect their CHROs to take the lead on these arrangements? Perhaps their procurement officers should lead? Or perhaps a combination of both (Boudreau, Swan, and Doyle 2016). Are HR leaders and their organizations prepared for such leadership? In many cases today, such issues fall outside the HR function or in the white spaces between today's HR job descriptions (Boudreau and Ziskin 2011).

Looking Ahead

The opportunity for the HR function to add value is great, but at this time, it is more promise than reality. For promise to become reality, HR executives need to develop new skills and knowledge, and HR needs to be able to execute HR management and administrative activities effectively. Doing the basics well is the platform on which the HR organization needs to build its role as a business partner. This is critical, because it demonstrates the capacity of the HR function to operate effectively as a business, and it potentially can provide the information that enables HR to be an effective business partner and strategic contributor. But it is not enough; HR must also make strategic contributions to the organization.

Indeed, the context for HR management increasingly requires boundaries that span the HR function, the organization, and the dynamic environment within which the organization operates. As organizations adopt definitions of sustainable effectiveness that include the social and environmental impacts of organizations and face the need to embrace constant and dynamic change, even today's aspirations for HR as a business partner that contributes to a human capital-based competitive advantage will change (Lawler and Worley 2011). Consider the following six trends that have been identified as pivotal to the future of HR (Boudreau and Ziskin 2011):

- Hero leadership to collective leadership
- Intellectual property to agile co-creativity
- Employment value proposition to personal value proposition
- Sameness to segmentation
- Fatigue to sustainability
- Persuasion to education

These trends illustrate the complexity and breadth of issues that organizations will face in the future. Where will expertise arise to help organizations craft a point of view and framework for sustainability, agility, co-creation with multiple constituents, mass-customized value proposition and talent segmentation, and the evolution of leadership as vested in a top team to something that pervades the entire organization? These are not "HR issues"; they are strategy and organizational design issues that will be central to the success of most organizations and vital topics for all businesses. And they draw on the unique disciplines that traditionally underlie HR, including psychology, political science, anthropology, values, culture, and engagement.

The need for a new business model for HR has been accepted and acknowledged by most HR executives, but the function still appears to be at the very beginning of the changes that are needed in order for it to become a reality. Our study establishes that the change process is slower than it should be. It identifies a clear action agenda that can yield an HR function capable of adding more value to the business. We believe there will be enormous change in the design and operation of HR functions, but we are not sure when it will occur. We have said it before, and we say it again: the HR function needs to look seriously at reinventing itself. The old approaches and models are not good enough. If they are not changed, the HR function will become a minor player in tomorrow's organizations.

REFERENCES   Bersin, J. 2016. "Predictions for 2016: A Bold New World of Talent, Learning, Leadership, and HR Technology Ahead." Bersin by Deloitte. http://www.bersin.com/Practice/Detail.aspx?docid=195 01&mode=search&p=Human-Resources.

Bersin, J., D. Agarwal, B. Pelster, and J. Schwartz. 2015. "Global Human Capital Trends 2015." Deloitte. https://www2.deloitte. com/content/dam/Deloitte/at/Documents/human-capital/hc-trends-2015.pdf.

Boudreau, J. W. 2010. *Retooling HR*. Boston: Harvard Business School Press.

Boudreau, J. W. 2012. "Decision Logic in Evidence-Based Management: Can Logical Models from other Disciplines Improve Evidence-Based Human Resource Decisions?" In *The Oxford Handbook of Evidence-Based Management,* edited by D. Rousseau, 13:223–48. New York: Oxford University Press.

Boudreau, J. W. 2014. "Will HR's Grasp Match Its Reach? An Estimable Profession Grown Complacent and Outpaced." *Organizational Dynamics* 43 (3): 189–97.

Boudreau, J. W. 2015. "What the Talent Lifecycle Looks Like in a World 'beyond Employment.'" ReWork, Cornerstone On Demand Online.https://www.cornerstoneondemand.com/rework/ what-talent-lifecycle-looks-world-%E2%80%9Cbeyond-employ-ment%E2%80%9D.

Boudreau, J. W. 2016. "HR at the Tipping Point: The Paradoxical Future of Our Profession." *People + Strategy* 38 (4): 46–54.

Boudreau, J. W., and W. F. Cascio. 2017. "Human Resource Analytics: Why Aren't We There?" *Journal of Organizational Effectiveness, People and Performance* 4 (2): 119–26.

Boudreau, J. W., and R. Jesuthasan. 2011. *Transformative HR*. Hoboken, NJ: Wiley.

Boudreau, J. W., R. Jesuthasan, and D. Creelman. 2015. *Lead the Work.* Hoboken, NJ: Wiley.

Boudreau, J. W., and E. E. Lawler. 2014. "Stubborn Traditionalism in HRM: Causes and Consequences." *Human Resource Management Review* 24 (3): 232–44.

Boudreau, J. W., and P. M. Ramstad. 1997. "Measuring Intellectual Capital: Learning from financial History." *Human Resource Management* 36 (3): 34–56.

Boudreau, J. W., and P. M. Ramstad. 2003. "Strategic HRM Measurement in the 21st Century: From Justifying HR to Strategic Talent Leadership." In *HRM in the 21st century*, edited by M. Goldsmith, R. P. Gandossy, and M. S. Efron, 79–90. Hoboken, NJ: Wiley.

Boudreau, J. W., and P. M. Ramstad, 2005a. "Talentship and the Evolution of Human Resource Management: From `Professional Practices' to `Strategic Talent Decision Science.'" *Human Resource Planning Journal* 28 (2): 17–26.

Boudreau, J. W., and P. M. Ramstad. 2005b. "Talentship, Talent Segmentation, and Sustainability: A New HR Decision Science Paradigm for a New Strategy Definition." In *The Future of Human Resources Management*, edited by M. Losey, S. Meisinger, and D. Ulrich. Washington, DC: Society for Human Resource Management.

Boudreau, J. W., and P. M. Ramstad. 2005c. "Where Is Your Pivotal Talent?" *Harvard Business Review* 83 (4): 23–24.

Boudreau, J. W., and P. M. Ramstad. 2006. "Talentship and Human Resource Management and Analysis: From ROI to Strategic Organizational Change." *Human Resource Planning Journal* 29 (1): 25–33.

Boudreau, J. W., and P. M. Ramstad. 2007. *Beyond HR: The New Science of Human Capital*. Boston: Harvard Business School Press.

Boudreau, J. W., M. Swan, and A. Doyle. 2016. "The Big Disconnect in Your Talent Strategy and How to Fix It." *Harvard Business Review Online*. https://hbr.org/2016/12/the-big-disconnect-in-your-talent-strategy-and-how-to-fix-it.

Boudreau, J. W., and I. Ziskin. 2011. "The Future of HR and Effective Organizations." *Organizational Dynamics* 40 (4): 255–67.

Breitfelder, M. D., and D. W. Dowling. 2008. "Why Did We Ever Go into HR?" *Harvard Business Review* 86 (7–8): 39–43.

Brockbank, W. 1999. "If HR Were Really Strategically Proactive: Present and Future Directions in HR's Contribution to Competitive Advantage." *Human Resource Management* 38 (4): 337–52.

Brundtland, G. H. 1987. *Report of the World Commission on Environment and Development: Our Common Future*. New York: United Nations.

Cascio, W. F. 2000. *Costing Human Resources,* 4th ed. Cincinnati: South-Western.

Cascio, W. F., and J. W. Boudreau. 2011. *Investing in People: Financial Impact of Human Resource Initiatives,* 2nd ed. Upper Saddle River, NJ: FT Press.

Cascio, W. F., and J. W. Boudreau. 2012. *Short Introduction to Strategic Human Resources.* Cambridge: Cambridge University Press.

Cascio, W. F., and J. W. Boudreau. 2017a. "Evidence-Based Management at the Bottom of the Pyramid: Why Human Resources Standards and Research Must Connect More Closely." In *The Oxford Handbook of Strategy Implementation,* edited by Michael A. Hitt, Susan E. Jackson, Salvador Carmona, Leonard Bierman, Christina E. Shalley, and Douglas Michael Wright, 343–72. Oxford: Oxford University Press.

Cascio, W. F., and J. W. Boudreau. 2017b. "Talent Management of Nonstandard Employees." In *The Oxford Handbook of Talent Management,* edited by David G. Collings, Kamel Mellahi, and Wayne F. Cascio, 494-520. Oxford: Oxford University Press.

Cascio, W. F., J. W. Boudreau, and A. H. Church. 2017. "Maximizing Talent Readiness for an Uncertain Future." In *A Research Agenda for Human Resource Management: HR Strategy, Structure, and Architecture,* edited by C. Cooper and P. Sparrow. London: Elgar.

Csoka, L. S., and B. Hackett. 1998. *Transforming the HR Function for Global Business Success.* New York: Conference Board.

Galbraith, J. R. 2014. *Designing Organizations: Strategy, Structure, and Process at the Business Unit and Enterprise Levels.* San Francisco: Jossey-Bass.

Gates, S. 2004. "Measuring More Than Efficiency: The New Role of Human Capital Metrics." Research Report R-1356-04-RR. New York: Conference Board.

Green, D. 2016. "The 30 Best HR Analytics Articles of 2016." LinkedIn. https://www.linkedin.com/pulse/30-best-hr-analytics-articles-2016-david-green.

Gubman, E. 2004. "HR Strategy and Planning: From Birth to Business Results." *Human Resource Planning* 27 (1): 13–23.

Huselid, M. A., B. E. Becker, and R. W. Beatty. 2005. *The Workforce Scorecard.* Boston: Harvard Business School Press.

Kassim, I., and M. Nagy. 2017. "The State of Workforce Analytics in Europe." http://ny.workforceanalyticssummit.com/the-state-of -workforce-analytics-research-report/.

Lawler, E. E. 1995. "Strategic Human Resources Management: An Idea Whose Time Has Come." In *Managing Human Resources in the 1990s and Beyond: Is the Workplace Being Transformed?* edited by B. Downie and M. L. Coates, 46–70. Kingston, Canada: IRC Press.

Lawler, E. E. 2008. *Talent: Making People Your Competitive Advantage.* San Francisco: Jossey-Bass.

Lawler, E. E. 2017. *Reinventing Talent Management: Principles and Practices for the New World of Work.* Oakland, CA: Berrett-Koehler.

Lawler, E. E., and J. W. Boudreau. 2009. *Achieving Excellence in Human Resource Management.* Stanford, CA: Stanford University Press.

Lawler, E. E., and J. W. Boudreau. 2012. *Effective Human Resource Management: A Global Analysis.* Stanford, CA: Stanford University Press.

Lawler, E. E., and J. W. Boudreau. 2015. *Global Trends in Human Resource Management: A Twenty-Year Analysis.* Stanford, CA: Stanford University Press.

Lawler, E. E., J. W. Boudreau, and S. A. Mohrman. 2006. *Achieving Strategic Excellence: An Assessment of Human Resource Organizations.* Stanford, CA: Stanford University Press.

Lawler, E. E., A. Levenson, and J. W. Boudreau. 2004. "HR Metrics and Analytics: Uses and Impacts." *Human Resource Planning Journal* 27 (4): 27–35.

Lawler, E. E., and S. A. Mohrman. 2000. *Creating a Strategic Human Resources Organization.* Los Angeles: Center for Effective Organizations.

Lawler, E. E., and S. A. Mohrman. 2003. *Creating a Strategic Human Resources Organization: An Assessment of Trends and New Directions.* Stanford, CA: Stanford University Press.

Lawler, E. E., S. A. Mohrman, and G. S. Benson. 2001. *Organizing for High Performance: The CEO Report on Employee Involvement, TQM, Reengineering, and Knowledge Management in Fortune 1000 Companies.* San Francisco: Jossey-Bass.

Lawler, E. E., D. Ulrich, J. Fitz-enz, and J. Madden. 2004. *Human Resources Business Process Outsourcing.* San Francisco: Jossey-Bass.

Lawler, E. E., and C. G. Worley. 2006. *Built to Change: How to Achieve Sustained Organizational Effectiveness.* San Francisco: Jossey-Bass.

Lawler, E. E., and C. G. Worley. 2011. *Management Reset: Organizing for Sustainable Effectiveness*. San Francisco: Jossey-Bass.

Lev, B. 2001. *Intangibles: Management, Measurement, and Reporting*. Washington, DC: Brookings.

Mohrman, A. M., J. R. Galbraith, E. E. Lawler, and Associates. 1998. *Tomorrow's Organization: Crafting Winning Capabilities in a Dynamic World*. San Francisco: Jossey-Bass.

Mohrman, S. A., and E. E. Lawler. 2014. "Designing Organizations for Sustainable Effectiveness: A New Paradigm for Organizations and Academic Researchers." *Journal of Organizational Effectiveness: People and Performance* 1 (1): 14–34.

Mohrman, S. A., J. O'Toole, and E. E. Lawler. 2015. *Corporate Stewardship: Achieving Sustainable Effectiveness*. Sheffield, UK: Greenleaf Publishing.

O'Toole, J., and E. E. Lawler. 2006. *The New American Workplace*. New York: Palgrave Macmillan.

Rasmussen, T., and D. Ulrich. 2015. "Learning from Practice: How HR Analytics Avoids Being a Management Fad." *Organizational Dynamics* 44 (3): 236–42.

Sage-Gavin, E., and K. Foster-Cheek. 2015. "The Transformation of Work: Will HR Lead or Follow?" *People + Strategy* 38 (3): 8–10.

Ulrich, D. 1997. *Human Resources Champions*. Boston: Harvard Business School Press.

Ulrich, D., and W. Brockbank. 2005. *The HR Value Proposition*. Boston: Harvard Business School Press.

Ulrich, D., W. Brockbank, D. Johnson, K. Sandholtz, and J. Younger. 2008. *HR Competencies: Mastery at the Intersection of People and Business*. Alexandria, VA: SHRM.

Ulrich, D., J. Younger, W. Brockbank, and M. Ulrich. 2011. *The New HR Competencies: Business Partnering from the Outside-In*. Provo, UT: RBL Group.

Ulrich, D., J. Younger, W. Brockbank, and M. Ulrich. 2012. *HR from the Outside In: Six Competencies for the Future of Human Resources*. New York: McGraw-Hill.

Worley, C. G., T. Williams, and E. E. Lawler III. 2014. *The Agility Factor: Building adaptable Organizations for Superior Performance*. San Francisco: Jossey-Bass.

APPENDIX A
Research Partners

United States

Conference Board–USA
Rebecca L. Ray, Executive Vice President—Knowledge Organization Human Capital Lead
James O'Hern—Executive Director, Member Engagement

Executive Network
Mike Dulworth, President and CEO
John Jay Koriath, Community Technologist

SHRM/Human Resources Planning Society
Alexander Alonso, Senior Vice President—Knowledge and Development
Brian Calvary—Manager, CHRE Engagement

Institute for Corporate Productivity
Kevin Oakes, Chief Executive Officer
Erik Samdahl, Director of Marketing

Australia

Australian Human Resources Institute
Dana Grgas, Manager—Development and Research
Femi Hardwick-Slack, Development and Research Consultant

Canada

Conference Board of Canada
Ruth Wright, Director—Leadership and Human Resources Research
Shannon Jackson, Associate Director—HR Transformation Research

China

Institute of Organization and Human Resources, School of Public Administration, Renmin University of China
Chaoping Li, Professor of Organizational Behavior and Human Resource Management

Tongji University
Yan Shumin, Professor—School of Economics and Management

CEIBS (China Europe International Business School)
Katherine Xin, Professor of Management
Jian Han, Associate Professor of Management

United Kingdom/Europe

Corporate Research Foundation/Strategic Dimensions

Mike Haffendon, Cofounder

Viktorija Verdina, Research Executive

CIPD

Peter Cheese, CEO

Stephen Pobjoy, Head of Events—Design and Development

Wilson Wong, Head of Insights and Futures

MarkAllen Group

Sian Harrington, Publishing Director

Katie Jacobs, Editor of *HR Magazine*

Amanda Woozencroft, Marketing Manager

APPENDIX B
Research Design

Our study examines the extent to which the design and activities of the HR function are actually changing by analyzing survey data from 1995, 1998, 2001, 2004, 2007, 2010, 2013, and 2016. We examine the use of practices that are expected to represent the new directions that human resource organizations must take in order to fit with the changes that are occurring in the organizations they serve. We also examine how these changes are related to the strategic role of HR, its effectiveness, and the effectiveness of organizations. Finally, we examine the impact of how the HR function is designed and operates on its effectiveness. It focuses in depth on eleven areas:

1. *HR activities.* In order to assess how HR has changed, questions were asked about how the activities of HR have changed. Of particular interest is whether HR is doing less administration and more strategic work.

2. *HR role and activities.* Because of changes in the business environment, it is reasonable to expect that the HR function may have changed. A major focus of the study is to learn to what extent the HR function is changing, particularly with respect to becoming a strategic partner. It also looks at which organizational designs and HR practices are associated with HR being a strategic partner. Of particular concern is whether attention to strategic services, such as organizational design and development, is related to the effectiveness of the HR function and organizational effectiveness. We also focus on finding out how much increase or decrease there has been in the emphasis on traditional HR functions such as HR planning, compensation, recruitment, selection, and HR information systems. Of particular interest is whether HR is doing less administrative and more strategic work.

3. *Decision science for talent resources.* Numerous books and articles that discuss talent have highlighted the fact that organizations are increasingly competing for human capital and that their ability to successfully compete can be a source of competitive advantage. They also need to effectively manage the talent. Our study therefore focuses on whether organizations have developed a decision science for their important talent decisions and whether this is related to how effectively they manage it and to organizational effectiveness.

4. *Design of the HR function.* We examine whether changes have occurred in the way the HR function is organized in order to increase the value that it delivers. Because of their role in determining the balance between efficiency and customer-focused support, we look at the adoption of shared services and centers of excellence. We also look at the use of self-service and HR generalists.

5. *Information technology.* Human resource information systems (HRISs) can potentially radically change the way HR services are delivered and managed. Thus, the study examines how companies are using information technology in their HR functions. It also focuses on how effective organizations consider their HRISs to be in influencing employee satisfaction and providing strategic information.

6. *Metrics and analytics.* It is important to know both what measures HR organizations collect and how they analyze them. Thus, our study looks at what metrics are being collected and used and how effectively metrics and analytics are being used.

7. *Sustainable performance.* Organizations are increasingly being asked to perform well not just financially but socially and environmentally as well. This raises the question of what HR can and should do to ensure that organizations perform well in all three areas.

8. *HR skills.* Critical to the effectiveness of any HR function are the skills of the HR professionals and staff. Thus, the study examines how satisfied organizations are with their HR professionals' skills in a variety of areas. It also looks at the importance of the skills HR professionals need in order to serve as true business and strategic partners.

9. *HR effectiveness.* The effectiveness of the HR function is a critical issue. Particular emphasis in our study is placed on the effectiveness of the HR function in doing many of the new activities that are required in order for it to be a business and strategic partner. These include managing change, contributing to strategy, managing the outsourcing of HR, and operating shared service units. Perhaps the crucial issue with respect to effectiveness concerns what practices lead to an effective HR organization. Thus, the study focuses on what HR structures, approaches, and practices are associated with the effectiveness in an HR organization.

10. *Organizational performance.* The effectiveness and structure of the HR function is just one of many influences on an organization's overall performance, but it can be a significant influence. Human capital is an important driver of organizational performance in most organizations. Thus, the relationship between organizational performance and how the HR function is designed and operates is an important focus of the study.

11. *International.* In our first five surveys, we gathered data only from U.S. corporations. The economy has become increasingly global since we began this research in 1995, and thus it is particularly important to consider how HR functions in different countries. For the first time in our 2010 survey, we collected data from corporations in five countries in addition to U.S. corporations.

Method

This is the eighth in an every-three-year study examining whether change has occurred in the HR organizations of large and medium-sized corporations and what makes HR function effectively. In the first study in 1995, surveys were mailed to HR executives at the director level or above in 417 large and medium-sized service and industrial firms. The executives chosen had broad visibility to the HR function across the corporation. We received responses from 130 companies (response rate 19.6 percent). In the second study, done in 1998, we mailed surveys to similar executives at 663 similar firms; 199 usable surveys were returned (response rate 17.9 percent) (Lawler and Mohrman 2000). In the third survey, done in 2001, 966 surveys were mailed and 150 usable surveys were received (15.5 percent response rate; Lawler and Mohrman 2003). For the 2004 study, surveys were again mailed to HR executives with corporate visibility of the HR function in large and medium-sized companies (Lawler, Boudreau, and Mohrman 2006).

For the 2007 survey, questionnaires were once again mailed to HR executives in medium-size and large companies. For the first time, data were also gathered by using the Internet. The Institute for Corporate Productivity (i4cp) created a web-based version of our survey and used it to collect data from 43 companies, giving us a total sample of 106 companies. All of the 2010, 2013, and 2016 survey data were collected using the Internet. HR executives were given a link and asked to respond.

For the first time in 2004, data were collected from non-HR senior managers. In 2007, 2010, and 2013, data were again collected from non-HR senior managers in U.S. corporations. A cover letter to the HR executives in the United States asked that the survey be distributed to individuals who were not in HR but were in a position to evaluate the function. In 2010, the manager's questionnaire was made available by a link, and the questions were answered online. A complete copy of the 2010 manager survey with frequencies, means, and variances for the United States is in Lawler and Boudreau (2012). For this study, as for 2013, no data were collected from managers.

For the first time in 2010, data were collected from more than one country. In addition to the United States, data were collected from HR executives in Australia, Canada, Europe, the United Kingdom, and China. For the 2013 study, we added India to the list of countries, but in 2016 we did not collect data from India because we could not find a research partner.

In all countries except China, the survey was in English. In China, it was in Mandarin. Access was provided by the organizations listed in appendix A, which also identifies the individuals who worked with us in each country.

Sample

As in our past surveys, data were collected from HR executives in companies with one thousand or more employees. Responses were received from Australia ($n = 34$), Canada ($n = 36$), China ($n = 98$), the United Kingdom and Europe combined ($n = 37$), and the United States ($n = 114$).

The median company in the U.S. sample had fourteen thousand employees, and the median company in the international sample had five thousand-employees. The revenue of the U.S. firms was also greater: $4.5 billion (median) versus $1.4 billion (median) for the international sample.

The companies in our sample are in a wide variety of industries. Among the least common are mining and art/entertainment. The international and U.S. samples have relatively similar profiles with respect to industries.

Staffing of the HR Function

In the U.S. firms studied, the average number of employees in the HR function was 249. The ratio of total employees to HR employees was 100 to 0.98. This ratio is similar to that found in 2001 (1.11), 2004 (1.00), 2007 (0.94), 2010 (0.88), and 2013 (0.91).

Despite the introduction of information technology and the downsizing of corporate staff groups, there has been no significant decrease in the size of the HR function relative to the rest of the organization. Why this is true is unclear. It may reflect the increased importance of the function and an increase in its workload or simply that it is a well-institutionalized part of most organizations that is difficult to reduce in size.

The respondents were asked to state the background of their current HR heads (1.8 percent did not have a chief HR officer). In 80.7 percent of U.S. companies, the top HR executive came up through the HR function. In the other 17.5 percent of cases, these executives came from other functions, including operations, sales and marketing, and legal. This result is similar to the findings of the 2001, 2004, 2007, 2010, and 2013 surveys. The percentage of chief HR officers who come from HR varies significantly on a country-to-country basis. The low is 70.6 percent in Australia, and the high is 80.7 percent in the United States.

Some firms continue to place executives who are not traditional HR executives in charge of the HR function for three likely reasons. First, these executives are being put in charge of HR in order to develop them because they are candidates for the CEO job. Second, they are being put in charge of HR in order to make it run more like a business and be more of a business partner. Third, failed line managers are being put into HR because it is a "safe" preretirement job. The survey did not ask why this is being done, so we can only speculate that in the majority of cases, it is done in order to change the HR function or develop an executive. In today's business world, it is too important a position to use as a dumping ground, but it may happen.

Measures

The 2016 HR survey is a slightly altered version of the previous surveys. Our surveys have covered fifteen areas:

- General descriptive information about the demographics of the firm and the HR function
- The organizational context that the HR function serves, including its broad organizational form, management approach, and the amount and kinds of strategic change and organizational initiatives being carried out by the company (expanded in 2007 and some items changed in 2010)
- The amount of work that is done by other than traditional employees and how it is carried out and managed (new in 2016)
- The changing focus of the HR function measured in terms of how much time it is spending in different kinds of roles compared with five to seven years ago
- The degree of emphasis that a number of HR activities are receiving and the involvement of HR in business strategy
- The HR function's use of various organizational practices to increase efficiency and business responsiveness and the extent to which it is investing in a number of initiatives to support change
- The use of outsourcing and its effectiveness (altered in 2007 and 2010, not asked in 2013 and 2016)
- The use of information technology and its effectiveness (new in 1998, expanded in 2001, reduced in 2007)
- The use of HR metrics and analytics, as well as their effectiveness (new in 2004, expanded in 2007)
- HR's role in sustainability programs--what it is and what it should be (new in 2013)
- How the effectiveness of HR programs and activities is measured (new in 2004, expanded in 2007)
- How HR leaders and business leaders make decisions that involve human capital (new in 2004)
- The skill requirements for employees in the HR function and satisfaction with current skills
- The perceived effectiveness of the HR function and the importance of a variety of HR activities
- Overall organizational performance in comparisons to competitors

A complete copy of the 2016 survey with frequencies and means for each item in the U.S. sample is in appendix C.

Method Limitations

Survey research of the type used in this study has a number of limitations. The following are among the most important:

- The data for each company are provided by only one individual. Participants are asked to respond to a number of questions that require broad knowledge of the company in order to answer effectively. Clearly not all individuals answering the survey could reasonably be expected to have the breadth of knowledge that is required to give an accurate answer to each question. In some cases, individuals skipped questions when they presumably did not know the answers. In any case, their responses are best looked at as guesstimates by individuals rather than as fully informed data-based information. Because there is only one respondent per firm in most cases, it is impossible to check the interrelatedness of the responses.

- It is impossible to accurately calculate the response rate to the survey. Because of the method we used to distribute the survey, we are unable to determine how many people were actually asked to respond. In any case, it is safe to assume that the response rate is very low. The survey is long, and it is not something that everyone who got a chance to respond would be able to respond to accurately and be interested in spending the time required. Although this is a limitation of our study, it does not mean that the data are misleading. In the case of most countries, we have a reasonable number of responses so that we have at least some idea as to what things are like in those countries.

- It is hard to determine whether the samples from the different countries are comparable. Clearly there are differences in organization size and, most likely, the kinds of industries that were sampled. This reflects the reality that the countries typically have different size organizations and concentrations in different industries. Thus, to some degree, the comparisons between countries reflect differences in the size of the company and industry, as well as the country it is in. Given this, it is important to be cautious in interpreting the country comparison data. The best conclusion about the methodology is to regard the data as providing good starting points for thinking about how HR functions over time in different countries. This information is not definitive, but these are the only data of their kind that exist and so warrant serious consideration. They certainly provide a much better guide to what is happening with respect to HR than many of the articles that are written based on interviews with a few heads of HR about what they are doing in their companies.

- The same words can mean different things to different people, particularly if they are from different countries and speak different native languages. Since we used English in virtually all of our surveys, the data may be compromised to some degree by the different meanings being attached to the same words by people in different countries or, for that matter, by people in the same country. There are large cultural differences between and within countries, which may make people think differently or interpret words like *quality, frequency, often,* and so on differently. Words can also change their meaning over time, so someone responding to a question in 1995 may not make the same response to the same question in later years because the terms used have gradually evolved or been redefined. This may be particularly true in the case of management terms, which seem to constantly be redefined by the ongoing, highly active literature in the field of management. Overall, this means that we must be careful in interpreting changes or lack of changes in longitudinal data.

2016 HR Global Study:
U.S. Results (*N* = 114)

THIS SECTION ASKS QUESTIONS ABOUT YOUR COMPANY AND HR IN YOUR ORGANIZATION.

	Mean	S.D.*
1. What is the annual revenue of your company (in $billions)?	$13.7	$24.2
2. Approximately how many employees are in your company?	25,420.9	51,796.4
3. Approximately, how many full-time equivalent employees (FTE's, exempt and nonexempt) are part of the HR function? (This number should include both centralized and decentralized staff).	249.0	470.4

4. What is the background of the current head of HR (CHRO)? (please check one response)	
80.7%	Human Resource Management
17.5%	Other Function(s), which one(s):
1.8%	Do not have a CHRO

5a. Who does the CHRO report to?	
83.3%	CEO
4.4%	COO
2.6%	CAO
7.9%	Other
1.8%	No CHRO

5b. Do you have a COO?	
47.4%	Yes
52.6%	No

*S.D. = Standard Deviation

6. How would you gauge your company's performance, relative to its competitors ...	Much Below Average	Somewhat Below Average	About Average	Somewhat Above Average	Much Above Average	Mean	S.D.
a. Societal and environmental sustainability performance.	0.0	8.0	33.6	38.1	20.4	**3.71**	.88
b. HR function performance.	1.8	13.3	26.5	40.7	17.7	**3.59**	.99
c. Overall company performance.	0.9	6.2	23.9	49.6	19.5	**3.81**	.85

7. To what extent do these describe how your organization operates?	Little or No Extent	Some Extent	Moderate Extent	Great Extent	Very Great Extent	Mean	S.D.
a. Bureaucratic (hierarchical structure, tight job descriptions, top-down decision making).	14.9	32.5	28.1	19.3	5.3	**2.68**	1.11
b. Low-cost operator (low wages, minimum benefits, focus on cost reduction and controls).	29.2	34.5	23.0	10.6	2.7	**2.23**	1.07
c. High involvement (flat structure, participative decisions, commitment to employee development and careers).	10.6	23.9	29.2	30.1	6.2	**2.97**	1.11
d. Global competitor (complex interesting work, hire best talent, low commitment to employee development and careers).	23.0	23.0	28.3	20.4	5.3	**2.62**	1.20
e. Sustainable (agile design, focus on financial performance and sustainability).	3.5	15.0	36.3	39.8	5.3	**3.28**	.91

8. To what extent is each of the following strategic initiatives present in your organization?	Little or No Extent	Some Extent	Moderate Extent	Great Extent	Very Great Extent	Mean	S.D.
a. Building a global presence.	23.9	12.4	18.6	31.9	13.3	**2.98**	1.40
b. Acquisitions.	17.7	16.8	21.2	23.0	21.2	**3.13**	1.40
c. Customer focus.	0.0	4.4	8.8	33.6	53.1	**4.35**	.82
d. Technology leadership.	3.5	15.0	27.4	34.5	19.5	**3.51**	1.08
e. Talent management.	0.9	9.7	28.3	41.6	19.5	**3.69**	.93
f. Knowledge / intellectual capital management.	6.2	16.8	42.5	23.9	10.6	**3.16**	1.03
g. Sustainability.	6.2	18.6	31.9	31.9	11.5	**3.24**	1.08
h. Innovation.	4.4	13.3	31.9	27.4	23.0	**3.51**	1.12
i. Achieving a broad social purpose	10.6	20.4	28.3	22.1	18.6	**3.18**	1.26
j. Growth	0.0	5.3	16.8	48.7	29.2	**4.02**	.82
k. Agility	3.5	15.9	28.3	34.5	17.7	**3.47**	1.07

9. For each of the following HR roles, please estimate the percentage of time your HR function spends performing these roles. Percentages should add to 100% for each column.

	Currently	5–7 Years Ago
a. **Maintaining Records** (Collect, track and maintain data on employees)	13.2%	25.7%
b. **Auditing/Controlling** (Ensure compliance with internal operations, regulations, and legal and union requirements)	12.1%	17.3%
c. **Providing Human Resource Services** (Assist with implementation and administration of HR practices)	26.6%	30.4%
d. **Developing Human Resource Systems and Practices** (Develop new HR systems and practices)	20.0%	13.0%
e. **Strategic Business Partnering** (Member of the management team; involved with strategic HR planning, organization design, and strategic change)	28.2%	13.6%
TOTAL	100%	100%

10. Which of the following best describes the relationship between the Human Resource function and the business strategy of your corporation? (Please check one response.)

Mean = 3.19; S.D. = .81

3.5%	Human Resource plays no role in business strategy (**if checked, go to Question 12**).
14.2%	Human Resource is involved in implementing the business strategy.
41.6%	Human Resource provides input to the business strategy and helps implement it once it has been developed.
40.7%	Human Resource is a full partner in developing and implementing the business strategy.

11. With respect to strategy, to what extent does the HR function . . .	Little or No Extent	Some Extent	Moderate Extent	Great Extent	Very Great Extent	Mean	S.D.
a. Help identify or design strategy options?	10.9	22.7	35.5	24.5	6.4	**2.93**	**1.08**
b. Help decide among the best strategy options?	8.2	24.5	30.9	27.3	9.1	**3.05**	**1.10**
c. Help plan the implementation of strategy?	1.8	9.1	22.7	41.8	24.5	**3.78**	**0.98**
d. Help identify new business opportunities?	24.5	34.5	29.1	11.8	0.0	**2.28**	**0.97**
e. Assess the organization's readiness to implement strategies?	2.7	14.5	29.1	35.5	18.2	**3.52**	**1.04**
f. Help design the organization structure to implement strategy?	0.9	9.1	16.4	37.3	36.4	**3.99**	**0.99**
g. Assess possible merger, acquisition, or divestiture strategies?	12.7	20.0	27.3	31.8	8.2	**3.03**	**1.17**
h. Work with the corporate board on business strategy?	18.2	19.1	33.6	21.8	7.3	**2.81**	**1.19**

Your company's HR organization:

12. To what extent does each of the following describe the way your HR organization currently operates?	Little or No Extent	Some Extent	Moderate Extent	Great Extent	Very Great Extent	Mean	S.D.
a. Administrative processing is centralized in shared services units.	7.0	21.1	30.7	28.1	13.2	**3.19**	**1.13**
b. Transactional HR work is outsourced.	40.4	36.8	11.4	9.6	1.8	**1.96**	**1.03**
c. Centers of excellence provide specialized expertise.	8.8	13.2	20.2	42.1	15.8	**3.43**	**1.17**
d. Decentralized HR generalists support business units.	16.7	8.8	15.8	36.0	22.8	**3.39**	**1.37**
e. People rotate *within* HR.	19.3	25.4	25.4	20.2	9.6	**2.75**	**1.25**
f. People rotate *into* HR.	42.1	36.8	14.9	4.4	1.8	**1.87**	**.95**
g. People rotate *out of* HR to other functions.	43.0	38.6	14.9	2.6	0.9	**1.80**	**.85**
h. HR practices vary across business units.	27.4	38.1	22.1	9.7	2.7	**2.22**	**1.04**
i. Some transactional activities that used to be done by HR are done by employees on a self-service basis.	8.0	31.0	31.0	23.0	7.1	**2.90**	**1.07**
j. HR information and advice are available online for managers and employees.	8.8	28.3	24.8	27.4	10.6	**3.03**	**1.16**
k. There is a low HR/employee ratio.	6.1	23.7	37.7	25.4	7.0	**3.04**	**1.01**
l. There is a data-based talent strategy.	13.3	28.3	33.6	20.4	4.4	**2.74**	**1.07**
m. There is a human capital strategy that is integrated with the business strategy.	7.0	20.2	26.3	31.6	14.9	**3.27**	**1.15**
n. Provides analytic support for business decision-making.	7.1	30.1	31.9	25.7	5.3	**2.92**	**1.03**
o. Provides HR data to support change management.	8.8	18.6	35.4	30.1	7.1	**3.08**	**1.06**
p. HR is involved in decisions about whether and where to use project-based, freelance, and platform gigs in order to get work done.	14.2	29.2	28.3	20.4	8.0	**2.79**	**1.16**
q. Provides direction and services for workers who are not covered by a traditional employment relationship (e.g., contract, gig, platform workers).	21.9	28.9	25.4	18.4	5.3	**2.56**	**1.18**
r. Drives change management.	1.8	16.7	27.2	32.5	21.9	**3.56**	**1.07**
s. Makes rigorous data-based decisions about human capital management.	10.6	28.3	29.2	24.8	7.1	**2.89**	**1.11**
t. Uses social networks for HR activities such as recruiting, performance management, and work assignments.	7.0	28.9	28.1	25.4	10.5	**3.04**	**1.12**
u. Uses mobile technology to support HR activities such as recruiting, self-service, communication, etc.	14.9	30.7	29.8	16.7	7.9	**2.72**	**1.15**
v. Uses software as a service (SaaS) model (subscription based, hosted in the cloud).	14.0	26.3	22.8	23.7	13.2	**2.96**	**1.27**
w. Incorporates artificial intelligence.	73.7	17.5	4.4	3.5	0.9	**1.40**	**.81**

13. Here we ask about the HR technology your company uses. This encompasses all technology used to manage people, including technology for the core HR information system, payroll, and specific HR processes such as talent acquisition, learning, and performance management, whether the budget and management for the technology are located in HR, IT, or other functions.

	0% to 20%	21% to 40%	41% to 60%	61% to 80%	81% to 100%	Mean	S.D.
a. About what percentage of the work of the HR function is conducted using HR technology?	6.2	37.2	33.6	19.5	3.5	**2.77**	**.95**
b. About what percentage of HR work that uses technology is conducted using a single integrated software suite, such as Workday, Success Factors, or Oracle HCM?	26.5	19.5	13.3	23.9	16.8	**2.85**	**1.47**
c. About what percentage of the HR transactions using HR technology are performed by employees and managers rather than by HR or IT staff?	27.4	32.7	23.0	12.4	4.4	**2.34**	**1.14**
d. About what percentage of the HR technology budget is for applications that are housed in the cloud?	27.4	27.4	10.6	23.0	11.5	**2.64**	**1.40**

14. To what extent does each of the following statements characterize your HR technology?	Little or No Extent	Some Extent	Moderate Extent	Great Extent	Very Great Extent	Mean	S.D.
a. It is mobile device enabled (usable over cell phones or tablets).	31.6	21.1	27.2	13.2	7.0	**2.43**	**1.26**
b. It makes an enterprise social media platform available to all employees.	35.1	25.4	17.5	13.2	8.8	**2.35**	**1.32**
c. It provides tools that permit deeper analysis of human capital issues.	23.9	30.1	28.3	10.6	7.1	**2.47**	**1.17**

15. Please check the one statement that best describes the current state of your HR Information technology:

Mean = 2.26, S.D. = .72

11.5%	Completely integrated HR information technology system.
55.8%	Most processes are information technology based but not fully integrated.
28.3%	Some HR processes are information technology based.
4.4%	There is little information technology present in the HR function.
0.0%	There is no information technology present. **(If checked, skip to Question 17.)**

16. To what extent do you consider your information technology system to . . .	Little or No Extent	Some Extent	Moderate Extent	Great Extent	Very Great Extent	Mean	S.D.
a. Be effective.	2.6	27.2	37.7	28.1	4.4	**3.04**	**.92**
b. Satisfy your employees.	7.9	31.6	37.7	19.3	3.5	**2.79**	**.96**
c. Improve HR services.	6.1	20.2	32.5	31.6	9.6	**3.18**	**1.06**
d. Reduce HR transaction costs.	7.0	22.8	30.7	28.9	10.5	**3.13**	**1.10**
e. Provide new strategic information.	16.7	24.6	36.0	16.7	6.1	**2.71**	**1.12**
f. Speed up HR processes.	4.4	22.8	30.7	30.7	11.4	**3.22**	**1.06**
g. Reduce the number of employees in HR.	22.8	33.3	26.3	12.3	5.3	**2.44**	**1.13**
h. Integrate HR processes (e.g., training, compensation).	14.2	28.3	34.5	16.8	6.2	**2.73**	**1.10**
i. Measure HR's impact on the business.	33.3	25.4	25.4	13.2	2.6	**2.26**	**1.14**
j. Improve the human capital decisions of managers outside HR.	21.1	29.8	33.3	14.0	1.8	**2.46**	**1.03**
k. Create knowledge networks.	37.7	37.7	14.0	7.0	3.5	**2.01**	**1.06**
l. Offer a positive user experience.	14.0	22.8	38.6	17.5	7.0	**2.81**	**1.10**
m. Represent a state-of-the-art solution.	23.7	29.8	27.2	14.0	5.3	**2.47**	**1.15**
n. Use the most advanced technology.	25.4	31.6	21.9	16.7	4.4	**2.43**	**1.17**
o. Analyze and optimize social networks.	50.0	23.7	19.3	6.1	0.9	**1.84**	**1.00**

17. Does your organization currently . . .	Yes, Have Now	Being Built	Planning For	Not Currently Being Considered	Mean	S.D.
a. Measure the business impact of HR programs and processes?	28.9	22.8	38.6	9.6	**2.29**	**.99**
b. Collect metrics that measure the cost of HR programs and processes?	37.5	24.1	27.7	10.7	**2.12**	**1.04**
c. Have the capability to conduct cost-benefit analyses (also called utility analyses) of HR programs?	25.4	17.5	27.2	29.8	**2.61**	**1.16**
d. Use HR dashboards or scorecards?	51.8	22.8	19.3	6.1	**1.80**	**.96**
e. Measure the financial efficiency of HR operations (e.g., cost-per-hire, time to fill, training costs?)	47.4	23.7	23.7	5.3	**1.87**	**.96**
f. Measure the specific effects of HR programs (such as learning from training, motivation from rewards, validity of tests)?	27.2	22.8	27.2	22.8	**2.46**	**1.12**
g. Benchmark analytics and measures against data from outside organizations (e.g. Saratoga, Mercer, Hewitt)?	44.7	18.4	19.3	17.5	**2.10**	**1.16**
h. Measure the quality of the talent decisions made by non-HR leaders?	14.0	22.8	26.3	36.8	**2.86**	**1.07**
i. Measure the business impact of high versus low performance in jobs?	17.5	19.3	25.4	37.7	**2.83**	**1.12**

18. How effective are the information, measurement, and analysis systems of your organization when it comes to the following?	Very Ineffective	Ineffective	Neither	Effective	Very Effective	Mean	S.D.
a. Connecting human capital practices to organizational performance.	1.8	30.6	35.1	29.7	2.7	**3.01**	**.89**
b. Identifying where talent has the greatest potential for strategic impact.	2.7	21.6	27.9	41.4	6.3	**3.27**	**.96**
c. Predicting the effects of HR programs before implementation.	3.6	36.9	32.4	24.3	2.7	**2.86**	**.92**
d. Pinpointing HR programs that should be discontinued.	3.6	28.8	36.9	27.9	2.7	**2.97**	**.91**
e. Supporting organizational change efforts.	3.6	9.0	23.4	52.3	11.7	**3.59**	**.94**
f. Assessing and improving the HR department operations.	1.8	14.4	26.1	47.7	9.9	**3.50**	**.92**
g. Contributing to decisions about business strategy and human capital management.	2.7	7.2	35.1	46.8	8.1	**3.50**	**.85**
h. Using logical principles that clearly connect talent to organizational success.	2.7	15.3	36.9	37.8	7.2	**3.32**	**.91**
i. Using advanced data analysis and statistics.	12.6	27.0	36.0	19.8	4.5	**2.77**	**1.05**
j. Providing high-quality (complete, timely, accessible) talent measurements.	4.5	26.1	31.5	33.3	4.5	**3.07**	**.98**
k. Motivating users to take appropriate action.	3.6	23.4	43.2	27.0	2.7	**3.02**	**.87**
l. Capitalizing on "big data".	18.2	35.5	26.4	18.2	1.8	**2.50**	**1.05**

19. To what extent are these statements true about your organization?	Little or No Extent	Some Extent	Moderate Extent	Great Extent	Very Great Extent	Mean	S.D.
a. We excel at competing for and with talent where it matters most to our strategic success.	5.5	18.2	35.5	33.6	7.3	**3.19**	**1.00**
b. Business leaders' decisions that depend upon or affect human capital (e.g. layoffs, rewards) are as rigorous, logical and strategically relevant as their decisions about resources such as money, technology, and customers.	4.5	22.7	27.3	31.8	13.6	**3.27**	**1.10**
c. HR leaders have a good understanding about where and why human capital makes the biggest difference in their business.	1.8	15.6	26.6	36.7	19.3	**3.56**	**1.03**
d. Business leaders have a good understanding about where and why human capital makes the biggest difference in their business.	1.8	22.7	30.9	28.2	16.4	**3.35**	**1.06**
e. HR systems educate business leaders about their talent decisions.	18.3	24.8	33.0	19.3	4.6	**2.67**	**1.12**
f. HR adds value by ensuring compliance with rules, laws, and guidelines.	0.0	13.6	25.5	47.3	13.6	**3.61**	**.89**
g. HR adds value by delivering high-quality professional practices and services.	1.8	8.2	24.5	50.9	14.5	**3.68**	**.89**
h. HR adds value by improving talent decisions inside and outside the HR function.	3.6	10.0	26.4	37.3	22.7	**3.65**	**1.05**

20. How much does your Corporation's Board call on HR for help with the following?	Little or No Extent	Some Extent	Moderate Extent	Great Extent	Very Great Extent	Mean	S.D.
a. Executive compensation.	6.4	8.3	8.3	27.5	49.5	**4.06**	**1.22**
b. Addressing strategic readiness.	18.3	14.7	30.3	26.6	10.1	**2.95**	**1.25**
c. Executive succession.	6.4	6.4	19.3	22.9	45.0	**3.94**	**1.22**
d. Change consulting.	17.4	19.3	29.4	22.9	11.0	**2.91**	**1.25**
e. Developing board effectiveness/corporate governance.	31.2	14.7	29.4	22.0	2.8	**2.50**	**1.22**
f. Risk assessment.	15.6	15.6	40.4	22.0	6.4	**2.88**	**1.12**
g. Information about the condition or capability of the work force.	9.2	12.8	22.0	33.9	22.0	**3.47**	**1.23**
h. Board compensation.	23.9	15.6	17.4	18.3	24.8	**3.05**	**1.52**
i. Sustainability.	36.7	13.8	27.5	15.6	6.4	**2.41**	**1.30**

Regarding the skills and knowledge of your organization's current HR professional/managerial staff:

21. How satisfied are you with current HR professional/managerial staff in each of these areas?	Very Dissatisfied	Dissatisfied	Neutral	Satisfied	Very Satisfied	Mean	S.D.
a. Team skills.	0.9	10.9	19.1	50.0	19.1	**3.75**	**.92**
b. HR technical skills.	0.9	17.3	16.4	44.5	20.9	**3.67**	**1.02**
c. Business understanding.	3.6	16.4	27.3	38.2	14.5	**3.44**	**1.05**
d. Interpersonal skills.	0.9	5.5	7.3	54.5	31.8	**4.11**	**.83**
e. Cross-functional experience.	5.5	21.1	34.9	28.4	10.1	**3.17**	**1.05**
f. Consultation skills.	0.9	12.7	34.5	41.8	10.0	**3.47**	**.88**
g. Leadership/management.	1.8	4.5	24.5	50.0	19.1	**3.80**	**.87**
h. Global understanding.	7.3	21.8	39.1	22.7	9.1	**3.05**	**1.05**
i. Organizational design.	4.5	19.1	27.3	42.7	6.4	**3.27**	**1.00**
j. Strategic planning.	6.4	25.5	21.8	41.8	4.5	**3.13**	**1.05**
k. Information technology.	1.8	24.5	39.1	31.8	2.7	**3.09**	**.86**
l. Change management.	0.9	13.6	35.5	38.2	11.8	**3.46**	**.91**
m. Metrics and analytics.	6.4	34.5	28.2	29.1	1.8	**2.85**	**.98**
n. Sustainability.	3.6	19.1	46.4	28.2	2.7	**3.07**	**.85**
o. Social media.	3.6	25.5	45.5	20.9	4.5	**2.97**	**.89**
p. Globalization.	12.7	17.3	35.5	30.0	4.5	**2.96**	**1.08**
q. Risk management.	4.5	16.4	30.9	40.0	8.2	**3.31**	**.99**
r. Organizational culture.	1.8	7.3	24.5	43.6	22.7	**3.78**	**.94**
s. Workplace branding.	4.5	10.9	33.6	40.9	10.0	**3.41**	**.97**

22. What percentage of your company-wide HR professional/HR managerial staff possesses the necessary skill set for success in today's business environment? (Circle one response.)

None 0%	Almost None 1–20%	Some 21–40%	About Half 41–60%	Most 61–80%	Almost All 81–99%	All 100%	Mean	S.D.
0.0	0.9	16.4	32.7	32.7	16.4	0.9	**4.50**	**1.01**

23. Please rate the following activities on a scale of 1 to 10 or not applicable. In view of what is needed by your company:

How well is the HR organization meeting needs in each of the areas below?	Not Meeting Needs	2	3	4	5	6	7	8	9	All Needs Met	Not Applicable	Mean	S.D.
a. Providing HR services.	0.0	0.0	1.8	0.0	1.8	7.3	24.8	40.4	20.2	3.7	0.0	**7.73**	**1.21**
b. Providing change consulting services.	1.8	3.7	1.8	5.5	16.5	17.4	19.3	19.3	11.0	3.7	0.0	**6.49**	**1.98**
c. Being a business partner.	0.0	0.9	3.7	4.6	7.3	10.1	23.9	19.3	21.1	9.2	0.0	**7.31**	**1.85**
d. Improving decisions about human capital.	2.8	0.9	3.7	6.4	6.4	13.8	21.1	21.1	17.4	6.4	0.0	**6.94**	**2.07**
e. Managing outsourcing.	4.0	3.0	7.1	9.1	13.1	14.1	17.2	13.1	15.2	4.0	0.0	**6.20**	**2.31**
f. Operating HR centers of excellence.	2.9	1.9	6.8	2.9	7.8	15.5	13.6	22.3	20.4	5.8	0.0	**6.86**	**2.22**
g. Operating HR shared service units.	4.0	5.1	5.1	4.0	8.1	16.2	26.3	14.1	14.1	3.0	0.0	**6.37**	**2.24**
h. Helping to develop business strategies.	3.7	2.8	5.5	8.3	10.1	18.3	16.5	17.4	12.8	4.6	0.0	**6.36**	**2.23**
i. Being an employee advocate.	0.9	0.9	0.0	0.9	9.3	8.3	14.8	23.1	26.9	14.8	0.0	**7.81**	**1.76**
j. Analyzing HR and business metrics.	2.8	1.8	9.2	10.1	12.8	17.4	18.3	14.7	7.3	5.5	0.0	**6.10**	**2.16**
k. Working with the corporate board.	3.0	5.9	6.9	5.0	5.9	5.0	12.9	13.9	30.7	10.9	0.0	**7.01**	**2.61**
l. Preparing talent for the future.	1.8	1.8	5.5	3.7	13.8	14.7	21.1	18.3	16.5	2.8	0.0	**6.64**	**2.01**

24. Please indicate your agreement or disagreement with the following statements about your company's environmental and social sustainability activities:

	Strongly Disagree	Somewhat Disagree	Neither Disagree or Agree	Somewhat Agree	Strongly Agree	Mean	S.D.
a. Sustainability performance and competences *are* explicitly built into HR processes such as selection, rewards, and development.	18.3	22.9	17.4	31.2	10.1	**2.92**	**1.30**
b. Sustainability performance and competences *should be* explicitly built into HR processes such as selection, rewards, and development.	3.7	11.9	15.6	38.5	30.3	**3.80**	**1.11**
c. HR *is involved* in the design of sustainability initiatives and programs.	10.2	20.4	20.4	35.2	13.9	**3.22**	**1.22**
d. HR *should be involved* in the design of sustainability initiatives and programs.	2.8	5.5	23.9	36.7	31.2	**3.88**	**1.01**
e. HR *provides* support and expertise in organization design issues that impact sustainability.	6.5	3.7	24.3	46.7	18.7	**3.67**	**1.04**

25. Please indicate what HR's role is in your company's sustainability activities.

No role	6.6%
Minor role	42.5%
Active support	31.1%
Major support	9.4%
Leader	10.4%
Mean	**2.75**
S.D.	**1.07**

26. What proportion of the work in your organization is:

	0% to 20%	21% to 40%	41% to 60%	61% to 80%	81% to 100%	Mean	S.D.
a. Designed as projects and tasks that are done by other than traditional employees?	46.2	33.0	11.3	8.5	0.9	**1.85**	**.99**
b. Is location and time flexible rather than limited to a particular place and time?	35.8	31.1	19.8	10.4	2.8	**2.13**	**1.11**
c. Detached from the traditional employment relationship through contracts, platforms, etc.?	65.1	24.5	7.5	1.9	0.9	**1.49**	**.80**
d. Carried out through collaborations and connections that cross your organizational boundary, such as alliances, borrowing and loaning talent from other organizations?	64.2	16.0	12.3	7.5	0.0	**1.63**	**.97**
e. Rewarded immediately upon task completion rather than on a traditional periodic or calendar basis?	70.8	14.2	10.4	2.8	1.9	**1.51**	**.93**
f. Rewarded in an individualized way rather than by similar rewards for all employees?	46.2	24.5	16.0	10.4	2.8	**1.99**	**1.14**
g. Rewarded with elements, beyond the traditional rewards of money, benefits, stocks recognition, etc.?	59.0	21.0	8.6	9.5	1.9	**1.74**	**1.08**

These tables are based on the entire data set for 2016 (both U.S. and Global Responses)

In which country is your company based? (Percentage of total)					
0.0	Argentina	0.6	India	1.2	Switzerland
10.5	Australia	0.0	Ireland	0.0	Thailand
0.0	Austria	0.0	Israel	0.0	Turkey
0.3	Belgium	0.0	Italy	0.0	United Arab Emirates
0.0	Brazil	0.0	Japan	5.9	United Kingdom
11.1	Canada	0.3	Mexico	35.3	United States of America
0.0	Chile	1.2	Netherlands	0.0	Other
29.7	China	0.0	New Zealand		
0.0	Czech Republic	0.0	Norway		
0.0	Denmark	0.0	Poland		
0.0	Egypt	0.0	Portugal		
0.3	Finland	0.3	Russia		
0.3	France	0.0	Saudi Arabia		
1.2	Germany	0.0	Singapore		
0.3	Greece	0.0	South Africa		
0.6	Hong Kong	0.0	South Korea		
0.0	Hungary	0.3	Spain		
0.0	Iceland	0.3	Sweden		

Please select the industries below that match your firm's primary businesses. (Percentage of total)			
3.5	Agriculture/forestry	8.8	Manufacturing (consumer)
9.6	Business and professional services	19.3	Manufacturing (industrial)
5.3	Communications/broadcasting/publishing	0.9	Mining
12.3	Computers/technology/software	4.4	Services/hospitality/arts
1.8	Construction	4.4	Transportation and warehousing
4.4	Energy	5.3	Utilities
9.6	Financial services	11.4	Wholesale and retail trade
10.5	Health care	1.8	Other
5.3	Government/public administration/nonprofit		